The Dynamics of Bride Price in Zimbabwe and the UK Diaspora

Ottis Mubaiwa

Series in Sociology

VERNON PRESS

www.vernonpress.com

In the Americas:
Vernon Press
1000 N West Street,
Suite 1200, Wilmington,
Delaware 19801
United States

In the rest of the world:
Vernon Press
C/Sancti Espiritu 17,
Malaga, 29006
Spain

Series in Sociology

Library of Congress Control Number: 2020936557

ISBN: 978-1-64889-226-4

Also available: 978-1-62273-817-5 [Hardback]; 978-1-64889-058-1 [PDF, E-Book]

Cover design by Vernon Press using elements designed by Tatutati from Pixabay.

To my family, this book is dedicated to you because I couldn't have done it without you.

Table of contents

List of Figures and Tables

List of Figures

List of Tables

Abbreviations and Glossary

BP	Bride Price
Danga	Refers to the livestock that is given to the bride's father
FGM	Female Genital Mutilation
GBV	Gender Based Violence
GoZ	Government of Zimbabwe
NGO	Non-Governmental Organisation
Roora	Bride Price
Lobola	Bride Price
UK	United Kingdom
UN	United Nations
VAWG	Violence Against Women and Girls

Abstract

My book, which is a product of my doctoral research, examines different discourses on the practice of Bride Price. I explore the historic, cultural and traditional constructions of the practice and contrast these with feminist interpretations that see it as harmful. I then compare these discourses with how men and women today view the practice. Furthermore, I seek to understand if and how Bride Price intersects with gender. To what extent does it help to enforce unequal patterns of power that render women inferior and vulnerable to abuse? I do this by exploring contentious debates within and between the Zimbabweans in the diaspora (in Birmingham) and those at home (in both rural and urban settings). I examine questions of gender inequalities to elucidate how debates on African marriage were influenced by shifting ideas of urbanisation and migration. Existing studies of African marriage focus on local macro-studies: my research is the first to place these questions within a transnational frame, examining perceptions and experiences of the practice across three different contexts. This represents an important original contribution to the scholarship and provides essential context for current debates.

This research consists of a literature review examining the current discourses on Bride Price. The literature review then informed the subsequent data collection. My findings reveal multiple contradictions. Many felt the practice is out-dated but still stated they would observe it, while others held to its centrality as an expression of cultural identity. Some supported feminist arguments that link the practice with gender inequalities. Clearly, expectations around Bride Price have intensified with globalisation and migration. Diaspora Zimbabweans now face the highest Bride Price bill, with couples having to raise the money jointly. My analysis revealed that Bride Price intersects with religious beliefs on marriage which are in turn founded on patriarchal ideology that sees wives as the property of their husbands. As such, my book supports feminist arguments that practices such as Bride Price are harmful and represent barriers to the empowerment of women.

Acknowledgements

This project would not have been possible without the help of many people. Firstly, I would like to thank my PhD supervisor Professor Tamsin Bradley for her continuous support, encouragement and generosity of time. Thank you to Dr Lana Chikhungu for always being available to answer my questions. Thank you to my family for their support and understanding and thank you to my friends for supporting and entertaining me throughout the write-up. Finally, I would like to offer sincere thanks to all of the participants who took part in the research. In particular, thank you to the families who shared their experiences with me.

Chapter 1

Introduction

I wish my feminist-lite friends who still support the patriarchal practice of having *Lobola* paid for them will listen!

(Chimamanda Ngozi Adichie)

In this chapter, I outline and introduce the general context of the book. The chapter takes the following structure: the importance of Bride Price is highlighted followed by the justification of pursuing this research, which includes highlighting my interest in this area of study. Next, the contextual background of my study is outlined which helps set the tone, which is followed by an overview of the patterns of migration, beginning with rural to urban areas within Zimbabwe and then from Zimbabwe to Birmingham. Understanding the migratory and global dimensions to my study is important as it represents a central part of its originality. In this introduction, I also present a justification for my use of a feminist perspective, which I argue helps me to explore the realities and experiences of women. The contribution to knowledge made by this research is also presented, particularly with regard to the theoretical element, which to some extent challenges the critique of post-colonial feminists who have claimed that the emphasis on culture and its overuse as an explanation for the abuse of women in developing contexts is unhelpful. My argument asserts that culture is central to understanding why Bride Price continues but is not the only dimension. The originality of this research will be made clear in this introduction.

1.1 Importance of Bride Price

Bride Price payment is one of the most highly cherished and highly regarded practices, not only in Zimbabwe but also in many other African countries. The practice is performed in order to formalise and solemnise a marriage before the partners can be recognised as husband and wife. According to Hague, Thiara and Turner (2011), Bride Price is widely practised and used as the basis to validate customary marriages in African countries. It is paid by the groom's family to the bride's family and it acts as a contract between the two families. Bride Price involves the exchange of material gifts like livestock, cash, goats, and sheep, depending on the particular community. Recently, due to the influence of modernisation and Westernisation, other new and 'modern' gifts like land titles, electronics, furniture, cars and other items have been introduced into the process alongside the so-called 'traditional' items. However, these new and modern products - the 'modern' way of paying Bride Price - has in some cases led to Bride Price being seen as a showy affair that has resulted in the payment of "astronomical" amounts (Moore, 2013). The expectation that exorbitant amounts will be paid puts huge pressure on prospective grooms with small incomes.

In recent years in Zimbabwe, the practice of Bride Price has generated a great deal of debate and has faced criticisms from feminists, women's rights activists and some politicians, who have condemned it as an out-dated practice that promotes male domination and gender inequality, subjecting women to abuse and reducing their decision-making powers. It has also been criticised for being commercialised and commoditised in recent times, thus raising issues of affordability and equating women to purchasable commodities. This has prompted some women's rights activists in Zimbabwe to petition the constitutional court seeking abolition of the practice, but the case was lost in 2012. As I write this book, some female members of parliament and NGOs are battling with a bill in parliament that seeks to abolish the practice (Muzulu, 2014).

Despite the above arguments made by feminists and politicians, the voices of the most important stakeholders have been missing; the men and women at the grassroots level who are more affected by the practice of Bride Price. There are few studies that capture the voice of those actors, especially in cities and rural areas, and fewer still seek to explore perspectives across generations and transnationally. This study, therefore, attempts to fill this gap by analysing the views and experiences of those members of society. Accordingly, the main objective of this research is to provide a theoretically sound and informed study, based on a set of interrelated conceptions, of people's perceptions and experiences of Bride Price. Thus, the study is guided by the following heading: The Dynamics of Bride Price in Zimbabwe and the UK Diaspora.

This heading is based upon the assumption that Bride Price is in some way a gendered practice reinforced by feelings of masculinity and femininity in societies. It is also a class issue that, in some respects, conforms to forces of modernisation and modernity but at the same time resists those forces. This is geared to influence the way people perceive Bride Price, its process, and the experiences and outcomes of it for men and women. This book is based on months of field study with the Shona and the Ndebele ethnic groups in Birmingham, UK, and in urban and rural Zimbabwe.

1.2 Justification for the Research

Bride Price custom has existed for a long time, though with gradual changes and modifications that sometimes bring its relevancy and legitimacy into question. It is a common assumption that once modernisation occurs in a society, there would be a corresponding reduction in the level of traditional practices held by the society. However, in Zimbabwe, the Bride Price custom has tended to defy this assumption and is instead is gaining more momentum. This research seeks to ascertain if changes have occurred in how and why it is practised, and also considers if any changes reflect shifts in family structures and the respective roles of married men and women.

There are few documented studies that provide reasons for the continuation of the practice or that seek to understand wider shifts in marriage patterns and gendered expectations. As such, this book is situated in a clear knowledge gap, but my decision to focus on Bride Price is also because it represents a vehicle through which changes in patterns of gender relations within family structures and more widely across society can be addressed. This, of course, involves looking at the shifting make up of families across the settings of this study as well as probing the ways in which Bride Price is observed today.

There is a lot of debate in Zimbabwe about the relevancy of Bride Price payment; women's rights activists, legal professionals, religious leaders and other members of civil society often contribute to these debates. But there is limited empirical evidence to substantiate the different claims made by the groups in the debate. This study therefore tests theory in order to generate evidence-based knowledge about the dynamics of Bride Price payment and people's perceptions about it. The knowledge produced will contribute to informing academics, human rights activists, family scholars, legislators and other policymakers on how best to debate or legislate on reform in relation to the practice.

I also chose to focus on Bride Price because it is useful and important in terms of trying to understand changes within marital and household structures and the patterns of relationships within them. If I can capture changes in the way in which Bride Price is practised, that would also be an indicator of change within gender relations. Bride Price is central to marriage and so it offers a useful focus in terms of capturing shifts in how marriage is viewed and gendered; for example, in the respective expectations placed on women and men once married. If no changes are found in either or both Bride Price practices and gender relations, this would also highlight how embedded the practice is and how central certain ideas about gender are. Feminist literature on Bride Price such as Walby (1990), Tong (1993) and Lundgren (1995) argue that Bride Price maintains an unequal gendered hierarchy through marriage. Women are effectively bartered and sold at the point of marriage rendering them inferior to their husbands and vulnerable to violence and their autonomy and life opportunities are reduced. I want to explore the extent to which Bride Price still operates to instil unequal patterns of gender even after urbanisation and migration and in the context of a Westernised and global world.

1.3 Reasons for My Interest in this Area of Research

I recognise at the outset that the issue of Bride Price is not straightforward and that it is considered by many to be an important traditional cultural practice of considerable value, with a long history in various parts of Africa. However, since modernisation and globalisation have brought economic, social and cultural changes - both negative and positive - the need to reassess the practice in terms of these changes in the 'modern' age has been widely suggested to be necessary. Whilst acknowledging the historical significance and benefits of Bride Price to family and community integrity, conducting this enquiry in contemporary times is considered to be important, timely and highly relevant (Dery, 2015).

My interests lie in understanding individual experiences and the implicit meanings connected to Bride Price. I am also interested in capturing and putting on paper the viewpoints of those that are affected positively and negatively by the practice. It would have been interesting to gather the views of non-African women on Bride Price to determine the discourses that shape outer perceptions of the practice. However, the ambitions of my book were already great. In this respect, I sympathize with Grounded Theory, developed by Glaser and Strauss (1967) who emphasise the development of theory from empirical data in contrast to approaches which analyse data from 'a theoretical point of view'. My approach probably owes much to my cultural-anthropological background with its 'traditional' emphasis on ethnographic detail and reluctance to generalise as there may always be a counter-example in empirical reality. This has been pointed out by, amongst others, anthropologists such as Fishburne Collier and Yanagisako (1987) and post-colonial thinkers like Oyewùmí (2002, 1997).

I was conscious throughout, nevertheless, of the historical importance of Bride Price and of the significance of upholding African cultural beliefs in the contemporary era. It is particularly appreciated that 'cultural' rituals are not frequently universally advantageous or detrimental and that it is the changing nature of 'culture' that results in its prolonged existence (Dery, 2015). I therefore explored the link between culture and Bride Price by considering the adverse and the valuable features of it as experienced by my participants.

In deliberating on Bride Price in Zimbabwe and Birmingham (U K), it was critical to avoid the possible stigmatisation of African societies and beliefs as backward and not to take the continuation of the practice as evidence of this. Nevertheless, in many other cultures such as India and Greece, restructuring of customary systems has happened in more recent years (Dekker & Hoogeveen, 2002). This research is part of that trajectory. In the words of a senior church leader:

> Cultural practices usually have a good root - people generally do seek good. But then it can get distorted; as in this case by male dominance and particular views of women's sexuality. So, one needs to think it through - what is its value - its roots? How can one get rid of the parts that discriminate against women and hurt them?

> (Dekker & Hoogeveen, 2002, p. 55)

One very important aspect of Zimbabwean marriage is that families transfer goods and services on the occasion of marriage. Dowry and Bride Price are the two types of transfer that are present in Indian marriages. These two types of payments are not mutually exclusive, rather they can occur simultaneously (Rao, 1993). Dowry, which is the dominant practice between the two, has received wide attention from social scientists at large, whereas Bride Price has been examined to a lesser extent.

1.4 Intimate Partner Violence in Zimbabwe

Links between marriage practices and violence have been identified, in relation to dowry, for example (see e.g., Bradley, 2011). There is a high level of intimate partner violence in Zimbabwe with domestic violence on the increase according to police records which show that some 40,500 cases were reported between January and September 2016 alone as compared to 36450 during the same period in 2015. Speaking during the commemorations of the international day of gender-based violence (GBV) in Harare, UN resident coordinator Bishow Parajuli said there was a spike in cases of abuse, especially against women and girls. GBV is a grave violation of human rights with the problem deeply rooted in gender inequality and discrimination.

There are still many thousands of cases of GBV not being reported across the country and we know that even one case, is one too many. The UN believes that when GBV and gender inequalities are reduced, more children will go to school, families will be healthier, agricultural productivity will improve and incomes will increase. Parajuli further said that violence against women has serious consequences for development; it poses significant threats to households' economic welfare as it impacts scarce public resources for essential health, security and infrastructure services. Reports further indicated that one in every three girls in Zimbabwe experiences sexual violence before they turn eighteen years of age and 78 percent of women report that their husband or intimate partner is the perpetrator. In addition, women are in a worse position than men in terms of literacy in Zimbabwe despite being the majority with 48.7 percent of adult women having reached at least a secondary level of education compared to 62 percent of men (UNICEF, 2016).

The latest Zimbabwe Health Demographic Survey shows that, in terms of health, women are severely disadvantaged with a HIV prevalence rate of 18 percent between ages 15-49, compared to 12 percent among men.

(a) Prevalence Data on Different Forms of Violence against Women:

1. Lifetime Physical and/or Sexual Intimate Partner Violence: 35 percent. Proportion of ever-partnered women aged 15-49 years experiencing intimate partner physical and/or sexual violence at least once in their lifetime.

2. Physical and/or Sexual Intimate Partner Violence in the last twelve months: 20 percent. Proportion of ever-partnered women aged 15-49 years experiencing intimate partner physical and/or sexual violence in the last twelve months (Zimbabwe National Statistics Agency and ICF International, 2016; Zimbabwe Demographic and Health Survey, 2015).

Child Marriage: 34 percent. Percentage of women aged 20 to 24 years who were first married or in union before age 18 (UNICEF, 2016).

3. Gender Inequality Index Rank: 126.

The Gender Inequality Index is a composite measure reflecting inequality between women and men in three different dimensions: reproductive health (maternal mortality ratio and adolescent birth rate), empowerment (share of parliamentary seats held by women and share of population with at least some secondary education), and labour market participation (labour force participation rate) (UNICEF, 2016).

What is original about my book is the in-depth focus on Bride Price across generations and across context (from rural to urban Zimbabwe and from urban Zimbabwe to Birmingham). I wanted to understand the transnational dimension of Bride Price and how it may emerge differently in different contexts. Bride Price has been at the heart of marriage in these communities, influencing how gender relationships are structured. I wanted to understand if and how this is still the case and if so, how it influences gender relations more widely and in particular the position of women. In order to do so, I considered the following questions:

- How important is Bride Price in shaping marriage and gender relationships across these three contexts?

- Has the amount given gone up or down over time and what might this tell us about the continued importance of the practice?

- Does it become more important after migration/urbanisation? And if so why?

- Does Bride Price in any way shape the expectations then placed on men and women after marriage?

- Can Bride Price lead women to be abused?

Overall, my data shows that Bride Price is still as strong as it used to be; with globalisation and commodification, expectations have increased in terms of what might be given. Consumer goods and cash are now expected. The main difference across settings is that in both urban settings people contradict themselves - on one hand, they might say they think Bride Price is not necessary and in fact is not good for women as it projects them as inferior, while on the other hand, they say it must go on as it is fundamental to their cultural identity. In the rural site, however, people were clear that Bride Price is central to marriage and no contradictions were recorded. Furthermore, in the rural areas, the economic dimension of Bride Price is still acknowledged as important and across settings the link between Bride Price and cultural identity is strong. The importance of culture challenges some of the post-colonial feminist narratives that argue that culture should not be over emphasised in explanations of gender inequality. I argue it is more complex; Bride Price is seen as cultural and central, and it is also underpinning a gender ideology that renders women inferior and open to abuse.

1.5 Book Structure

This book consists of six chapters, plus this introductory chapter. This introduction lays out the theoretical dimensions of the research and the types of marriages in Africa and introduces the research topic, and the context of the subject. The chapter presents an overview of the book as a whole and provides the motivation behind the project, the research objective and the organization of the book. The rest of the book is organised as follows.

Chapter Two: Approaches to Researching Bride Price

This chapter not only outlines the methodology, but also discusses how the methodology is part of the originality of this book. I present my methodology which spans three different contexts and also pulls out inter-generational differences in order to understand shifting patterns in Bride Price and how different family members might view it. In order to do so, I have conducted qualitative interviews and focus group discussions, in rural and urban Zimbabwe and urban UK.

Chapter Three: Contextualising Bride Price: from the Global to the Local

In this chapter, I give the context of Bride Price, discussing what it is and where it is practised. I summarise the global literature around Bride Price which enables me to evidence the originality of my research. My review clearly shows that there is very little research on Bride Price in Zimbabwe and even less that seeks to take such a contemporary and transnational perspective.

Chapter Four: Analytical Framework: Post-colonial Theories, the Ecology Model & Bride Price

In this chapter, I present the critique by Uma Narayan in which she highlights the overuse of culture as the explanation behind abuse against women in African and Asian contexts. She describes cultural representations as Eurocentric and imperialist, reinforcing colonial power relationships. In my data analysis, I test out the extent to which culture is a key dimension or not in the continuation of Bride Price and also how it may feed into other forms of abuse. My book goes on to simultaneously agree and disagree with Narayan's critique. Culture and religion are given over and over as the most dominant dimension behind Bride Price.

The chapter also focuses on applying one tried and tested model, the ecology approach, developed by Lori Heise. This model is well known and has been used extensively within research on violence against women and it offers a useful way of unpacking how different economic, social, cultural, religious and political factors create an environment that sanctions particular constructs of gender that in turn may be oppressive or empowering. In other words, this model presents a way of unpacking how our environment is gendered at various levels and spheres from individual behaviours and mind-sets through to the social norms and views that then shape the relationships and institutions within which we live. I used this model in order to understand how and where Bride Price fits into constructing (or not) the gendered society of my research sites. It is also a helpful tool for comparing my three contexts.

Chapter Five: Cultural, Religious and Gendered Dimensions of Bride Price

One of my key findings draws out the dominance of religious and cultural beliefs and values in promoting the continued need for Bride Price despite the changing global contexts in which it is observed. The link between Bride Price, religion, culture and marriage is strong, and clearly feeds into wider gender relationships and the expectations for men and women in terms of duty and roles. The analysis here draws out the significant differences between the rural and the two urban settings, but these differences are not so pronounced between the two urban settings, despite one being in Zimbabwe and the other among the diaspora living in Birmingham (UK).

Chapter Six: Comparing the Three Contexts: Bride Price and Harm

In trying to answer the question of why Bride Price is still so strong and what its links with identity I found that it is not just a practice that structures marital and family relationships, it is integral to how people see the world and their place in it. This chapter explores the contradictions emerging from the data. Whilst people support Bride Price there is significant acknowledgement that it is not good for women. The 'harmful practice' category has been around for some time, but Bride Price has not always been considered within that category in the same way that FGM or honour crime has. What I am arguing through my research is that it should be. The harm it causes is complex and largely indirect; the practice in itself is not harmful but, I argue, it has harmful consequences. Capturing those harmful consequences is challenging because, as I found out, people see it as an integral part of their cultural identity and necessary in order to transition into married life. This chapter highlights the challenge facing activists who wish to see an end to Bride Price because of its role in reinforcing patriarchal gendered relations.

1.6 Conclusion: The Dynamics of Bride Price

In my conclusion, I return to my central argument; Bride Price should be seen as harmful because it does embed inequality that ultimately limits life opportunities for men and women. The economic element to the practice is lessening (in so far as families are not reliant on it for their wealth) but the explanations in terms of amount and type of price given has not; if anything, it has increased. The giving of Bride Price is still linked to honour and status: the more you give, the higher your standing. The pressure this puts on men and women is intense and this in itself could be seen as a harmful consequence of the practice.

***

While the introductory chapter has here presented an outline of the whole book, chapter two is rooted in the methodology of the research. This includes, but is not limited to, the choice of and justification for the methods applied and the reasons for discounting other potential methods. The originality of my book lies in its methodology, and particularly its application spanning three different contexts.

Chapter 2

Approaches to Researching Bride Price

This chapter describes and explains the methodology deployed in this study and the literature which informed my choice of methods. I outline the research strategy, research approach, the type of data analysis, the ethical considerations and the limitations of the research. By presenting the stages of study and methods deployed as well as the different locations in which the research was conducted, I set the scene for the subsequent chapters and justify why I used semi-structured interviews and focus groups for my fieldwork. The purpose of conducting the interviews in three different contexts is to answer the core research question which is whether urbanisation, modernisation and migration have an impact on Bride Price. To answer this question, it is important to understand women's (and men's) experiences of the importance and effect of Bride Price in contemporary times. Also outlined are the aims and methods of the study, the research questions, the data collection tools and the justification of those choices. Finally, I also highlight my unique position as an insider researcher; as a male researcher, my position is also unusual as this kind of research tends to be done by women.

In this chapter, I highlight the originality of my book by presenting my methodology which spans three different contexts and also pulls out inter-generational differences in order to understand shifting patterns in Bride Price and how different family members might view them differently.

2.1 Aims and Methods

The main focus of this book is to fill the gap left by a lack of an investigative study or methodical information on the subject of Bride Price. This is especially important because of the contradictions associated with the practice. On one hand, the practising communities acknowledge that the practice contributes to gender inequality and gender-based violence and on the other hand, they want the practice to continue. In other words, I intended to present new data that explores the extent to which Bride Price is harmful to women. I also wanted to understand the extent to which men and women still believe Bride Price to be central to marriage and to the formation of kinship networks and family life. The aim of the research was to explore the role that Bride Price has in people's lives today. I explored this across a number of contexts relating to Zimbabwe - rural, urban and diaspora - in order to determine the impact of the context on the nature and relevance of the practice. The objective was to consider how harmful Bride Price is to the pursuit of gender equality and more specifically for the aspirations and well-being of women. Furthermore, this book looks at how Bride Price payment has changed from a simple cultural practice into a highly commercialised venture, and how this has affected men and women. My aim was to provide an in-depth qualitative narrative of identity and belonging and to consider how the communities establish themselves around traditional practices that in turn legitimise these customs and secure their continuation. Furthermore, I considered how and if different practices are linked. For example, I assess whether FGM, which is shrouded in secrecy in Zimbabwe, is linked to Bride Price and if so, what implications this has on and for women's lives?

I used both semi-structured and open-ended questions in interviews that also aimed to capture women's views on whether Bride Price triggers gender-based violence and whether it is a contributory factor to their inferior status. These interviews also involved both men and women and were inter-generational, including with grandparents, parents and children, so as to capture societal and community influence. Four or more members per family were interviewed per site. I used the intersectional approach to ascertain how time of migration, ethnicity, race, age, socio-economic background in certain groups affect people's views of Bride Price. I wanted to capture both inter and cross-generational change. I asked questions around the impact of migration and urbanisation on the lives of women and men. I wanted to understand changes specifically around patterns of gender and how they shape family relationships across time and space. I also sought to capture changes in family structures, and a focus on Bride Price helps here because it is central to marriage negotiations and to the ceremony itself. In summary, I used Bride Price as a focus of my inquiry because it is at the heart of marriage practices; marriage practices are, in turn, at the heart of family structures and are fundamentally gendered.

My original methodology attempts to render visible subtle differences within the families spread across the three different contexts. I use this to draw out insights into how positioning affects how people see and regard the cultural practice of Bride Price. Additionally, I explored the extent to which living in Harare or Birmingham influences the expectation for Bride Price to take a commercial form.

2.2 The Analytical Approach and its Theoretical Motivations

A concern when working in a socio-cultural setting other than your own is the 'problem of ethnocentrism'. I have developed my analytic approach with this in mind. Gender is a theoretical and analytical concept, which is extremely informed by socio-cultural and political context. These political connotations and socio-cultural meanings may constitute major blind spots that manifest when an outside researcher writes about women from his or her own socio-cultural context. This may become more obvious and infused with a political power dimension when researching in a socio-cultural context which has been colonised.

The analytic approach is thus theoretically, methodologically and subjectively informed in that it reflects the choices I have made - sometimes, but not always clearly formulated - when approaching and interpreting the material (which includes how the interviews were conducted). This project uses gender, gender-meanings and relations, and gender-related power and structure as analytic tools to understand the role Bride Price still plays in the lives of Zimbabweans. However, in doing so, I do not deny the agency of my participant's. The analytical concept of 'agency' is more ontological in character. 'Agency' has a basic definition of intentionality in people's acting on and/or attempting to change their situation or relations. This intentionality is not seen as necessarily conscious or one-dimensional; it can encompass several dimensions.

The first analytical concepts presented below, 'the analytical trinity', gender, gender-meanings and relations and gender-related power, which will be used in the interpretations of the interviews will be further developed in the interpretation-process. I attempted to develop an approach that did not close the interpretation in relation to specific theories and/or my own socio-cultural frame of reference, but instead enabled the analysis to be as open to the interview material as possible. This approach does not presuppose a 'blank' interpreter with no frames of reference but aims to allow the interpreter to be flexible in approaching the material. The analytical terms are thus used as searching tools in approaching and interpreting the text. The analytical trinity has been developed also as a consequence of an insight developed throughout the analysis: that gender as a theoretical category should not be separated from gender-related power.

This insight came about when I started to look for 'gender meanings' connected to Bride Price in the interview-texts. My approach stressed that we need to 'think power' as soon as we 'think gender' in order not to lose important dimensions of the empirical material. But this does not mean that there is a one-dimensional relationship, only that gender and gender-related power must be 'held together' analytically. Gender is seen empirically as both a cultural construction (with cultural meaning) and a social power relation. Thus, the first three analytical terms discussed - gender, gender-related power, and gender meanings and relations - should not be seen as analytically separate but as interrelated analytical terms focusing different dimensions of the empirical material (Anderson, 2007).

2.3 Gender

A problem in the sex/gender definition, which can also be connected to problems in feminist theory in general, is whether gender should be seen as an over-contextual/universal category or alternatively as determined by context and as situational. By making a clear distinction between sex and gender and by defining sex as biology and beyond socio-cultural relations, gender easily becomes an over-contextual analytical category with definable 'contents' even if the contents are seen as socio-culturally constructed: masculinity is rationality, femininity is emotionality. With the above definition of gender as a socio-cultural construction of sex and the distinction made between sex and gender, gender can also be analysed as contextual 'content'; different organisations may, for instance, be analysed as having different definitions of masculinity and femininity. The extreme end of the contextualisation of gender in feminist theory is the post-modern feminist theories in which the subject and subjectivity is seen as fluid, fragmented and at the same time determined by the subject's positions in relation to different discourses (Dorow, 2006).

I used gender as an 'open' analytical concept without a predefinition. This was to avoid related problems with predefinitions of gender as purely positional in local contexts and in discursive positions and as an over-contextual category. There is one premise for being able to use 'gender' as an open analytical term and that is that there is a socio-cultural categorisation and distinction made between men and women in the society studied. But not that this distinction is founded in biology (although to some extent it is dependent on the socio-cultural use of anatomical differences in making a distinction between two socio-cultural categories of people) and/or dichotomously essentialised into two different kinds of beings. This premise also includes an understanding of gender as an important part of the sociocultural organisation of society.

Bride Price payment and some of the procedures and experiences involved are heavily influenced by notion of masculinity and femininity and are highly gendered in nature. McClintock (2013) looks at gender as constituting:

> an institution that establishes patterns of expectations for individuals, orders the social processes of everyday life, is built into the major social organisation of society, such as the economy, ideology, family and politics and is also an entity in and of itself

> (McClintock,2013, p. 1)

Still, in line with the notion of masculinity, Bride Price payment is used to reinforce those feelings, especially in the amount one is able to pay. One participant stated that a groom's handsomeness is not reflected on his face or physical appearance but in his wallet. That is to say, how much property or cash he is able to pay for the bride. So, even if a man is considered ugly or too old, he is likely to get a beautiful young bride as long as he has a lot of property in order to pay. Some parents have gone further in trying to match their daughters to wealthy men even if it meant withdrawing their daughters from school; some men with less income, in trying to prove their 'handsomeness', have resorted to fundraising, selling land or acquiring bank loans in order to pay hefty amounts and prove their worth. Here, we see a society that is mixing Bride Price and marriage with economics rather than with romantic love, as well as a belief that money and wealth belong to males and not necessarily females. For this reason, men sometimes tend to shy away from marriage.

In terms of femininities and Bride Price, it was observed that girls are socialised from childhood to grow up as 'good' girls and become 'good' women/brides so as to attract responsible husbands capable of paying good amounts; this practice cements girls' femininities. They are taught how to dress well, sit well, respect elders and boys, how to walk, talk and even how to 'perform well in bed after marriage' and never to annoy the husband even if he wrongs her (Tamale, 2009). Among the Shona and Ndebele tribes where this study was rooted, this role is normally done by paternal aunties, locally known as *kurairwa* (well mannered). On the day of Bride Price payment, this paternal aunt is always at hand to lead and guide the niece so that every step she makes is done 'well'.

It can be observed that such processes and socialisation of the girls and brides into what is referred to as 'behaving well as a woman' tend to reinforce the gender stereotypes of what a 'good/proper' woman should be or how they should behave, and it is this socialisation that perpetuates femininities and masculinities. Such stereotypes and views of women have further encouraged societies, especially in Africa, to develop rigid customary laws and practices that have translated into social structures that promote the subordination of women (Schmidt, 1991; Mama, 1996; and Musisi, 2002). As Musisi put it:

> As a wife if you don't submit to your husband, it will be like two lions in the same house, so there will be always quarrels, there will always be fights. So, one has to submit, so that there would be that unit, that peace in the marriage and in the family.
>
> (Musisi, 2002, p. 45)

In some extreme cases, a woman is perceived as having a weak mind; she should always be guided and guarded in her actions and should even be owned like any other household possession (Tamusuza, 2002). In the discussions I had, that perception featured prominently. Women who take up these constructed identities of a woman end up behaving in a way that conforms to the socially allocated feminine roles. However, with the increasing campaigns by feminists and other activists and with modernisation, such perceptions are changing. This is further elaborated below in relation to intersectional analysis.

2.4 Intersectionality

The concept of intersectionality has gained popularity, especially in feminist scholarship, and is seen as having potential to analyse peoples' problems and experiences from a multidimensional point of view which guards against the danger of being monolithic and shallow in inquiry. It looks at the interaction of multiple and intertwined identities, experiences of exclusion, subordination or oppression. Rather than focusing on gender as a singular entity, it instead focusses on issues of difference and diversity among women (and also men) while giving clear attention to issues of race, class, power, sexuality, status, financial status, disability, and heteronormativity along with gender, depending on the prevailing characteristics of people under study (Davis, 2008).

Brah and Phoenix (2004) while emphasizing the need for an intersectional approach, argue that studies need to analyse how social class and intersections with gender and race or sexuality operate simultaneously to affect one's social positioning and daily experiences, and how analysing their intersections leads to a more complex understanding of reality than focusing on a single characteristic. They emphasize the issue of multiple, intersecting and relational nature of realities and subordinations (Brah & Phoenix, 2004, p. 77). Verloo (2006) also argues that while studying gender experiences or when formulating gender equality policies or studies, it is advisable to focus on the multiplicity of inequalities rather than assuming similarity of inequalities at the structural level. Thus, there is a need to focus on and compare the specific sets of inequalities or experiences of class, race, ethnicity, sexual orientation and gender. This calls for attention to structural and political intersectionality in order to analyse issues of multiple discrimination and the dynamics and processes that constitute them. The assumption of 'one size fits all' is thus discouraged (Verloo, 2006, p. 211).

In line with the above argument, and as reviewed in the previous chapter, Mohanty, Russo and Torres (1991) counsel feminist scholars in their production of knowledge about women to avoid generalisation and homogenisation of women and their experiences as a homogeneous category of analysis, on the assumption that women are 'an always -already constituted group', they instead argue that not all women (or women in the 'third world') are homogeneous, nor do they suffer subordination uniformly because they have diverse and multiple identities.

As the discussion above shows, the concept of intersectionality not only helped me to analyse the data but also to select the participants. For example, it helped me to select participants based on gender, sex, class, education level, financial status, and age, or position in the family or community. I also endeavoured to assess how some of these characteristics and forces overlap in certain individuals and how the responses, perceptions and experiences about Bride Price are influenced by or interact with some of those characteristics. But most importantly, this approach facilitated a greater understanding of the interrelationships of the concepts of gender, masculinity, class and modernisation in relation to Bride Price.

Notions of gender, masculinities, social class and modernisation do influence people's experiences and perceptions of Bride Price; each notion is not in isolation, but instead, all interact at some level to create multiple levels of perceptions, experiences, outcomes and even masculine or feminine identities. While studying phenomena such as those that are gendered, it is imperative to analyse the multiplicity of cases or inequalities instead of assuming similarity at all levels. This calls for comparison of the specific sets of experiences of class, race, ethnicity and gender while attending to the intersectionality of processes and dynamics that influence or constitute them (Verloo, 2006).

2.5 The Research Approach

In Stage One, initial (pilot) interviews were held with Zimbabweans in Birmingham. Discussions were held with key experts in the United Kingdom and in the African diaspora, which was followed by an international field trip to Zimbabwe. In Stage Two, data was collected from three locations to assess women's perceptions of the impact of Bride Price. A short questionnaire was also completed with all participants to collect socio-demographic data. The majority of these interviews were tape-recorded with the participant's agreement, as well as notes being taken by the researcher. All interviews were then transcribed. Additional sets of individual and group interviews were conducted in the UK. Following an initial analysis of the qualitative data, a thematic analysis was further developed (across all the data-sets) was developed for Stage Three. The thematic analysis emphasizes pinpointing, examining, and recording patterns (or 'themes') within data. 'Themes' are patterns across data sets that are important to the description of a phenomenon and are associated to a specific research question. A process of critical reflection also took into consideration the challenges and achievements of the research. Information gathered as part of this participative process, along with all data gathered, was then fed into the final book.

I interviewed a wide range of women and men, including some newly married couples. These interviews numbered thirteen in total and they included thirty-seven women and thirty-one men from the Shona and the Ndebele tribes, although the Shona were the most numerous. The interviewees had a wide-range of occupations, but the majority were professionals in their own right. Four focus group families were interviewed in Birmingham and these included husband and wife, their parents and where possible their grandparents. The families were then traced in Harare, where four family focus groups were also held, and these families were then also traced back to their rural homes, where four more family interviews were conducted. Tracing families from Birmingham to Harare then to the rural areas and interviewing in these three sites represents one of the original contributions of my book.

Table 2.1. Participants (Birmingham, UK).

Location	Method	Occupation	Age	Gender	Marital Status	Tribe
Birmingham	Women focus group	Social Worker	46	Female	Single	Ndebele
		Radiographer	36	Female	Married	Ndebele
		Social Worker	34	Female	Married	Ndebele
		Nurse	28	Female	Married	Shona
		Teacher retired	66	Female	Married	Shona
		Care Assistant	32	Female	Married	Shona
Family B	Family focus group	Research Assistant (daughter in law)	26	Female	Married	Shona
		Pilot (Son)	28	Male	Married	Shona
		Nurse (mother)	46	Female	Married	Shona
		Lecturer (father)	47	Male	Married	Shona
		Retired Nurse (grandmother)	68	Female	Married	Shona
		Retired Teacher (grandfather)	72	Male	Married	Shona
Family A	Family focus group	Care Assistant (daughter)	24	Female	Married	Ndebele
		Student Nurse (son in law)	25	Male	Married	Ndebele
		Teacher (father)	54	Female	Married	Ndebele
		Social Worker (mother)	59	Male	Married	Ndebele

Family C	Family focus group	Paediatrician (daughter)	30	Female	Married	Shona
		Civil Engineer (son in law)	34	Male	Married	Shona
		Director: Nursing Agency (mother)	59	Female	Married	Shona
		Director: Nursing Agency (father)	60	Male	Married	Shona
Family D	Family focus group	Social Worker (daughter in law)	27	Female	Married	Shona
		Pharmacist (son)	29	Male	Married	Shona
		Nurse (mother)	48	Female	Married	Shona
		Accountant (father)	52	Male	Married	Shona

Table 2.2. Participants (Bulawayo & Harare, Zimbabwe).

Location	Method	Occupation	Age	Gender	Marital Status	Tribe
Bulawayo Zimbabwe Family A	Family focus group	Receptionist/Secretary (sister)	26	Female	Married	Ndebele
		Footballer (brother in law)	28	Male	Married	Ndebele
		Lawyer (aunt)	49	Female	Married	Ndebele
		Car sales Trader (uncle)	53	Male	Married	Ndebele
		Retired Lawyer (grandmother)	74	Female	Married	Ndebele
		Retired Teacher (grandmother)	78	Male	Married	Ndebele
Family B **Harare**	Family focus group	Housewife (daughter in law)	28	Female	Married	Shona
		Pastor (brother)	35	Male	Married	Shona
		Social Worker (aunt)	57	Female	Married	Shona
		Electrician (uncle)	61	Male	Married	Shona
Family C	Family focus group	Vendor (daughter in law)	20	Female	Married	Shona
		Vendor (son)	24	Male	Married	Shona
		Teacher (aunt)	47	Female	Married	Shona
		Teacher (uncle)	50	Male	Married	Shona
		Housewife (grandmother)	72	Female	Married	Shona
		Member of Parliament (grandfather)	74	Male	Married	Shona

Family D	Family focus group	Teacher (daughter in law)	38	Female	Married	Shona
		Businessman Motor spares trader (son)	42	Male	Married	Shona
		Retired Teacher (mother)	61	Female	Married	Shona
		Retired Teacher (father)	68	Male	Married	Shona

Table 2.3. Participants (Rural Zimbabwe).

Location	Method	Occupation	Age	Gender	Marital Status	Tribe
Rural areas (**Near Bulawayo**) Zimbabwe Family A (**Near Harare**)	Family focus group	Vendor (brother)	22	Female	Married	Ndebele
		Vendor (sister in law)	28	Male	Married	Ndebele
		Housewife (aunt)	51	Female	Married	Ndebele
		Truck driver (uncle)	59	Male	Married	Ndebele
		Subsistence-Farmer (grandmother)	83	Female	Married	Ndebele
		Subsistence-Farmer (grandfather)	91	Male	Married	Ndebele
Family B	Family focus group	Student teacher (sister)	21	Female	Married	Shona
		Student teacher (brother in law)	24	Male	Married	Shona
		Teacher (aunt)	43	Female	Married	Shona
		Teacher (uncle)	48	Male	Married	Shona
		Housewife (grandmother)	70	Female	Married	Shona
		Pastor (grandfather)	79	Male	Married	Shona
Family C	Family focus group	Nursery Teacher (daughter in law)	21	Female	Married	Shona
		Builder (son)	30	Male	Married	Shona
		Farmer-Cattle rancher (aunt)	55	Female	Married	Shona
		Farmer-Cattle rancher (uncle)	60	Male	Married	Shona
		Subsistence-Farmer (grandmother)	82	Female	Married	Shona
		Subsistence-Farmer (grandfather)	89	Male	Married	Shona

		Housewife (daughter)	23	Female	Married	Shona
		Bus driver (son)	27	Male	Married	Shona
Family D	Family focus group	Retail-Businesswoman (aunt)	54	Female	Married	Shona
		Retail-Businessman (uncle)	61	Male	Married	Shona
		Subsistence-Farmer (grandmother)	87	Female	Married	Shona
		Subsistence-Farmer (grandfather)	90	Male	Married	Shona

I chose qualitative research over quantitative research data collection tools since the primary concern of the research was to understand in detail the beliefs, feelings and perceptions of participants, and so a more open-ended and detailed approach was necessary. Chambers (2007) notes that a qualitative approach allows researchers to explore situations where little is known. It is adequate in exploring sensitive issues and for allowing participants to speak for themselves. Denscombe describes this approach to data collection as follows:

> Qualitative research is an umbrella term that covers a variety of styles of social research, drawing on a variety of disciplines such as sociology, social anthropology and social psychology.

(Denscombe, 2010, p. 207)

Although the research presented in this book is derived from analysed data, the use of qualitative research would support Corbin, Strauss and Strauss (2014) who suggest that the use of qualitative information is vital to a researcher as it gives them the scope to derive new theories from the data collected. I used Grounded Theory as a method of analysing the data collected. Grounded Theory is a general research method (which is not owned by any one school or discipline), which guides matters of data collection and can be applied to quantitative data or qualitative data of any type) (Glaser & Strauss, 2009). Strengths associated with qualitative research are that it has no set rules on what method of data analysis to use as compared to quantitative research. Since this research includes a literature review it is worth noting that Corbin, Strauss and Strauss (2014) stress that analysis of data needs to be rigorous as it is the overall strategy of doing the research. The literature helped me to identify what has not been looked at/explored, to identify suitable approaches to data collection, to look at the ethics needed to frame the research and to consider how to analyse it how to analyse it.

As a researcher it is important to realise that although qualitative research would be appropriate for a project where in-depth inquiry is needed, particularly on a topic that is under-researched, there are limitations to this method; qualitative data has to be interpreted and here debate can ensue over which particular interpretation is the right one. The researcher's bias could lead or skew the analysis of data, this is particularly problematic when the research topic is emotive, and the researcher has an activist position in relation to it. Denscombe (2010) further states that the researcher's identity, background and beliefs have a role in the creation of data and its analysis. I was therefore in a position to understand both my own feelings and those of the participants. Having stated that Bride Price is a sensitive topic, care on how data was handled was of paramount concern to me.

2.6 Semi-Structured Interviews

Semi-structured interviews were chosen as the most appropriate data-gathering technique. This was because the research strategy intended to gather information concerning the interviewee's personal beliefs, and their considered opinions and insights, not just in relation to the practices under study. These may be difficult to obtain through structured interviews where rigid questioning prevents opportunities to pursue an interesting angle or call for elaboration. I felt that structured interviews were not the best for the topic of Bride Price because the use of rigid questions could limit the possibility of unexpected views emerging, and indeed runs counter to the use of a Grounded Theory. The semi-structured interview technique provides sufficient flexibility to gain insights that may otherwise be lost by the imposition of the 'next' structured question. However, at the same time it allows a list of questions to be given to participants as part of the process of gaining their consent and explaining the topic under study; doing away with questions altogether makes the ethical process difficult. Its goal is to elicit rich, detailed material that can be used in analysis and the production of a narrative drawn from the experiences and insights of participants (Lofland & Lofland, 2006).

Such interviews are best conducted face to face, as they can allow the researcher and participants to share a common understanding of the topic and circumstances, feel relaxed and build the trust and rapport needed when sensitive topics are looked at. I felt that it was important to use open-ended questions in conjunction with a checklist to guide me during interviews and to ensure uniformity, consistency of facts, opinions and unexpected insights. By conversing with the participants, I corrected any misinterpretations by repeating back the answers I thought I had heard. In practice, internal validity checks were conducted during the interviews by using prompts such as, "so what you are saying is…" or "is this a correct interpretation?". This interview method was useful in overcoming internal invisibility. Schein (1993) argues that interviewees cannot tell the researcher about the basic assumptions or how they are patterned because they have ceased to be aware of them.

The interview schedule was established around a number of key themes, informed by the literature. Bradley and Harrell (2009) suggest that this thematic structure will allow "people to answer more on their own terms than the standardised interview permits, but still provide a greater structure for comparability over that of the focused interview." Since the topic of Bride Price was viewed as controversial by many studies in the literature review, interviews were secured during the process of document review examination. According to Trochim & Donnelly (2010), interviews have a number of advantages and disadvantages as discussed below.

Interviews offer the ability to let the interviewee see, feel and/or taste a product. The researcher is offered the opportunity to target the population he may wish to interview. In so doing the researcher is able to identify the population that can stand prolonged interviews thus giving both the interviewer and the interviewee the opportunity to perceive each other's body language and non-verbal responses.

Semi-structured interviews yield the richest data, details and new insights and offer the researcher the opportunity and flexibility to probe further and obtain immediate responses. They allow the interviewees to 'speak their minds' and thus explore the topic in-depth. Nevertheless, there are draw backs with interviews too; they cost more in terms of time and finance than other methods. This is true of in-home interviews, where travel time is a major factor. Interviews offer no reflexivity; the interviewee may express what the interviewer wants to hear whether it is true or not and the researcher will not be in a position to dispute that. Therefore, requiring the researcher to probe further to verify the facts may result in the same question being asked several times.

The amount of information recorded during interviews may appear in large volumes, making it difficult for the interviewer to transcribe in fear of deleting important issues raised, thus resulting in inconsistencies across interviews. According to Denscombe (2010), the advantage of interviews is their validity. I tried to ensure the reliability and validity of the study by asking follow-up questions that also gave me an opportunity to interact further with the interviewees and to make sure that what they said was what they meant to say. During the interviews, there was direct contact with the interviewees, which means that data collected can be checked for accuracy and relevance. However, this may make it difficult to gain consistency and objectivity.

In data analysis, researches arrange and portray the data in ways that help detect patterns or problems, explore associations that exist in data, and generally see if the data are consistent with their hypobook or theories.

(Harris, Hoyle & Judd, 2002, p. 425)

Having collected data through the literature review and the qualitative semi-structured interviews, it was important to analyse the data. This data consisted of recorded information from written notes taken during the interviews. There are various computer programs that may be used to analyse qualitative data (Tesch, 1990; Dey, 2003); this project used colour coding. The researcher used colour coding in the classification of themes coming out of the interviews. Interestingly, some themes began to appear in most of the interviews which in turn allowed for a comparative analysis. Moreover, virtually all the themes came out in different questions.

The importance of coding to a researcher is asserted by Strauss (1987), any researcher who wishes to become proficient at doing qualitative analysis must learn to code well and easily. The excellence of the research rests in a large part on the excellence of the coding (1987, p. 27). Fuller & Petch (1995) recommend that whether data is to be analysed manually or by computer, it must be checked and coded, transformed into orderly and systematic categories. This involved assigning symbols for variables identified. Whilst conducting the interviews I recorded and took notes for coding and referencing. The relevant interview data was collected and analysed; potential regularities, patterns and explanations were flagged and placed into relevant categories that were conceptually linked to the thematic guides. The project is rooted in Grounded Theory which places an emphasis on how social researchers organise their qualitative data, how they code their material and interpret the data. However, its limitation is that it does not accept that qualitative research can 'speak for itself' (Denscombe, 2010). There are no specific units that are used when analysing data, this depends on the research being carried out. In this research, the data matrix consisted of each individual involved in the study as they have their different values relating the themes identified throughout the interview schedules (see Appendix).

Having analysed the different methods of data collection that I used and those that I discounted in this research, I conclude that qualitative research is best suited for this kind of project. This is further reinforced by the fact that qualitative research is useful for studying a limited number of cases in depth and for describing complex phenomena. Furthermore, it is useful for conducting cross-case comparisons and analysis, which in this case was useful for making comparisons between the responses recorded from all the focus groups. Qualitative research is also useful in providing an understanding and description of people's personal experiences of phenomena and can describe phenomena in rich detail as they are situated and embedded in local contexts.

2.6.1 Focus Group

"...focus groups are small, homogeneous groups representative of the target population and of key informants brought together to discuss pertinent issues. In needs analysis, focus groups are conducted to discuss community needs and priorities."

(Alston & Bowles, 2003, p.136)

Home (1997, p.128) also equates that focus groups are a data collection method in which people reflect together on a topic that matters to them. He further says focus groups harness rather than control the group process and are especially apt when participants are knowledgeable about the topic and interested in it. Denscombe (1996) reiterates this by stating that focus groups are useful in exploring attitudes on non-sensitive, non-controversial topics. Although contrarily, this topic is both of the above I feel with a focus group the researcher would be in a position to elicit reliable information from the participants taking into account their attitudes towards the practice. The researcher should be knowledgeable about power differences when conducting group work and should be able to diffuse the situation while at the same time valuing each individual's opinion. Furthermore, focus groups were chosen because they encourage people to interact and share experiences. Focus groups do not discriminate against those who cannot write, and they encourage participation from all group members cross-culturally. This makes focus groups a data collection technique particularly sensitive to cultural variables-hence it is used in cross-cultural research and work with ethnic minorities. Nevertheless, the downside of focus groups is that the articulation of group norms may cause group dynamics.

2.7 Ethical Issues

Ethical issues were of particular importance as there were some cultural differences to consider, not least between the researcher and some of the communities under study. The topic of harmful cultural practices is highly sensitive in nature and could potentially provoke a range of emotional responses. However it should be noted that the participants interviewed were not asked directly their views on the practices rather, the focus was on understanding the influence that migration and urbanisation might have in shaping the mind-sets of the communities in relation to the practice, as well as their wider views on any possible change in Bride Price and the implications that it has on and for the lives of men and women. As the aim of this research was to explore change in Bride Price and its implications, it was important to approach the participants who were recruited through my network in a non-discriminatory manner.

In focus groups, issues of confidentiality automatically arise as people may disclose personal accounts which they do not want to be exposed to the general public; ground rules were therefore set at the beginning which included confidentiality and respect. As Lee & Renzetti note:

> Ethics has to do with application of a system of moral principles to prevent harming or wronging others to promote the good, to be respectful and to be fair.

> (Lee & Renzetti, 1993, p. 15)

Sieber (1992) states that a prerequisite of ethical problem solving is accurate assessments of the potential for risks, which could include invasion of privacy, breach of confidentiality and embarrassment, equitable treatment of the parties that are involved and safety of the individuals. These risks have been identified in the focus group schedule. Cultural sensitivity was of great importance whilst carrying out ethical research; the researcher reflected and evaluated himself and others around him. He maintained an open mind and avoided judging any disclosures made. The research was submitted to the University of Portsmouth's ethics committee for ethical screening and clearance, upon which the committee mentioned that it is important for the researcher to respect the rights and the dignity of the participants of the research and that it must be of benefit to the participants given their vulnerability.

The researcher ensured confidentiality and anonymity by not disclosing either the project or the participants interviewed to outsiders. Participants were advised that there would be a possibility for some of the data collected to be looked at by authorised persons from the University of Portsmouth. Data may be looked at by authorised people to check that the study is being carried out correctly. Consent was sought from all participants and the questions were shown to all potential interviewees before the interviews, giving participants the time and opportunity to decide on whether to continue or withdraw. The participants were approached to confirm that they understood what was required of them. The researcher ensured that the language used was simple English and avoided using jargon.

I also acknowledged my position in the Zimbabwean community, where I am well known due to my late father's high- profile political position. The risk here was that people might have been hesitant to enter into an open conversation with me worried about my thoughts over their responses. My father was well respected, and people looked up to him. There was a possibility that people would hold back from sharing information that may (in their view) place them in a bad light. I did not want my participants to feel inferior to me, this was obviously not the case, but I felt this might make them feel uneasy. I mitigated this by making sure they felt comfortable and understood the research process and protocols around confidentiality. I also maintained awareness through the process and would have stopped the interviews if I felt people were feeling uncomfortable.

Due to the respect that my father had in the Zimbabwe diaspora community, I was concerned that participants would feel obligated to take part in my research. To mitigate this, I set out a very lengthy three-month process of meeting different families and talking to individual family members to ensure that they understood what my study was about and to ensure that they felt comfortable with the questions. These informal discussions also helped to inform my research through the establishment of informal connections; it required time to build such trust. And only once I was confident that they were happy to participate did I move forward. I did not feel, however, that my standing in the community affected or inhibited the focus groups because the questions that I was asking were neither deliberately sensitive nor likely to provoke arguments or tensions. It was a conversation about family structures and change over time, which is a very common conversation held in diaspora households.

I did not interview women, I instead worked with a female researcher who is a trained community development worker. The peer ethnographer conducted one female focus group in Birmingham; I did the rest of the data collection which included four family focus groups in Birmingham, four family focus groups in Harare and four family focus groups in the rural areas. She did not use my data for her research, nor did I use her data for my research. She collected the data for me for my research due to the sensitivity of the issues. She was working on an FGM topic whilst I was working on Bride Price.

2.8 Research Locations

The research was located in Birmingham (UK), and in Harare, rural Mashonaland and Bulawayo and also some rural areas in Matabeleland in the south of Zimbabwe. Although the limited research focus restricted the study to these Districts, were selected for the following reasons: Bride Price takes specific forms in Mashonaland and Matabeleland that need particular examination and investigation. In addition, it was easier to travel around Harare and Bulawayo Districts due to reliable communication and transport networks which helped me to facilitate the research which otherwise might have been very difficult. In order to avoid possible bias, the research areas were carefully selected to include rural areas in Mashonaland and Matabeleland. Bride Price customs operate differently in other parts of Zimbabwe, an obvious example being Bulawayo where it is still a token of appreciation, although it can reach high levels of expenditure. The findings and recommendations which this research aimed to unearth were likely to have relevance across Zimbabwe and internationally.

H Harare
B Bulawayo

Figure 2.1. Map 1. Administrative Map of Zimbabwe.

Birmingham, United Kingdom:

The Zimbabwean community in the UK consists of people who have migrated from Zimbabwe and those born in the United Kingdom. They represent a diverse community, comprised of people from all walks of life and of different racial, ethnic and political affiliations. They include those seeking political asylum, those who came to work, students, unrecorded migrants, and those who have acquired British citizenship.

The migration of Zimbabweans to the UK is categorised into three stages by the International Organisation for Migration (IOM). The first surge of migration of Zimbabweans to the UK began with white Zimbabweans who left Zimbabwe after the country gained its independence from Britain in 1980.The second main wave, from 1989 until 1998, was triggered by the collapse of the economy and subsequent hardship that followed the programmes that were designed by the International Monetary Fund (IMF) and the World Bank (2017) to restructure the economy: the Economic Structural Adjustment Programme. Before November 2002, Zimbabweans did not require a visa when they travelled to the UK, and this presented a route through which to claim political asylum. It has been difficult for Zimbabweans to travel and seek political asylum in the UK since November 2002 when the British Government launched visa requirements for Zimbabweans wish to enter the country. The number of political asylum claims made by Zimbabweans fell as a result and growing numbers have since been going to South Africa to seek asylum. The number fell from 185,950 before the introduction of the visas in November 2002 to 35,350 after (IOM, 2018).

Most of the Zimbabweans in the UK are first-generation immigrants. According to the UK Census of 2011, there were 9,850 Zimbabwean-born people living in the country in 1971. This number increased to 18,340 in 1981 and to 95,720 in 1991. The 2001 Census registered 195,995 Zimbabwean-born people living in the UK. Unofficial figures that estimate the population vary considerably (Wintour, 2009). The figures for Zimbabweans living in the UK are rough and based on estimates. However, the 2001 census recorded a 205 percent increase from the 1991 count. The Zimbabwean British population, including those born in the UK to Zimbabwean parents, is also unclear, with estimates also varying considerably. Many papers have put the population at one million, and an estimate of 700,000 was reported by *The Independent* in 2005. Some community groups and leaders assert that the population is in the range of 600,000 to 800,000.

Regardless of the lack of clarity regarding exact numbers, the Zimbabwean population has spread across the UK, and the majority of the Zimbabweans are found in the large cities and towns. The table below shows the geographic spread of Zimbabwean people in the UK in 2006, based on estimates by the IOM and community leaders (IOM, 2018). The influx of Zimbabweans to the UK was partly contributed to by the enlargement of the National Health Service (NHS) which attracted many Zimbabwean doctors and nurses, and the economic and political collapse in Zimbabwe also contributed to the increase in refugee numbers. There is no explicit tribal integrated information for different groups of Zimbabweans in the UK. But in recent research carried out among a thousand Zimbabweans in the UK, most interviewees identified themselves as black and Shona. Eighty percent spoke Shona fluently while fifteen percent were fluent in both Shona and Ndebele. Twenty percent of those interviewed were monoglot white English-speaking Zimbabweans (IOM, 2018).

Most of the Zimbabweans live in Birmingham, Leeds and London and its northern commuter towns such as Luton, Milton Keynes and Slough. Zimbabweans who are settled in the UK are dispersed as a result of the strategy by the British Government of spreading refugees across the country and also partially due to the local significance of care work, for instance in coastal and other retirement centres (Humphris, 2010). The UK received an increased number of Zimbabwean asylum seekers around 1999, when 12,050 applications for asylum were made compared to only 2350 in 1998. The number of applications increased in correlation to the scope of violence and economic and political instability in Zimbabwe. The UK Border Agency also received a considerable increase of asylum applications between 1999-2005 as Zimbabwe's situation deteriorated, and this culminated in country becoming UK's top asylum-seeking nation (Mbiba, 2012).

The imposition of visa requirements for Zimbabweans visiting the UK in December 2002 reduced the number coming to the UK. In spite of the restrictions, Zimbabwe still remained the UK's top asylum-seeking nation. To counter this obstacle, Zimbabweans coming to the UK resorted to using either Malawian or South African passports (McGregor, 2009). In the long term, this led to the reduction of asylum applications from Zimbabweans in the UK as authorities tightened the entry requirements. Nonetheless, the intensifying violence in Zimbabwe between 2007-2010 saw the country retain its top spot on the UK's asylum-seeking nations list. The number of asylum claims from Zimbabwe was double that of the second-ranked asylum-seeking country in the UK (Home Office, 2009a). There were also large numbers of unescorted children from Zimbabwe seeking asylum in the UK in 2000, though the number of unaccompanied children is small as measured against the overall number of asylum claims from Zimbabwe (Mbiba, 2012).

Transnational Ties:

Zimbabweans in the UK retain consistent and continued social, economic, political and cultural international links with their folks back home and in the wider diaspora (Bloch, 2008). For instance, they take part keenly in transnational diaspora politics. Zimbabweans in the UK describe transnational diaspora politics as:

giving financial support to the MDC, as an alternative democratic space from the shrinking and repressive conditions in the homeland as internationalising the Zimbabwean crisis and as an avenue for permanent settlement.

(Pasura, 2010; McGregor, 2011, p. 202)

Besides the transnational diaspora politics, huge links connecting diasporas with their native country are expressed principally by way of remittances, and factual or symbolic connections are articulated via music, language and food at social and religious get-togethers in the host country. For instance, IOM argues that:

Zimbabweans have strong social and economic ties to Zimbabwe and the inter-connectedness of these ties is evidenced by regular contact with family members in Zimbabwe and the sending of regular monetary remittances.

(IOM, 2018, p. 1)

The IOM's study shows that seventy percent of the interviewees support their families and relatives back home through economic remittances.

Although settlement and the idea of return provide both purpose and contradiction in people's lives, Zimbabweans in Britain are eager to participate in their country's reconstruction. As the Zimbawe-IOM 2012 survey indicates seventy percent of respondents in her study would like to contribute to their country's development, that is, if the following changes are made: opening of the political space; voting rights in Zimbabwean elections; economic opportunities; and dual nationality. Hence, the full potential of the diaspora can only be realised if a mutual and trusting relationship exists between the diaspora and the homeland government. If diaspora capital is to be tapped, then it is important for the government to engage the diaspora in productive ways that are designed to rebuild the country.

The migration of Zimbabweans to Britain, has engendered a proliferation of diasporic media. As Mano and Willems (2008) point out, the emerging media provided the space for interaction between the diaspora and the homeland. It became the conduit to express socio-cultural, economic and political transnational ties between the diaspora and the homeland and those in the wider diaspora. The diasporic media surfaced to challenge the community's representation in Britain's mainstream media as well as providing news for Zimbabweans abroad and those in the homeland. For Zimbabweans in

Britain, immigration status can be understood as creating class divides, as it shapes the opportunity structures for migrants as well as determining their everyday lives. Although the classical conception of diaspora is underscored by homogeneity, in reality, the Zimbabwean diaspora in Britain is fractured and fragmented.

Table 2.4. The Geographical Distribution of Zimbabweans in the UK in 2013.

Location(s)	Estimated Zimbabwean Population
London, Birmingham, Leeds	50, 000 each
Manchester, Luton, Leicester	40, 000 each
Liverpool, Sheffield	35,000 each
Coventry, Glasgow, Wolverhampton	30, 000 each
Edinburgh, Bristol	20,000 each
Swansea, Milton Keynes	10, 000 each
Cardiff, Oxford, Slough	5,000 each

2.9 Sampling

Due to the negative impact and the controversy associated with Bride Price, I used purposive sampling (in all the three sites) to select the participants ensuring they were comfortable with the topics and questions. I was careful not to frame the questions in a way that might cause harm or arguments, or that could put all concerned in a difficult position, as this was not the purpose of the research. Equally, participants were not asked direct questions regarding the practice. However, they were asked how migration and urbanisation affect the practice. Purposive sampling enables the researcher to carefully select specific people who are seen as likely to produce valuable data the population is selected with a specific purpose in mind and the rationale reflects the criteria of selecting the sample (Densecombe, 2010).

Interviews were conducted at different venues; the participants' homes, the Birmingham Women's Aid offices and the United Nations Association of Zimbabwe (UNA-Zimbabwe) offices. The interviews were directed by the interview guide, and flexibility was accounted for. All the interviews were audio-recorded and were intended to average one hour in duration. Thematic content analysis was adopted as it is an appropriate method for analysing qualitative data (Chambliss & Schutt, 2006). After completing all interviews, the transcribed data was analysed using tables to summarize all the information on each of the different issues that formed the focus of the interviews. Important categories in the data were also identified.

The study was conducted with the four family focus groups in Birmingham, four from the same families in Harare, and then four from the same families in the rural areas of Zimbabwe. I administered questionnaires with both open-ended and semi-structured questions to assess the impact of urbanisation and migration on Bride Price. The interviewees were assured of confidential treatment of their responses as well as anonymity. They were asked not to write their names or any identifying information on the questionnaire and participation was voluntary. I collected the questionnaires immediately after they were completed and data was tabulated to show frequencies and subjected to evaluative analysis.

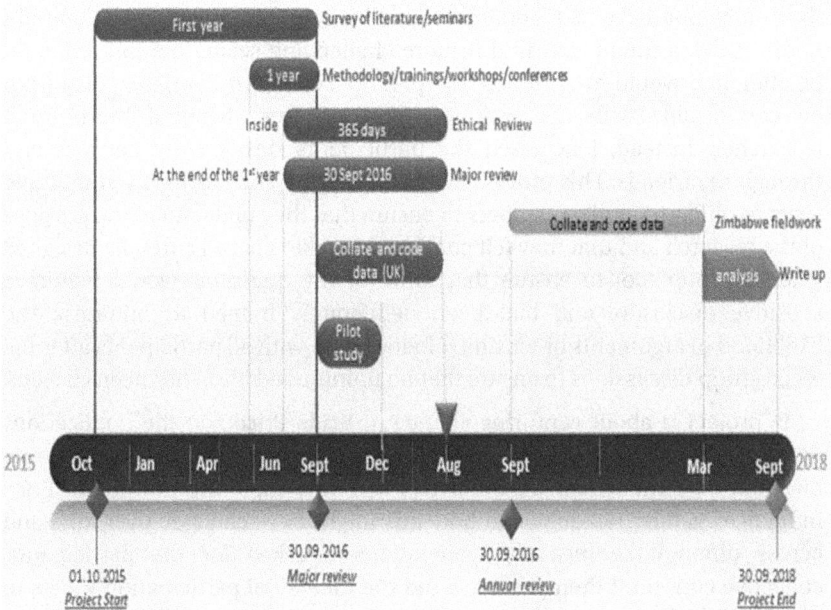

Figure 2.2. Research Timeline.

I interviewed three generations provided the third generation was above the age of eighteen. I did not interview children (anybody under 18 years of age) and neither were any children present in the room during focus groups. I interviewed cousins, grandfathers, grandmothers, mothers, fathers and their children over the age of 18 as an indication of how far I went to provide their adult age. It was also important to acknowledge that grandfathers and grandmothers may not be living in that house.

Grandfathers and grandmothers usually live in the towns or cities during their working life but migrate to rural areas upon retirement. In Birmingham, most families are made up of mothers, fathers and children; they are much smaller nuclear families. The third generation is usually below eighteen (and these would not be interviewed). I interviewed 4-6 people per family, though they were unlikely to be living under one roof. But they were likely to live closer to each other for family networks and support such as child care. I wanted to capture the views of the children and their parents who were also unlikely to be living in the same house but would have agreed to come together in order for me to carry out the interviews. I took more of a generational approach rather than a physical approach in defining a 'household'.

The families I selected were not directly linked to me in terms of kin, neither were any of the participating families my friends. This was essential because they may not have felt comfortable talking to me if we shared family. Additionally, a friend may find it more challenging seeing me in a different position and would not feel able to open up. For that reason, they might not be comfortable with me swapping position from being a friend to a researcher. Instead, I accessed the participants through my network and through my friends. This process has been lengthy and has involved multiple visits to different family members to ensure that they understood the purpose of the research and that they felt comfortable taking part. I carefully designed a focus group tool to ensure that none of my questions would require a sensitive disclosure and had been deliberately framed to minimise the likelihood of arguments or tension. I followed up with all participants after the focus group discussions to ensure that no unintended harm has been caused.

My project is about capturing change in Bride Price and the implications that it has for the lives of men and women in Zimbabwe and the Zimbabwean diaspora in Birmingham. In other words, I was exploring how Bride Price influences gender relations and how this might have changed over time and across different settings and generations. I asked for the participants' collective consent. I then passed round the individual participation sheets to be signed before proceeding with the questions. I recorded the interviews after seeking permission from the participants and ensuring the participants were also comfortable with this arrangement.

2.10 Limitations

The reason for choosing only four family focus groups and tracing these to Harare and to rural Zimbabwe, with the addition of one female focus group (in Birmingham), was due to time and logistical constraints. This also may have limited the potential for expansion beyond the sample size that was proposed, which would have been unfeasible in terms of financial logistics even if it might have been possible. The interview numbers provided were only intended as a guide, and the interviews were set to continue until nothing new emerged from them and the saturation point was reached.

Another limitation is related to gender. It would not have been easy as a Zimbabwean man to spend long hours debating and holding discussions with women on issues to do with their personal lives, especially those who were either widowed or whose husbands might be unavailable or away at work in Harare. I endeavoured as much as possible to approach the topic from the perspective of the participants themselves in order to give space to the diversity of voices on Bride Price (Pellauer, 1991, p. 305; Sanders, 1995, p. 58). This study places the views of Zimbabwean women as the most critical perspectives that contribute to its conclusions as advocated by Oduyoye (1994).

In Chapter Five, I compare the perspective I am bringing to Bride Price to how other people actually view or observe it. I adopt this lens in my study, but I am essentially applying it in a critical manner to what is a fundamental part of my own culture which is quite an unusual position to put myself in. It is unique and interesting but also brings with it some struggles regarding how to manage being a researcher who is essentially applying a critical to lens to my own culture. I am uniquely positioned to be able to do this research as an insider as I am a Zimbabwean of Shona heritage, which is one of the tribes represented among those being interviewed. The advantages of my position is supported by Narayan (1997) who argues that:

> to avoid normative descriptive judgements that seem to replicate a colonist attitude of 'telling the natives what to do', has understandably entered into the range of current Western feminist concerns with power, representation, voice and marginality.

> (Narayan, 1997, p. 127)

My position is challenging but ultimately, I am able to make this critique whilst others may not be in a position to do so: my critique is made as an insider. This stance was further endorsed by Narayan- who describes the position and advantage of this type of inside status:

> The problem of 'Authentic Insider' is different from that of 'Mirror to the West' in that it permits more sustained attention to Third World

contexts and cultures without swiftly returning discursive attention to the West [...]

(Narayan, 1997, p.142)

My choice to study the lives of women was motivated by the overwhelming assumption that they are relatively oppressed by African patriarchy, as alluded to in this work. The choice of this tribal grouping was influenced by my own position as a Shona resident by birth and a descendent of the Shona chiefdom under the current Chief Zvimba. I am also comfortable in speaking the three languages - English, Shona and Ndebele. Additionally, the travel and accommodation logistics were made easier by the transport and communication links between cities and the rural area of Zvimba which is around sixty miles from Harare. The number of four family focus groups and one female focus group were deemed adequate for the purpose of this piece of work. Whether or not my work would have been enhanced by interviewing more men is worth considering. These issues do also affect them, but my work is solely focussed on the inequality that women experience in the name of culture.

Related to my position is a problem regarding translation. In the process of recording the interviews, this arose as the questions were written in English and then asked and answered in Shona and Ndebele, the native languages of the participants. There are Shona and Ndebele words that have no direct translation from English such as sara pa vana, chiredzwa, and kutsikisa vana mapoto. But as the researcher, I attempt to find the closest translation, while also aware that the words may lose their meaning in the process, thereby affecting the overall implication of is said. Asking the questions in Shona and Ndebele was done in order to accommodate some of the low literacy levels amongst the participants. No request was made to the university to write the book in Shona or Ndebele to avoid this translational problem. The interviews took place in the homesteads of the interviewees and at the Birmingham Women's Aid offices. Each interview was expected to take about an hour. Family focus groups and discussions helped me significantly in the clarification of some issues, and also allowed me to access some of the personal expressions of a cultural nature that may otherwise have appeared ambiguous in the formal questionnaire.

In this study, most of the participants in Zimbabwe worked in informal employment due to the economic crisis currently gripping the country and this made it impossible for them to secure time for interviews during the day. To solve this, I scheduled interviews in evenings and weekends for those who could not afford the time during working hours. In addition, many NGOs and government departments that conduct focus group discussions in the communities have been paying out allowances to participants thus contributing to the phenomenon known as the 'allowance syndrome'. Some participants (especially men) in family focus group discussions expected me to do the same. However, due to expert advice from UNA-Zimbabwe, I used their community mobilisation skills to clarify with the interviewees beforehand and during invitations not to expect participation allowance. I did, however, offer light refreshments during the discussions.

2.11 Self-reflexivity & Translation

I agree with Alvesson and Sköldberg (2017) who argue that reflexivity is a key part of good qualitative research. Social sciences should increase our understanding of society and be able to function as a resource in the quest for improving people's lives. In feminist research, the political dimension is often clearer than within 'mainstream' research. Thus, feminist research is sometimes accused of being ideologically based, and therefore biased, but the engagement in society and the wish to improve people's lives could also be seen as an asset, particularly in the important activity of reflexivity. Just as any person who would like to make improvements in their personal life needs to make an honest assessment of herself and the situation, social scientists need to do the same in order to do good research. A wish to improve people's lives may help in keeping our feet on the ground and helping us to not tread too far away from reality in our analytical and theoretical work.

Reflexivity has been discussed from several angles in the social sciences: critical theory problematises the influence of ideology on theory, feminist theory has pointed out male bias in research, and post-modern thinkers have also discussed the narrative aspects of scientific representation, to name a few. Together these broad critiques have raised an important consideration: how should we be reflective about our own individual academic work? For feminist researchers, the solution has sometimes been to make a 'confession' in the beginning of their work as to their class and background - a solution which may not really add anything of analytical importance to the overall study. Sometimes personal accounts of, for example, fieldwork, have been presented in separate anthologies. The separation of such work from the academic analysis probably reflects the strong dichotomization between the personal and the scientific in the academic world, a dichotomization which in turn is inherited from a positivistic scientific framework. By far, the most difficult and frightening part of writing this dissertation has been to include a personal side to it. It is still not commonplace to be self-reflexive about academic work, although the positivistic view of science has been strongly criticised for its lack of reflexivity.

Additionally, I also faced challenges in creating a distance between myself and my data since I am interrogating my culture. Learning to keep that distance was an interesting exercise. The difficulty that I had to overcome in my methodology was the need to create a false barrier. I had to do so because my data is the evidence I am discussing, and my discussion is therefore confined to what my data tells me. I cannot use my existing knowledge of the culture or previous experience.

2.12 Conclusion

The originality of this book comes in the methodological approach - the application of both a feminist and an Afrocentric stance. Molefi Asante (2007, p. 34) asserts that, "it should be clear that Afro centrists too have recognized the inherent problems in [...] patriarchy" among other theoretical underpinnings that include Structuralism, Capitalism and Marxism. In light of this, my book discusses Bride Price as one of the aspects accountable for unequal gender relations, yet at the same time is still a central marker of what it is to be African. In order to remove the harmful consequences of Bride Price the inherent cultural importance of the practice needs to be navigated. This chapter highlighted and explained the methodology employed in this study and the research methods that informed my choice of approach. Additionally, the chapter outlined the research strategy, research approach, the type of data analysis, the ethical considerations and the limitations of the research. Having detailed the stages of the research and the methods employed, and having listed the three sites in which the study took place, I have set the scene for the rest of the chapters. I also justified the use of semi-structured interviews and focus group discussions for my fieldwork, which were ideal for this type of research and sought to explore people's experiences and perceptions. The chapter that follows goes on to review existing literature, through which I gathered, compiled and analysed the research available to date on the topic of Bride Price. This enabled me to show in my book how my study produces new knowledge and helps to develop a framework through which to analyse the findings of the study.

Chapter 3

Contextualizing Bride Price: From the Global to the Local

The previous chapter described and explained the methodology of this study and the research methods which informed my choice of approach. It also outlined the research strategy, research approach, the type of data analysis, the ethical considerations and the limitations of the research. This literature review chapter compiles and evaluates the research currently available on the topic of Bride Price. It provides an overview of Bride Price and presents a summary of the research to date on the practice. This enables me to demonstrate how my research supports new knowledge about the nature and gendered impact of the practice. This review also helped me to develop a framework through which I could analyse and present my research findings. The focus then was to highlight what is known globally about Bride Price and to assess where the critical gaps in knowledge lie. My book went on to attempt to fill at least some of those gaps. Additionally, this chapter serves to present a description of the cultural context of marriages and marriage transfers in Zimbabwe whilst providing an overview of the background literature on the topic that extends beyond contexts that observe the practice. My research also pays special attention to the definition and evolution of marriage transfers as captured in the literature. This chapter is concerned with understanding what has been documented about marriage transactions, in particular, the expansion, inflation and other factors affecting Bride Price.

The summary I present here of Bride Price practices across the globe helped me to draw out different and similar patterns and then to reflect on how they map out in the context of Zimbabwe. This process also enabled me to evidence that my work is original, not least because there is little written on the practice in Zimbabwe. In particular, little of the research that does exist is contemporary. The research approach used in the majority of the published work also has a single country and a single location focus. My approach is innovative in that it maps and compares across three sites and two countries. I also demonstrate through this chapter that more needs to be understood about the links between marriage and gender and different changing global contexts.

The first section of this chapter looks at the global literature on Bride Price, what it is and how it is practised. The main purpose is to review the international literature on Bride Price highlighting what has already been researched and published globally. This includes the general history of Bride

Price, a comparison with dowry, and also an analysis of the present situation in different contexts. The chapter then moves on to look at the context of Zimbabwe. This is done through exploring the country overview with a focus on the two main tribes in Zimbabwe, the Shona and the Ndebele and how they observe Bride Price. This is important because with Bride Price there are differences regarding what and how much is given at the ceremony between these two tribes. This section is followed by an exploration of the different functions of Bride Price as reflected in the anthropological literature. Identifying how early anthropologists viewed the practice helped me to analyse my data in terms of what and how the practice may have changed since these earlier studies. The chapter then moves on to explore the legal position of marriage in Zimbabwe which in turn helps illustrate how laws seem to reproduce patriarchal relationships. An example of this is that in Zimbabwe the Marriage Act prohibits boys below the age of eighteen marrying whereas girls as young as sixteen can marry: girls can marry before reaching adulthood, but boys cannot.

The latter part of the chapter looks at what the literature has captured in terms of the impact of modernisation and migration on Bride Price. A key focus of my research is seeking to understand how shifts in the global and national economy may have resulted in changes in the practice. This is followed by a section which introduces the main critical and feminist discourses on Bride Price. This includes literature on post-colonial feminist theory in which this book is rooted. I am utilising post-colonial feminist theory because it carefully argues that Bride Price maintains an unequal gendered hierarchy through marriage. Women are effectively bartered for and sold at the point of marriage, which renders them inferior to their husbands and vulnerable to violence and reduced autonomy and life opportunities. The chapter concludes by bringing out the gaps in knowledge and reiterates the originality of this research in relation to the literature.

3.1 The History of Bride Price: Where and Why it is Practised

The notion of Bride Price has been theorised by numerous researchers and authors as payment at the point of marriage. According to Oguli Oumo:

> Bride Price may be defined as payment made in kind, cash or material as demanded by custom of a group by a groom or his family to the family of the bride in order to make the union legitimate [...] this payment comprises of an agreement where material objects (usually cattle) or cash is given by the groom to the bride's family in exchange for the bride, her labour and her ability to bear children.

(Oguli Oumo, 2004, p. 69)

Dey (2003) describes Bride Price as, "the sum of cash or material goods or wealth paid by the groom or his family to the parents of the woman at the point of marriage of their daughter to the groom". The material gifts exchanged range from livestock to animals and cash, especially in rural areas. Radcliffe-Brown (1987) likewise describe Bride Price "as the situation where payment of goods and services is made by the bridegroom to the bride's family as a vital part of the formation of validity of marriage." In Urban areas where land for grazing livestock may not be available, cash or physical assets like furniture, machinery, electronics and other household items are exchanged instead. Traditionally, among most communities it is expected that if the marriage later fails, materials or gifts paid are supposed to be refunded to the groom's family, irrespective of the length of time the spouses have stayed together. However, in rural areas (though varying by ethnic/tribal group, tradition and culture), more traditional Bride Price practices such as duties for the bride after the ceremony remain traditionally common and tend to be accepted as the cultural norm.

Bride Price - which is called *roora* in Shona or *lobola* in Ndebele (these words will be interchangeably used in this book) - has undergone a radical transformation in Zimbabwe. Few studies have been done in Zimbabwe on *lobola* but they have mainly focused on how this practice is conducted and the cultural significance attached to it (Dery, 2015; Bourdillon, 1982 & 1993). For example, the work of Mvududu (2002), Kambarami (2006), and Chireshe and Chireshe (2010) focused on the effects of *lobola* in general without exploring its effects in its contemporary commercialised form. Yet, it is clear that *lobola* has assumed some new characteristics over recent years that need to be analysed to appreciate how the practice affects women today (Dery, 2015).

The approved Bride Price is commonly calculated to mirror the distinguished worth of the girl or young woman. In the view of Alupo this amount:

> comprises payment in cash or property by husband and his family to the Bride's family. It epitomises friendship but in actual fact it is the transfer of productive and reproductive service to the man's family.
>
> (Alupo, 2004)

Similarly, to Meekers (1992) Bride Price, "common in South African marriages, epitomises the transfer of the right of the girl's sexual and economic services to the husband". Wegh (1998) theorised Bride Price in line with Meekers perspective, to him, Bride Price "implies to the act of obtaining progressively and collection of an article [...] a component of saving". To Alupo (2004, p.35), *lobola* "is a representation aimed at exchanging, to enforce a cash sum of Bride Price". Anyebe (1985), in his analysis of Bride Price, explained that:

> Bride Price (bride-wealth) makes marriage lawful and authenticates the legitimacy of children. Furthermore, it is a reimbursement for loss to the woman's family of one of its members, a potential child bearer, it is marriage insurance to stabilize relationship and safeguard the wife.

> (Anyebe,1985, p.85)

In Islam, Bride Price was required in order to validate marriage (Bianquis, 1996). Traditionally in China, the negotiation of a Bride Price has also been necessary for the legitimacy of marriage, and this practice is still common today, especially in the rural areas of the country (Townsend, 2008). China is an example of a country where Bride Price and dowry coexist. Taiwan also follows the same practice of swapping marriage payments in the opposite direction (Parish & Willis, 1993). Burma, Indonesia and Thailand are the other countries in Southeast Asia, where Bride Price is practised (Cherlin & Chamratrithirong, 1988; Spiro, 1975). Bride Price is more commonly practised in rural areas of China and is rare in urban areas, and the same is in Thailand. Though the difference is that urban marriages in Thailand do still use other means payment such as electrical appliances.

Though it exists in these other contexts, Bride Price is predominantly practised in Africa where over eighty percent of societies recognise the practice (Murdock, 1967; Goody, 1973). It was popular in urban settings in Democratic Republic of Congo, Egypt, Iran, Syria and Uganda until the late 1970s, and for many practising societies, a marriage is not recognised until or unless Bride Price is paid. Wegh (1998) notes that "Bride Price helps in stabilizing of family alliance". The idea here seems to be that the fear of paying back Bride Price in the case of the marriage being dissolved may lead the family of the woman to do its part in ensuring that the marriage is successful. He observed that among the Tiv, the implication for children born in a situation where bride-wealth has not been paid is that such children are regarded as belonging to the woman's family rather than the family of the man. In this book, marriage could be conceptualized as a legal or legitimate unification of a man and a woman for the purpose of performing basic family functions, which is expected to endure for the rest of their lives.

Bride Price is a strongly rooted transaction that many African communities largely approve of because of its cultural value and role in the affirming of kinship. However, it has gradually become more commercial and its original meaning, which was as a symbol of appreciation and consensus between the two families (of the bride and groom), seems to have been eroded or transformed to include payment of expensive financial and material resources. In other words, the practice is now seen as a means of acquiring material goods. This has generated obstacles associated with raising such resources and the high prices may curtail the negotiating positions or agency of wives (especially poor women) in marital relationships. Some young men also face hurdles in trying to meet the demands of this practice, especially those with inadequate resources, and will try to find alternative ways of raising these amounts like selling off family property or getting bank loans (Dery, 2015).

Historically, Bride Price is assumed to have functioned helpfully, giving official identification to marriages, safeguarding wives against mistreatment, stabilising the union and merging the two families together (Goody, 1973). Nowadays though, the custom seems to have drifted from its customary position due to commercialisation and in turn has been losing importance (Oguli Oumo, 2004). These days the practice is also linked to status, there is pressure to give as much as possible and this links the amount to the status of the family.

As proposed by Cliff and Stoneman (1989), almost all traditional marriages in Zimbabwe are expected to include this ritual. Bourdillon (1993) asserts that in many African societies, the traditional marriage ritual of the Shona peoples is symbolised by the mediation and payment of Bride Price. It is worth noting that most of the literature on Bride Price is quite old and was gathered by anthropologists who were building knowledge over time. The payment of Bride Price within the Shona society, in which *roora* is the crucial element is the foundation of marriage and family commitments. There is general agreement in Zimbabwe (and within Africa) on what is involved in Bride Price.

Although Bride Price payment is practised and cherished in the whole of Zimbabwe, it tends to be more expensive among the Shona group in Mashonaland, and particularly so among the Vakaranga in Masvingo and the Manyika in Mutare (Dery, 2015). This is contributed to by the fact that these regions believe that they are the most educated in the country. As such, this study includes these groups and compares their perceptions with other tribal groups. The underlying reasons for the continuation of Bride Price will be explored through a critical intersectional analysis which will consider if and how constructs such as masculinity, gender, class, and modernisation all feed into the impact upon people's attitudes and support of Bride Price.

3.2 A Comparison with Dowry

Marriage transactions either in form of cash or kind made by the bride's family to either the bride or the newly married couple or the groom's family are broadly classified as dowries. The definition of dowry is important for research and policy purpose as policy implications may vary depending on the definition of the practice. Menski (2013) categorised dowry into three types based on its nature and the way it is presented and argued in writings that relate to the Indian context. The first is known as *stridhana*, which are gifts, jewellery, household goods and or other property that is given to the bride by her family during the marriage rituals. These payments are voluntary in nature and often viewed as pre-mortem inheritance. The bride enjoys the ownership right over these payments though this may not be the case if the bride herself is perceived as property by the groom and his family. The second form of dowry constitutes the expenditure that is made on the occasion of marriage celebration. Indian marriages are recognised for their conspicuous spending and families view this spending as a way to maintain their status. Neither the bride nor his groom or his family directly benefits from this second form of dowry. The third form of dowry is the payment of property in the form of cash or kind that is expected or demanded by the groom and his family as a condition of marriage. This third form of dowry can be described as 'Groom Price'. In Bride Price, the level of ownership is direct, the bride has been literally bought. That said, with dowry a bride is seen as bringing in money, but she has no control over how to spend it. If she brings in enough, she is safe, if she does not bring enough, she is not safe from violence.

Like dowry, Bride Price can also take different forms. Thus, considering who gets the payment, Bride Price can be seen as the opposite of Groom Price, but not dowry in general. In most economics literature of marriage transaction, where dowry is defined as the payment made by a bride's family minus the transfer made by the groom, dowry and Bride Price are considered as reverse of each other. Viewing negative dowry as Bride Price in the Indian context can be problematic as data on dowry does not distinguish whether the amount paid is *stridhana* or Groom Price or a combination of both. If dowry is consisted of *stridhana* in addition to Groom Price, the measure of dowry will be positively biased against Bride Price. In this book, I use the term dowry to refer to any payment made by a bride's family and the term net-dowry is used to refer to payments made by the bride's family less what is paid by the groom or his family.

3.3 The Anthropological Literature on Bride Price

Every society goes through different historic evolutions. The major factors that contributed to changes in the Shona and the Ndebele people occurred during the colonial era. The introduction of a cash economy to some extent commercialised the practice of Bride Price. In the past, the people of Zimbabwe regarded marriage as a cultural institution respected by both parties. Thus, Bride Price played a huge role in the recognition and legalisation of marriage.

Marriage was very communal. Bride Price was paid not by the groom but by his family to the family of the bride. Cattle were paid to the head of the bride's family and this was done in the presence of the extended family (Bourdillon, 1982). This validates the suggestion that marriage amongst the Shona and the Ndebele was a transaction between two families (May, 1983).

In the past, two cows and a bag of maize were used as Bride Price amongst the Shonas. Some prospective husbands paid Bride Price through providing labour by working either in the in-laws' fields or doing any tasks delegated by the in-laws (Janhi, 1970, p. 33). The payment was made in two parts, namely *rusambo* and *roora*. *Rusambo*, which gave a man sexual rights, was the first payment to be made and with this in mind, any form of adultery with a married woman remains a punishable offence (Bourdillon, 1982). However, this book acknowledges the problem associated with *rusambo* in that it was only payable when the bride was a virgin. Dery (2015) asserts that this payment was made whether a woman/girl was a virgin or not. However, the Ndebele people had a way of compensating for non-virgin brides. The Ndebele traditional society demanded that the father of a non-virgin bride pay a beast to make up for her daughter, protecting her from stigma and abuse. The second payment, *roora*, was a substantial payment in cattle and was associated with rights over children born to the woman (Bourdillon, 1982). This particular payment bestowed child ownership on the father. These children inherited their father's name and totem. This is the foundation of patrilineal nature of the Zimbabwean society.

Conversely, traditional marriage amongst the Ndebeles was quite different from the Shonas. The girl's father helped in setting up of the new home by giving his daughter a cow, just like dowry amongst the Ndebeles. This was intended to help the daughter lay the foundation of her new home as it multiplied. There were other rituals that were more or less the same as the ones practised by the Shonas. The bride was also showered with gifts by her extended family when she joined her husband. This was to show their blessing and participation in the whole process. Both the Shona and the Ndebele believed that a woman was 'incomplete' without a man and vice versa. Furthermore, child bearing was crucial in the survival of the marriage, but this has changed a great deal with modernisation and enlightenment. Couples are now able to decide how they want to live their lives without much interference from their parents or extended family unlike in the past when the families exerted pressure on the new couple, which included pressure to start a family (Janhi, 1970).

3.4 Context of Zimbabwe: the Shona and Ndebele People

Arguably, ethnicity has an impact on the shape of Bride Price and how it is practised, and the purpose of this section is to map out how the ethnic diversity of Zimbabwe affects the practice. There are differences between ethnic groups and the term Shona, in modern times, has been re-invented and used to bring together four ethnically and linguistically related groups in northern, southern and western Zimbabwe; namely the Manyika, Mandau, Zezuru, and Vakaranga (Dery, 2015). The term Ndebele refers to people who can be divided into two groups, the Ndebele and the Kalanga. These two groupings live in the south-western Zimbabwe. Though they have undergone some changes due to the effects of colonialism and modernization, the Shona are traditionally crop farmers whilst the Ndebele prefer livestock rearing with a strong preference for cattle due to the regional climate. Though the cattle are kept for economic reasons, one of the purposes is for use during settlement of Bride Price transactions. In addition, the Shona and the Ndebele societies like most African societies are deeply embedded in patriarchal families and relations with strong elements of hegemonic masculinities, female subordination, a strong preference for Bride Price payment, respect for marriage and a preference for many children. They were historically associated with strong taboos like prohibition of women from eating particular foods like eggs; modernisation has brought change to some of these beliefs (Dekker & Hoogeveen, 2002).

Zimbabwean society is stratified by an ethnic system and within each broad ethnicity there are sub-ethnicities. Prevalence of cross-ethnic marriages is very low in rural areas. Using a representative sample of rural Zimbabwe households of four major cities of Zimbabwe, Munshi and Rosenzweig (2005) found that inter-ethnic marriage was about fifteen percent for the rural Zimbabwean population in 1999. Using data from different surveys, they also found that inter-ethnic marriage was just below ten percent in Bulawayo in 2001 and six percent in the eastern city of Mutare in 2003.

The largest tribal group is the Shona which is comprised of the Karanga, Korekore, Manyika, Ndau, Rozwi and Zezuru, together constituting eighty-two percent of the population. The Ndebele are the second largest tribal group and is comprised of the Kalanga and the Ndebele, which makes up sixteen percent of the population. Most of the Shona people live in Mashonaland, Manicaland and Masvingo which is the eastern three-quarters of the country, whilst most Ndebele people live in the western quarter of the country which is termed Matabeleland. I chose these tribes because they tend to practise Bride Price differently. Women who were hitherto considered to be unfit for education are now accessing formal education and employment. In a similar vein, Bride Price that was hitherto just a custom to formalise marriages, has now changed: a lot of bargaining and negotiations have to be undertaken before a final 'price' can be agreed upon. With women now entering the workforce in greater numbers, a higher price can be asked for them as men are marrying women who will improve their household income.

Figures from the World Bank show an increase in the number of women in salaried employment in Zimbabwe from 22.2 percent in 2000 to 23.1 percent in 2016. Unemployed women went from 4.5 percent to 3.9 percent, and there was an increase in women in the service sector from 24.2 percent to 32 percent.

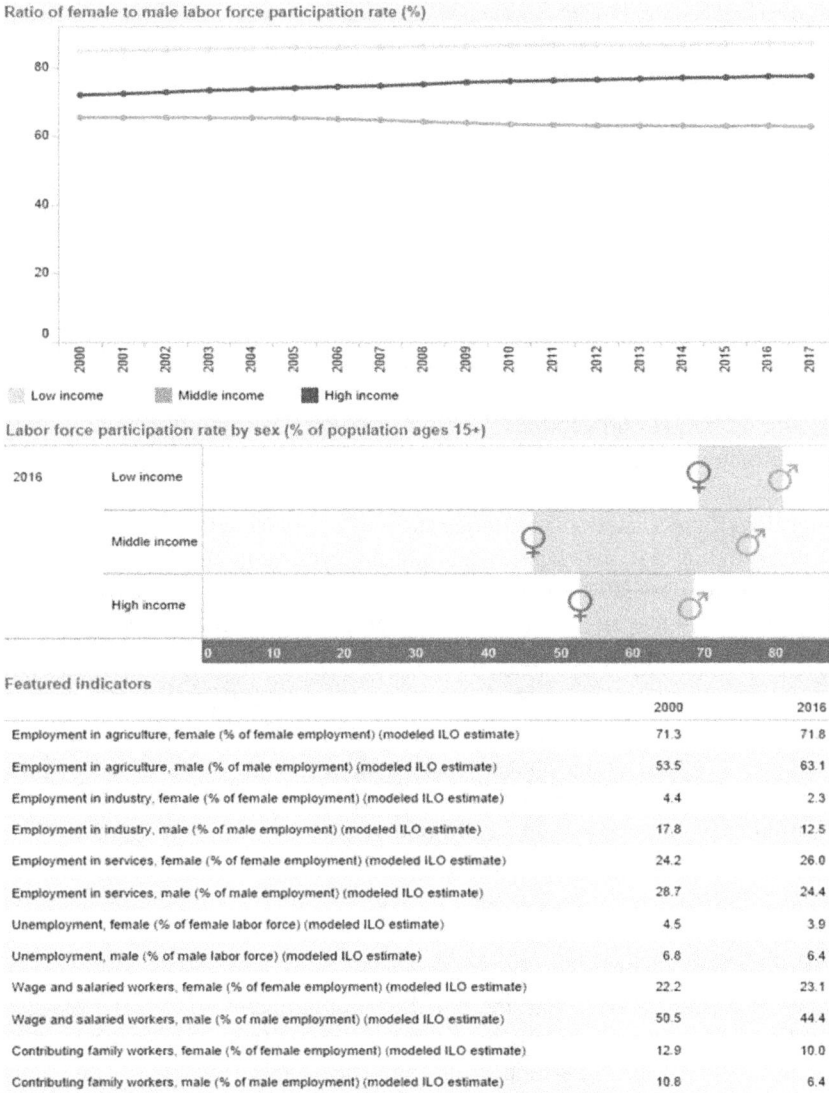

Ratio of female to male labor force participation rate (%)

Low income   Middle income   High income

Labor force participation rate by sex (% of population ages 15+)

Featured indicators

	2000	2016
Employment in agriculture, female (% of female employment) (modeled ILO estimate)	71.3	71.8
Employment in agriculture, male (% of male employment) (modeled ILO estimate)	53.5	63.1
Employment in industry, female (% of female employment) (modeled ILO estimate)	4.4	2.3
Employment in industry, male (% of male employment) (modeled ILO estimate)	17.8	12.5
Employment in services, female (% of female employment) (modeled ILO estimate)	24.2	26.0
Employment in services, male (% of male employment) (modeled ILO estimate)	28.7	24.4
Unemployment, female (% of female labor force) (modeled ILO estimate)	4.5	3.9
Unemployment, male (% of male labor force) (modeled ILO estimate)	6.8	6.4
Wage and salaried workers, female (% of female employment) (modeled ILO estimate)	22.2	23.1
Wage and salaried workers, male (% of male employment) (modeled ILO estimate)	50.5	44.4
Contributing family workers, female (% of female employment) (modeled ILO estimate)	12.9	10.0
Contributing family workers, male (% of male employment) (modeled ILO estimate)	10.8	6.4

Figure 3.1. Zimbabwe's female to male labour ratio: World Bank (2017).

Socio- economic variables such as the level of education of the bride and her family's social status have become deciding factors in determining Bride Price. In such cases where the bride attains higher education or is employed, Bride Price tends to be escalated and the groom or his family is expected to pay heavily in these circumstances. Further, most ethnic groups consider a female child to be a high value 'commodity', which when invested in properly can guarantee high financial or economic reward because they can be traded through the marriage market. Consequently, the groom or his family is required to offer the best possible price if they want to secure a highly-priced bride who, for example, is well educated and from a wealthy family (Fortunato, 2011).

3.5 Cultural Background of Marriage in Zimbabwe

Marriage is one of the most important events in the life of Zimbabwean men and women, marking the transition into adulthood. Zimbabwe is a country with a heterogeneous culture with respect to marriage practice, marriage and kinship structure, norms, ideology, gender roles and economic transactions surrounding marriage. The seminal study on kinship and gender in Zimbabwe by Dery (2015) spotlighted the regional differences, especially the North-South differences on gender, kinship and marriage related issues. According to Zimbabwean culture, "one is incomplete and considered unholy if they do not marry" (Dery, 2015, p. 35). Thus, an unmarried girl of marriageable age may face divine sanction and her family may be subjected to social stigma for not arranging her marriage at the socially preferable age. Using the 1982 census data, Dery (2015) reports that eighty percent of men are married by the age of twenty-five and for women, this proportion is reached by the age of twenty in rural areas.

The Shona-speaking people are the dominant ethnic group in Zimbabwe (Bourdillon, 1987; Gelfand, 1965; Gelfand, 1984). However, the Shona are a composite ethnic group composed of subgroups who speak dialects of the same language and who have strong cultural similarities: the Shona are patrilineal with an extended family system, and marriage is exogamous with the local residence. Normative Shona marriage, known as *roora* marriage, is a long process characterized by the payment of bride wealth from the family of the prospective groom to the family of the bride (Andifasi, 1970; Bere-Chikara, 1970; Dore, 1970; Gelfand, 1965 & 1984; Makamure, 1970; Tsodzo 1970).

Whereas most people from the practising communities observe the practice of Bride Price as a treasured part of 'African culture', many also regard it as an economic deal that essentially discriminates against women. This book therefore strives to clarify people's views and perceptions with reference to the discourses of 'equal rights' and 'culture' that are prevalent in urban areas and the diaspora communities. People from the practising community utilise these discourses in (re)negotiating the meaning of Bride Price, but the limitations of the discourses restrict the interpretations of Bride Price available to them.

Zimbabwe's constitution prohibits discrimination, but not explicitly on grounds of sex and, as in Lesotho, exempts Customary Law in matters of marriage, divorce and inheritance (Auret, 1990, p. 103). Additionally, Zimbabwe has attempted to reduce discrimination against women, and has ratified the Convention on the Elimination of Discrimination Against Women in 1991, although several laws still breach the convention (Essof & van der Wijk, 1996). While most Zimbabwean women are subject to Customary Law, all women over eighteen are accorded certain rights under the Legal Age of Majority Act (LAMA), passed in 1982. Bride Price is no longer a legal requirement of customary marriage, but the Customary Marriages Act assumes that, in most cases, Bride Price will be paid (Zimbabwe, Customary Marriages Act, 1996):

> While couples over 18 can choose to marry without Bride Price, this is rare: a survey in Harare in the 1980s revealed only five per cent of marriages to have been registered without Bride Price payments.

> (Cliffe & Stoneman,1989, p. 74)

In the past, social and cultural factors endorsed early marriage. This trend is gradually shifting with the increase of age at the point of marriage since 1980. The laws that concern marriage in Zimbabwe are biased against girls. The evidence is provided in Chapter 5:11 of the Marriage Act which asserts that a girl can legally marry between the age of 16-18 provided that her parents' consent, while girls under the age of sixteen are prohibited from marrying. But the Marriage Act prohibits a boy below the age of eighteen years from marrying. The Customary Marriages Act does not specify any age restrictions at all for one to marry, which in itself is a cause for concern. This contravenes the new Constitution of 2013, which entrenches the right of every boy and girl below the age of eighteen years to be treated equally before the law. Civil society has called for laws to be harmonised and the minimum age of marriage for both genders to be raised to eighteen.

This position is endorsed by anthropological studies that claim that there is a preference for younger brides in the marriage market, especially in rural areas. While addressing the existing preference for early age at marriage for girls in the society Caldwell, Caldwell and Reddy (1983) state the following reasons in reference to rural Karnataka:

> In many societies a young bride is preferred, so that her personality can be moulded by both her husband and his parents. This is important in

India, too, but traditionally it has not provided the main motivation for early marriage of women in the study area (rural Karnataka). That motivation was provided by divine sanctions against girls who failed to marry before menarche, and against the family that erred in this way.

(Caldwell, Caldwell, & Reddy, 1983, p. 345)

The ideal timing and age of marriage be it early or late, is typically decided by the parents, especially in rural areas. Parents not only decide the age at which to get married, but also choose the appropriate partners for their offspring. Selecting a partner for a son also means selecting a daughter-in-law who will play the vital role of reproducing the next generation for the family. Thus, finding a perfect partner of desirable qualities has its own importance and can be perceived as a challenging task, especially in rural areas. It is common for people to use social networks or matchmakers to locate a potential bride or groom of an appropriate match. Socio-economic status and most importantly religion and ethnic background, are frequently used as the basis for matching in the marriage market.

Generally, in those rural areas where marriages to people who are not known are not common, arranging matches between strangers without the couple meeting each other is also not uncommon. Parents and other relatives generally come to an agreement on behalf of the couple. Because parents do the matching, family traits rather than individual traits are likely to be given more importance. Marriage is treated as an alliance between two families rather than a union between two individuals (Dery, 2015, p. 15). There are reasons why family characteristics may play important roles in marriage-matching.

One big reason is the social norm of intergenerational co-residence, whereby parents and sons live together, coupled with the norm of patri-local (relating to a pattern of marriage in which the couple settles in the husband's home or community) exogamy. This means that when daughters in almost all regions of Zimbabwe marry then begin to live with their husband and his parents. Sons are the preferred source of old-age support for parents and are generally expected to co-reside with the parents even after marriage. This norm is particularly binding for the eldest son in most areas. A daughter, on the other hand, moves out of her patri-local residence after marriage and starts co-residing with her parents-in-law if her husband co-resides with them. Daughters-in-law are the preferred source of old-age personal care (Fortunato, 2011).

3.6 Patterns of Migration within Zimbabwe

There have been two main demographic and settlement patterns in Zimbabwe. Firstly, the acquisition of land for agricultural purposes by the colonisers until the 1950s and secondly, the colonial era, which led to industrialisation and, in turn, the creation of towns and cities supplying labour to the growing industries. Labour was supplied by men leading to the creation of the urban areas close to the industrial sites. Men seeking employment stayed in urban areas whilst women and children remained in rural areas. Although this gender imbalance in the urban areas no longer exists as there is more freedom in movement between urban and rural areas, most women still head households in rural areas. Most jobs continue to be found in the urban areas and employment income remain as the major pull factor (Mutizwa-Mangiza, 1986).

The majority of the people migrated into urban locations as the towns and cities expanded, exacerbated by migration of people moving in search of employment. For example, the population of Chinhoyi grew from 8,000 in 1961/1962 to 13,000 in 1969 and almost doubled to 24,000 in 1982. In 1992 it was 42,946 and rose to 49,603 in 2002 and almost doubled again to 77,929 in 2012. In Bulawayo, the population was 21,100 in 1961/1962 and shot up to 245,000 in 1969 and up to 414,000 in 1982. The trend is the same for other cities (GoZ, 2012). Initially, people would migrate for a short period of time to acquire money and commodities and would then return to the rural areas. This arrangement changed in the long term as people, especially working men, began to stay in urban areas for longer periods whilst leaving their families in the rural areas. These men would visit rural areas either at weekends, at month end, or during bank holidays and religious festivals such as Easter or Christmas. Movements between rural and urban areas were also a result of tribal violence, drought and the wish to move away from customary responsibilities. But scholars such as Kurebwa (2015) and Wekwete (1992) have argued that the economic factor in terms of migration from rural to urban areas far outweighs the other factors.

3.7 Functions of Bride Price in the Anthropological Literature

Traditionally, Bride Price charge was fixed at a fairly stable level. However, in present-day practising societies, this has changed (Hughes, 1985). In societies where marrying was the norm, the charge for Bride Price was relatively higher in a more distant relationship due to the husband gaining rights to a woman and children from a more distant lineage (Bianquis, 1996). In some societies, there was also a link between Bride Price and the ability to bear children. However, women who have been divorced and have children will command a lower Bride Price, while younger brides will command a higher Bride Price (Dekker & Hoogeveen, 2002; Mulder, 1995).

In central and southern Africa, the main reason for Bride Price was to establish a link between tribes (Dekker & Hoogeveen, 2002; Ekong, 1992). With this in mind, most members of the groom's extended family were involved in contributing towards the Bride Price. Big families also raised higher Bride Price and, accordingly, the expectations for the bride were also high. Educated women, according to Gaspart and Platteau (2007), also commanded higher Bride Price than their uneducated counterparts. This is explained by the demand and supply principle which dictates that since educated women were in short supply then the demand for them would be higher. Gaspart and Platteau (2007) further assert that:

> higher Bride Prices for educated women are only observed for arranged marriages: in the case of love marriages, there is no statistically significant difference between the Bride Prices paid for educated and non-educated women. To account for this differentiated result, the assumption of strategic behaviour is helpful. It indeed, suggests the following interpretation: when educated women are involved in love marriages, in which they obviously have more leeway to assert their concerns, they are better able to influence their parents so as to prevent the Bride Price from being set at a high level

> (Gaspart & Platteau, 2007)

Wegh (1998) believes that the rise in Bride Price payment is related to the economic matrix. In this matrix, money regulates a family's purchasing power. The cost of educating children is therefore considered in the matrix. The longer a girl child spent in education, the more the family will spend in her general upkeep and related educational costs. It is for this reason that Weigh (2003) argues that the bride's family include these costs when charging Bride Price. This part is regarded as a repayment of the money spent on raising and educating their daughter.

Early colonial interpretations of Bride Price in Zimbabwe equated it straightforwardly with the sale of daughters for cattle (Jeater, 1993, pp. 148-9), whilst "Protestant missionaries in the country similarly saw 'marriage with cattle' as commercial transactions, degrading women as mere chattels" (Murray, 1981, p. 126). This understanding was also held by colonialists regarding Bride Price, but before colonialism Bride Price was not understood to confer property rights (Schmidt, 1991). This is not to say that Bride Price did not serve material functions in pre-colonial Southern Africa. Materially, Bride Price has served to redistribute both scarce consumption resources (cattle as meat, or cash) and rights over productive resources: land, cattle and labour (Jeater, 1993, p. 14), including the immediate labour of the young people marrying and later the labour provided by their offspring. Through Bride Price, households secure both production and reproduction (Malahleha, 1986). The combination of such material functions implied by a particular transfer depends upon the economic context in which it takes place.

The types of commodities or gifts changing hands differ across time and space. Prior to colonialism the Bride Price payment for the Shona consisted of 1-3 heads of cattle and was complemented by other gifts like blankets, and baskets of grain. These types of gifts could allow a small accumulation of wealth. But with the coming of colonialism in 1890, cash payments began to emerge, Schmidt (2004) argues that this is the period during which the custom became commercialised. Due to the shortage of cattle, and a drop in crop prices around 1930 as a result of the credit crunch, people started to demand cash payments for Bride Price (Jeater, 1993). The introduction of the plough and the scotch cart, however, made cattle valuable as productive as well as consumption resources, and at times made them the preferred currency (Schmidt, 2004).

Although payment was sometimes made at least partly in cash, under colonial rule, Bride Price became formalised in terms of units of livestock (Ferguson, 1990). In pre-colonial Zimbabwe, the number of cattle demanded depended on wealth, and the poor paid only two or three cattle, plus calves, sheep and goats, while the rich might pay as many as forty cattle. Only at the end of the century did anyone note the 'conventional' expectation of 20 cattle, ten small stocks and a horse: a higher level than that expected in Zimbabwe, which has been attributed to the role of labour migration in the country (Murray, 1981). Among early observers who saw Bride Price as a material exchange of 'wives for cattle', the 'wife' side of the bargain implied the transfer of rights over a woman's productive and reproductive capacities. Bride Price payments were apparently higher in societies (such as Zimbabwe) where female agricultural labour was at a premium (Lowes & Nunn, 2017). While such interpretations have persisted to some degree, they have increasingly been challenged as over-simplistic, and have been criticised for their representation of those participating in Bride Price transfers as simple bearers of productive and reproductive capacities (Guy, 1990).

Bride Price should not be seen as relating exclusively to women's role in rural production. Following ethnographic work in Zimbabwe in the 1970s, Murray argued that

> it is often more realistic in contemporary practice to represent marital transactions as the result of bargaining conducted by senior women over the earning capacity of men, than as the result of bargaining conducted by senior men over the productive and reproductive capacities of women.

(Murray, 1981)

Through marriage and payment of Bride Price, in pre-colonial Zimbabwe, a son would be granted land and could thereby be transformed into a productive asset (Malahleha, 1986). *Lobola* has been interpreted as a means by which Shona elders extracted labour from junior men (Jeater, 1993). In pre-colonial times junior men would work for their own lineage to 'earn' the cattle they gave in Bride Price. Any deficit in the Bride Price payment would entitle the father-in-law to call upon his son-in-law for labour when needed (Gelfand, 1973).

Even if, as Guy (1990) argues, the principle function of Bride Price in pre-capitalist societies was the control of female labour, in the contemporary context, he accepts it should be seen as "part of a wider system of accumulation based on wage labour" (Guy, 1990). By the late nineteenth century, men's labour for payment in white-owned farms, factories and mines was already of greater value than their labour on the land, and it was this earning capacity that was valued by rural households. This is particularly true of Zimbabwe, where productive land became scarce and my work became lucrative. By the 1980s, Murray was able to assert that in Zimbabwe:

> bride wealth is not the 'same' institution in the latter part of the twentieth century as it was in the middle of the nineteenth century [...] High levels of *roora* today reflect the importance of access to able-bodied manpower.

> (Murray, 1981, p. 45)

A theme that has run through the changing patterns of Bride Price payment in Zimbabwe has been the transition from a primarily inter-lineage to a more intergenerational transfer of wealth (Ferguson, 1990). Nowadays, Bride Price serves as a means whereby elders can make claims on the next generation, specifically the earnings of potential sons-in-law. Insisting on high Bride Price provides for comfortable subsistence, or, in the event of default, affords entitlement to a daughter's children. The vested interest of the older generation in Bride Price partly accounts for the strong opposition of parents, particularly fathers, to the Legal Age of Majority Act in Zimbabwe, which permits young people to marry without payment of Bride Price (Murray, 1981).

It is believed that African marriage carries with it a lineage function in bringing families together. Bride Price received for a girl child was often set aside and used by his male siblings when they marry. The bride produced children for her husband's lineage and Bride Price cattle for her brother, enabling him to father children for her natal lineage. Other kin would also be involved in raising the Bride Price: debts that would need to be reciprocated. The bond created between lineages has been widely reported to result, in part, from the persistence of Bride Price debt (Gay, 1982). Bride Price rarely takes place at the same time but is usually linked to significant events like the birth of a child or responds to the needs of the father-in-law and the ability of the son-in-law to meet his financial obligations. In Zimbabwe, full payment of the Bride Price takes between ten and twenty years and, in some cases, it is never paid up. Murray (1981) asserts that should the husband die before fully settling Bride Price, then his sons are expected to assume responsibility of the debt:

> Marriage should be regarded as a process in time and not as a single point of transition between the unmarried and the married state. Affinity never ends.

> (Murray, 1981, p. 119)

Commercialisation of the practice from the late nineteenth century has resulted in the custom being an individual transaction conducted between two men, unlike the previous era in which extended family members were involved. Additionally, a new trend has emerged which requires the groom to settle the 'charge' in payment. Besides being a transfer of wealth between lineages, Bride Price serves a function within the lineage. Transfers are both horizontal and vertical, creating a 'web of lineage connections and kinship links.' While in pre-colonial times Bride Price enabled lineage heads to make advantageous alliances with other lineages, such alliances became less important; Bride Price reinforced the power of elders within individual lineages. In particular, the integrity of the Shona household, in the face of the dramatic centrifugal effects of labour migration, has been attributed to the redistribution of labour migrants' earnings through Bride Price, thus bonding the migrant to the rural homestead, and enabling the rural household to make claims upon absent earners (Cliffe & Stoneman, 1989).

Bride Price is regarded as a payment for bearing children because it "brings about the absolute transfer of rights in a woman's procreative capacity from the woman's family to her husband's family" (Thelejane, 1983). This transfer in rights over children has never been straightforward, particularly in Zimbabwe, owing to the protracted hand-over of Bride Price payments. Different stages in the payment of Bride Price accord different levels of paternity. However, while Bride Price appeared to early observers to be a coherent set of formal rules, Murray (1981) points to the inappropriateness of such a positivist interpretation. Instead, he sees Bride Price as "the idiom for resolution of conflict" over paternity, wherein "the existence of a particular 'marriage' only comes into question in circumstances of dispute" (Thelejane, 1983).

Bride Price also functions to enable the exercise of social control at a number of levels by different actors. Its significance within the lineage has already been mentioned. Bride Price accords considerable control to the older generation over the younger. In pre-colonial Zimbabwe, Bride Price gave elders not only a degree of control over their new daughter-in-law, but also their son - they "controlled land, livestock, marriage and behaviour. The control that charging Bride Price gave elders over young women also facilitated their control of young men" (Bereng, 1982, p. 51). Thus, through Bride Price exchange, control was exercised over both men and women. However, men were able to exercise a certain amount of control in and through the transaction, while women had fewer options. In Zimbabwe, at least, women have no direct say in the Bride Price transaction. It takes place in men's space (the cattle *kraal*), using men's property (cattle). The exchange links the gift-givers, not the gifts; "women are conduits of a relationship, rather than partners to it" (Bereng, 1982, p. 90): the transaction accorded them no social power. Furthermore, even if pre-colonial thought did not conceive of Bride Price in terms of property rights, nineteenth-century Shona women did not have full rights to themselves: others could dispose of them through a Bride Price exchange. Women's bodies were never their own. With the colonial introduction of the idea of property rights, a woman was seen to pass from the "ownership" of father to that of husband. It is thus unsurprising that women were not accorded rights in court cases (Schmidt, 2004).

Colonial attitudes to Bride Price were somewhat ambiguous. While some missionaries sought to abolish Bride Price (usually on the basis that it was 'uncivilised' rather than 'immoral') other missionaries, and also the Rhodesian colonial state, defended it as a "partial check on immorality". Colonial authorities, particularly in Zimbabwe, actually used Bride Price as a tool of control. It was functional to capitalism since men would engage in labour migration in order to pay Bride Price. It also facilitated control over women, who were often seen as a threat by colonialists in the settler state. Elders' concerns about Bride Price encouraged them to control their daughters and preserve their status as potential wives; they impeded their daughters' education and migration to towns or work outside the immediate community (Schmidt, 2004, pp. 144 & 157).

Furthermore, as a result of Bride Price, all women could be married, hence, according to the colonial authorities, there were no 'surplus women' and chances of 'prostitution' were reduced (Jeater, 1993, pp. 74-75). In Zimbabwe, colonial authorities co-operated with local elders in including Bride Price as part of codified customary law. From the 1930s onwards, the Rhodesian colonial authorities ruled that payment of Bride Price gave men custody/guardianship over children, partly because they did not consider

African women suitable mothers unless they were themselves under male control (Schmidt, 2004, p. 110). State fears of women may have subsided, but Bride Price continues to facilitate control over young women by their elders and husbands. It restricts women's control over their own bodies, both sexually and in terms of their labour (Batezat, 1988). However, Bride Price is no longer universally seen as a stabilising influence within a marriage. Recent research suggests many Basotho girls and parents, as well as boys; oppose it because starting marriage in debt is seen to cause instability in marriage (Ansell, 2001). Furthermore, *lobola* payments are becoming increasingly erratic and difficult to enforce.

3.8 The Impact of Modernisation and Migration on Bride Price

In earlier times, the purpose of Bride Price in many African countries was to validate marriages and to safeguard women against mistreatment. Furthermore, it was used to stabilize relationships and to merge the two families. At present, Bride Price has become so highly commercialised that in numerous cases, it has lost its traditional value. In many countries, Zimbabwe included, the norm has thus changed especially in the urban areas where money or goods are used as a method of payment rather than livestock. However, the situation is slightly different in the rural areas (though this varies according to ethnic and tribal groups) where more traditional Bride Price custom remains common and is still acceptable as the norm.

A better way to grasp the shifting characteristics of Bride Price ritual like other customs is through evaluating the modernisation concept and the influence it may have on present-day society. The fundamental supposition that underpins modernisation that the current society is out-dated and the modern society is advanced and energetic (Townsend, 2008). Early studies are based on this claim, which depicts traditional society as regressive and static while the modern society is being characterised by "a high drive for progress and change, urbanisation, increased education and increased role of mass media and innovativeness" (Dery, 2015, p. 112). An additional trait of modernisation that tends to be opposed to traditional methods and beliefs is the rise of capitalism, the major motivation of which is the drive for profits, thus discarding some beliefs and practices that are deemed to be anti-profit and anti-modernity (Hardin, 2007). If the concept was to be trusted, it would be expected that one of the social practices that would fall victim to this push toward modernisation would be Bride Price. There is academic evidence which points to the weakening of the support for most of the traditional beliefs, especially among the younger generation which is linked to modernisation. The empowerment associated with the education of girls is at the heart of this change, following which it is believed that discriminatory practices relating to marriage will change or disappear. For instance, there is a greater inclination towards monogamous marriages, as well as young people deciding their own partners instead of their parents, which is accompanied by a reduced role of Bride Price in marriages (D'Hondt & Vandewiele, 1980; Barton & Pillai, 1998).

In addition, with the spread of modernisation, other family types or arrangements that do not conform to the so-called 'traditional' family structure (which is typically extended oriented and polygamous, with co-residence based on marital relationships between partners) are gaining strength. But as Nicholson (1997a) shows, this was not a natural development. The expansion of the 'nuclear' family was an imposition and it was paired with a discourse that depicted the working classes, the non-white, and the non-Western as inferior and backward. Instead, other 'alternative' family arrangements characterised by cohabiting partners without necessarily being married, single parents who choose not to marry, same-sex marriages or friends staying together without having marital or sexual relationships have gained ground (Nicholson, 1997b; Budgeon & Roseneil, 2004). Such family and marriage arrangements may not provide a conducive environment for Bride Price payments since they take a different approach altogether.

However, in contrast to the general rhetoric about the relationship between modernisation and Bride Price, there is evidence to support the opposite. For example, Anderson (2003), using studies from India, argues that whereas modernisation has led to increased wealth among the people, the caste-based societies have largely inflated Bride Price to greater amounts instead of reducing it as modernisation theorists might expect. Indeed, Zimbabwe no different; in almost all communities of Zimbabweans, Bride Price has seen great increases in the amounts and attention paid to Bride Price in the last decade, which may be due to economics and people's greed and profit motives that come with capitalism and modernisation. This is used to analyse how trends in modernisation influence the processes, trends, perceptions and experiences of Bride Price. Since modernity sometimes goes hand in hand with class, the two concepts are analysed together in relation to the subject.

In the same line, therefore, this theory of modernization is used to explore and assess how Bride Price custom has changed or evolved with the rise of modernization. It is also important to consider why it has not been phased out or declined as modernisation theory had predicted, as well as how modernization has affected the practice and the perceptions of it among the educated, the rich, the poor and others. Are the changing practices, especially the shift in the property exchanged from a few heads of cattle to sophisticated items like land, vehicles and electronics (and the associated preference for Western items) a result of modernisation, commercialization, or greed? Or is this just a normal part of social change? How do the processes, perceptions and outcomes of the practice change with the rise in the education, especially of women? The above aspects are not treated as independent variables, but efforts are made to establish their intersection with other concepts.

Traditionally in both Ndebele and Shona customs, what the bridegroom pays is supposed to be a token of appreciation and a sign of commitment. As Andifasi (1970) explains, Bride Price is "an outward manifestation of the young man's love for his fiancé and is a safeguard against groundless divorce" (Andifasi, 1970, p. 28). In a way, attaching a value to the woman was a way of according status. The Bride Price value also surpassed the outward expression of gratitude by the son-in-law; it generally compensated for the loss of a productive daughter. In present day, it becomes a compensation for the economic costs incurred in bringing up a daughter (Bourdillon, 1997). Anderson (2003) summarizes some of the values behind the payment of Bride Price with particular reference to Ndebele customs. Bride Price had both emotional and spiritual connotations; it was used to express a feeling, yet at the same time, it cemented ties between the children and their maternal ancestors through, for instance, the payment of *inkomo yohlanga* (cow given to the mother of the wife). In Shona culture, this cow is known as *mombe yeumai*. Anderson (2003) gives three reasons for Bride Price in traditional Ndebele societies, which are:

- *kuyisibongo somkhwenyana ethakazelela imuli aselayo ngenxa yabakwabozala.* (It is a thank you from the son-in-law appreciating the family that he now has, courtesy of the in-laws)

- *kulobugugu bakho kunxa zonke zobudlelwano. Kothethweyo lasebazalini bakhe yisibonakaliso sothando, kwenza indoda ingamthathi kalula umkayo.* (It is precious to both sides of the relationship. It is a sign of love to the wife and her parents; it ensures the husband respects his wife)

- *kufaka abantwana emasikweni abogogo bakanina. bangena emasikweni lawo ngenkomo yohlanga. inkomo yamalobolo ephiwa unina wentombi.* (It puts the children in the ways of their mothers and grandmothers. They get into these customs through a cow given to the mother of the wife)

(Anderson,2003, p.109)

The above debate shows that the custom of Bride Price is important to the Shona and the Ndebele: it was a principled act for these tribes. The initiation was the creation of a family and was a cultural necessity for the formation of each family. This book will thus take the position that, regardless of cultural importance of the procedure, there remain aspects that I feel are no longer compatible with today's world. That is not to say that I embrace everything that modernity means to Africans, but it is a way of demonstrating that some of our traditional customs have been corrupted. I also argue that in many respects, the paying of Bride Price is one of the ways in which patriarchy asserts its power over women. In most cases, men are in control of the proceedings. This control is a vital feature of gender relations in patriarchies.

3.9 Payment of Bride Price in Contemporary Zimbabwe

Bourdilon (1976) asserts that the life of both the Shonas and the Ndebeles has faced radical changes in the past three to four decades. It is important to highlight that what was permitted over a century ago might not be the case today. The previously communal society has changed a great deal, becoming more capitalist. There are many aspects of our lives where these changes are visible, one of which is the practice of Bride Price. Modernisation and external pressures have contributed to these changes. As capitalism gradually replaced the communal nature of society, a shift to a more individualistic viewpoint took place, and ultimately, this brought about the change in the payment of Bride Price. Less and less family members became involved in the process. On the one hand, there was no longer a requirement for the family of the marrying man to take part in the proceedings, while on the other hand, the bride's father became the sole benefactor of his daughter's Bride Price. This shift from a communal to a private function is one of the main indicators that the custom has changed considerably, and it is also a major contributing factor to the payment of Bride Price spiralling out of control (Ncube & Stewart, 1985).

As previously noted, in the past, the Shona and the Ndebele only used cattle which was a modest payment as a means of Bride Price. However, all this has changed due to capitalism. It is also unusual that though cash is used as a form of payment Bride Price, it is still quantified in terms of cows. Some of the major requirements of Bride Price such as *rusambo* and *roora* are retained, but some other features have been added, which includes groceries. The charges also vary depending on in which part of the country or continent the ceremony is held. It is believed that some in-laws are demanding electrical gadgets and cars as part of the Bride Price payment (Dery, 2015).

There is also a different charge for a girl who has graduated from university. Girls who are based abroad, such as in the United States, Australia and Canada, also command higher Bride Price than locally-based girls. This is due to the fact that men who marry girls who are based abroad will in time move abroad to join their spouses, therefore improving their own economic status.

The switch from communalism to capitalism, from traditional to modern, has seen the practice adopt exploitative tendencies. In this regard, we are forced to accept May's proposition that:

> Such a system is, of course, liable to abuse in an increasingly commercial society. Fathers demand unduly high amounts for educated daughters as a recompense for the money they have invested in educating their girls.

(May, 1984, p.48)

An educated girl attracts more money for two reasons; it is a compensation for the money invested in her education and it is believed that she would be of more value to the husband than an uneducated wife. In the old times, there was a facility to cater for the poor. Those who had no way of raising the necessary payment could arrange to work for the father-in-law instead of paying Bride Price (May, 1983). According to May, there are many poor men around Zimbabwe and yet there are no facilities through which they can pay Bride Price in this modern society. As a result, the urban poor have mostly moved away from traditional payment of Bride Price as they simply do not have the means, choosing instead to have families without going through the trouble of the practice (May, 1983).

Ncube and Stewart (1985) observed many families are cropping up without the payment of Bride Price being made mandatory, and that there are also many cases of cohabitation and 'living ins' around the country. People start a family and have children, with no effort made to 'legalize' the marriage. and as the world has shrunk into 'a global village', boys and girls now grow up to get married to people from other cultures that do not necessarily value Bride Price payment. Even the concept of marriage itself seems to be losing its traditional value. Some may decide simply to have children and raise them as single parents; women can be mothers without necessarily having men around them as husbands. Insisting on Bride Price payment can now bring challenges. As a society, we have moved far away from the village structure, within which it is relatively easy to regulate its payment. Both boys and girls have acquired a great deal of freedom of movement, often leaving the village for urban life. As such, parents cannot easily control the lives, especially the sexual behaviour, of their grown-up children (Ncube and Stewart, 1985).

3.10 Conclusion

The existing literature on Bride Price points to the idea that the practice has implications with regard to gender relations in many socio-cultural situations; it is a deeply-rooted custom that shapes a large part of African identity and specifically family life. Nevertheless, commercialisation has transformed the custom over time, changing to some degree the economic dimensions of the practice and its links to concepts of kinship. The literature further argues that many men struggle to raise the finances required to pay Bride Price, and because of the character of this custom it is alleged by many that it demeans women; most men believe that once payment they are owed respect and subservience from women. The few benefits of Bride Price are that it permits the exchange of wealth between families, whilst compensating the bride's family for the expenses incurred whilst raising their daughter. However, as I will show, fundamentally it renders women marginalised and vulnerable to abuse.

The next chapter presents an outline of the concepts and theoretical frameworks used in the study and their relevance to Bride Price. The main concepts explored are postcolonial feminist theory, in which this book is rooted, and the ecological model. Additionally, the chapter also discusses the four elements of intersectionality and how they interact to shape people's experiences and perceptions of Bride Price with reference to the field interviews, observations, focus group discussions and other methods used to collect data. The chapter also reviews the data sources and discusses the sample analysed, as well as defining and explaining the construction of the variables to be used in the analyses. Empirical models for estimation are also discussed in this chapter, which provides the theoretical framework in which this book is rooted.

Chapter 4

Post-colonial Theories, the Ecology Model & Bride Price

The previous chapter compiled and evaluated the available literature on Bride Price. This chapter presents my theoretical framework - an adapted post-colonial feminist lens, which I used to analyse my data. I was in effect testing out the feminist post-colonial critique that argues that culture has been over-used as an explanation for the marginalisation of women and the harm inflicted upon them in developing countries. My question in this regard is, to what extent can I see echoes of their arguments in the way my participants reflect on the practice? In this chapter, I review in detail the feminist post-colonial theories that I am going to apply in the subsequent chapters.

The first section of this chapter introduces post-colonial feminist theory and its critique in a general sense, as my book is also concerned with understanding how Bride Price may intersect with other dimensions that affect gender relations and identities. The next part focuses on applying the ecology approach, a tried and tested model developed by Lori Heise. This model is well known and used extensively within research on violence against women and offers a useful way of unpacking how different economic, social, cultural, religious and political factors contribute to creating an environment that sanctions particular constructs of gender that in turn may be oppressive or empowering. It presents a way of unpacking how our environment is gendered at various levels and spheres from individual behaviours and mind-sets through to the social norms and views that then shape relationships and institutions within which we live. I use Heise's model in order to understand how and where Bride Price fits in constructing (or not) the gendered society of my research sites. It also helps me to construct a comparison between the multiple different contexts of my study. In my book and through the data collected I am exploring whether Bride Price is more or less relevant in a rural setting compared to the capital in Zimbabwe, and how both of these compare to the context of the UK Zimbabwean diaspora. In order to do this, I need a solid framework. In developing my framework, marriage, culture and religion emerged as key dimensions, as did family law in Zimbabwe. For instance, Bride Price has to be understood within the concept of plural legal systems whereby laws are sanctioned by the state, and others are customary laws that guide the practices of the majority of people in the country.

Bride Price can potentially be used as an entry point into understanding how different dimensions come together to shape the gendered social worlds of men and women. As reviewed in the previous section, feminists have argued that Bride Price locks women and men into a rigid existence that leaves very little room for manoeuvre. As I come to show through my data, whilst men and women across my contexts agree with this, they also endorse the practice seeing it as a key expression of cultural identity that is linked to marriage and status. In this section, I also introduce the conceptual and theoretical framework of the ecology model, following which I present my own adapted ecology model that reflects the context of my research. Essentially, I am mapping the ecology model to each context - Harare, the rural areas of Zimbabwe and Birmingham, where most of the diaspora live.

I present information on work and income, what infrastructure is accessible in terms of church and community, education and health. In relation to Zimbabwe, I give detail on the legal context; i.e., Bride Price is not illegal but violence against women is. I address questions that include; what access to justice exists? How strong is civil society? Is there a women's movement and how effective is its reach? Does the women's movement stretch as far as the rural areas or are they only confined to urban areas? What are the issues they are working on? To what extent do they see Bride Price as a critical part of gendering society and embedding inequalities?

This chapter also presents the key challenges facing women in Zimbabwe and among the diaspora, and considers to what extent these challenges can be understood through the application of the ecology model. I consider the ways in which different gendered and intersectional strands are linked together and why Bride Price might sit within a complex web of competing and often contradictory values and beliefs. Essentially, in this book, I am presenting Bride Price through a feminist framework and as such regard it as a harmful cultural practice. I therefore need to confront and reflect upon how post-colonial narratives have argued that focusing on the cultural dimensions of gender inequality in the context of Africa can be both reductionist and often racist. My data enables me to listen to and reflect upon different voices of people (both men and women) who observe Bride Price and to consider whether their viewpoints can help to reinforce or challenge the different feminist readings.

I present the post-colonial critique as argued by Uma Narayan, which she highlights the overuse of culture as the explanation behind all abuse that women in the developing world suffer from. She describes 'cultural explanations' as Eurocentric and imperialist and as reinforcing colonial power relationships in unhelpful and deflecting ways. As discussed in my data analysis chapter later in this book, I test out the extent to which culture is or is not a key dimension of the continuation of Bride Price and also how it may feed into other forms of abuse. Understanding how this scholar views the linkages often made between religion and culture and violence against women is an important step in the development of my argument, and my data seems to both agree and disagree with the post-colonial argument. It is important also to highlight that most of Narayan's work is based on the Indian context, which to some extent differs from the context of Zimbabwe.

Before exploring the meanings of the critical concepts mentioned above, it is important to interrogate the meaning of the concept of Bride Price itself; where it was derived from, what it means, and what its significance is with regard to the debate on women's reproductive, sexual and other rights. The concept will be examined from the feminist perspective which allows how the practice of Bride Price affects women to be shown. This framework helps in the development of a critical understanding of the social relations within which the practice of Bride Price operates and the way it structures women's sexual and reproductive rights.

4.1 The Post-Colonial Feminist Lens

My study has been informed by a feminist perspective. Feminist research explores realities and experiences of women (Townsend, 2008). There are diverse feminist perspectives which include radical, liberal, and Marxist/socialist perspectives. However, for the purpose of this study, the feminist approach is based on the common conviction that cuts across the various perspectives, that is, a commitment to investigating the experiences of women in society and to try to view the world from the perspective of women. The feminist approach affords women a safe realm within which to tell their stories and, in so doing, validates and empowers them. The feminist perspective also entails a critique of patriarchy, which is the institutionalization of men's power over women within economic, religious, social, political, and marital relations (Penfold, Rotunda & Williamson, 2004).

The feminist model is a critical part of explaining how Bride Price commodifies women and renders them inferior, and for this reason, it is at the heart of this study. Violence against women, in this case, domestic violence, is a matter of male power over women (Townsend, 2008; Tsanga, 1999). The 'control-over component' gives patriarchy a propensity to violence (Tracy, 2007, p. 282) and, according to feminist theories, patriarchy is the ultimate cause, the key construct which ultimately leads to violence against women (Tracy, 2007). As such, from a feminist perspective, violence against women is a critical tool in the maintenance of male hegemony. The feminist perspective on female subservience and patriarchy provides an appropriate framework for studying women's experiences of domestic violence. A feminist theory is being used in this book as a central part of a social system that devalues women. From a feminist viewpoint, the practice is therefore essential in shaping the social system.

I also test out the relevance of post-colonial feminism to see whether or not the claims around practices such as Bride Price emerge in my data. In particular, I was looking at the differences between people's perceptions of this practice and what the critics of the practice might say. Emerging evidence of contradictions in my data included the tendency for people to criticise Bride Price one minute and support it the next.

This book is informed by a post-colonial feminist lens that carefully argues that Bride Price carries negative implications for women in that it commodifies them and renders them inferior to their husbands and other male family members. At the same time, this lens seeks to understand first-hand experiences of the practice in order to challenge negative assumptions about the effect it may (or may not have) on the lives of women. In other words, it seeks to challenge any lasting colonial assertions that Bride Price reflects backward mind-sets. It was common in colonial accounts to focus on the harsh treatment of women, evidencing this claim by highlighting the practices that were labelled as barbaric and backward. I considered the negative impact that Bride Price has on and for the lives of both women and men and how it may have changed over time, in particular as the result of urbanisation and migration. In doing so, I draw on the theoretical work of Mohanty (1988), Mohanty & Russo (1991), Anzaldúa & Moraga (2015), Rosaldo (1980) and Narayan (1998) who all agree that essentialising the lives of African women in negative demeaning language is unhelpful and unethical.

I drew out the complexities of how men and women inside and outside of Zimbabwe position themselves in relation to each other and the world around them and how and why traditional practices like Bride Price now fit into a global and modern way of life. It is important to highlight that most of the work on Bride Price is quite old, conducted in the 1950s to 1970s. It was primarily conducted by anthropologists who produced dense descriptions of family, kinship and community relations. They viewed Bride Price as a vital part of the African culture and accumulated most of their data through ethnographic studies. But so much has changed since these early studies. For example, Zimbabwe has seen massive urbanisation and migration, and understanding how new dimensions like this may intersect with traditional practices such as Bride Price is under-researched. As such, it is of great interest to a range of development stakeholders (Sustainable Development Goal 5 focuses on gender equality and empowerment of women, for example). In this book, I explore how and if changes have occurred in the practice of Bride Price over time and the implications these changes may bring for the lives of men and women. I also wanted to find out why people continue to use or give cows at the point of marriage and why the practice continues even after urbanisation and migration.

For Zimbabweans, Bride Price is at the heart of the marriage system which is in turn at the heart of community structures and social relationships. In designing this study, I was seeking to understand something about gender relations and gender equality among Zimbabwean society, so I focused on Bride Price and people's views around it. It is an entry point to other wider questions and there is very little written about it. The chapter also looks at what Bride Price is whilst exploring the different perspectives from feminism through to the more traditional insider perspective of Bride Price. This includes looking at religious views around it, which also enables me to situate myself in terms of the view point that I take.

Feminists have argued that Bride Price equates to buying a wife as if she is a commodity, which results in the abuse of the wife if she does not fulfil her value or if she attempts to leave a relationship and the Bride Price cannot be repaid (Matembe, 2004; Ndira, 2004). Domestic violence, abuse of women's rights, divorce and poverty among newly married couples have all been found to be associated with high Bride Price (Matembe, 2004; Oguli Oumo, 2004). As these have serious implications for the stability of families, especially among newly married couples.

Using the conceptualizations of gender, masculinity/femininity, class and modernisation, this book argues that despite its popular support, Bride Price payment cements the already existing gender inequalities because, after payment, some husbands feel that they have 'bought' the wife into their household; a feeling that creates male dominance and feelings of 'total manhood' and reinforces their hegemonic masculinities. It this craving for the feeling of 'total manhood' that encourages the majority of men to insist on paying even when Bride Price is not demanded. Some would argue that the practice makes women feel loved and respected in their role, which boosts femininities. However, with increased modernization, Bride Price has become a demonstration of class, highly commercialized and commoditized which leads to affordability problems for the poor.

Despite Zimbabwe's current strides towards modernization and the subsequent decline of several customs and practices, Bride Price - an age-old practice - has instead continued to gain more prominence in terms of attention given to it and the amount of resources exchanged during the process. Some activists have claimed that it has changed from a procedure to solemnise marriages to a highly commercialised and expensive transaction. Currently in Zimbabwe, there is an extensive debate between women's rights activists and other actors as to whether Bride Price has genuine positive outcomes or whether it is a dehumanising tool that reduces women to purchasable commodities, thus lowering their position, decision making powers, and other negative outcomes in marital relations. The debate continues with few signs of a consensus being reached amidst a lack of documented facts. Despite the debates and perceptions, a large percentage of the population still supports the practice. This study therefore analyses peoples' experiences and perceptions of Bride Price, grounding itself in the notions of migration, urbanisation, gender, masculinity, class, and modernisation/modernity and the intersections between them.

Although the patriarchal nature of society, and not necessarily Bride Price, is largely to blame for issues of women's subordination and domestic violence, its payment may serve to reinforce or act as a contributing factor to men's power over women. While some supporters of the practice view Bride Price as a form of protection for women within marriages by providing them respect, status and acknowledgement within society, other viewpoints argue that the process may contribute to women's subordination to husbands which may then lead to wives being vulnerable to abuse. On the other hand, defaulting men could lose status and respect from wives and society because they were not able to pay Bride Price (Hague, Thiara & Turner, 2011). There are increasing concerns about the negative effects of Bride Price on women in Zimbabwe as it is argued that it renders them as purchasable commodities. This leads to negative effects on women, children, family life and general community development. Women activists such as Mifumi and scholars such as Lowes, & Nunn, (2017) and Dery (2015) have accused Bride Price of having a high correlation with domestic violence, the degradation of women's dignity and the violation of human rights. They thus call for its reform (Matembe, 2002; Hague & Thiara, 2011).

The impact of Bride Price particularly on women has led to a heated debate among activists and feminists, to the extent that some have called for its abolition, though with little success. This lack of success is largely because it carries such deep cultural roots and is sanctioned by religious leadership as a critical entry point for marriage (see discussion later in the book). Despite the on-going debates, little scholarly studies have been conducted to assess how people perceive it or why it thrives, despite its negative publicity by several feminists. Studies such as this research project are required to generate reliable knowledge and evidence that can be used as a basis for the debates by activists, academics and policy makers. According to Abrahams, Baluku, & Crispus, (2012), "Bride Price, a historic custom has not been well documented and is one of the most crucial social mechanisms by which women are forced into a subordinate position compared to men". Globalisation coupled with a neo-liberal economic system has opened up Zimbabwe to new markets and imports which in turn has driven new consumer demand for high-tech goods.

This has brought about a change in the nature of what is given and expected as payment for Bride Price.

4.2 Applying the Critiques of Narayan to Feminist Debates on Bride Price

I am adapting a feminist stance because I believe that Bride Price is harmful. I also believe that these linkages which are suggested by feminist scholars such as Uma Narayan who argue that as much as Bride Price is part of 'our culture' it ought to be questioned. She thus asserts:

> I would argue that what differentiates my accounts from those of my mother has less to do with her 'cultural purity' or with my Westernisation than with certain contingent features of our respective histories that mark the space between generations.

(Narayan, 1997, p. 12)

In my framework, this feminist link between patriarchy and a gendered construction of what it is to be either a man or a woman. The inequalities built into these constructions leave women vulnerable to different forms of violence. I am taking this set of linkages and I am trying to see the extent to which that particular understanding is shared by the people that I have interviewed. I am positioning Bride Price as a key dimension in shaping gender relationships.

Uma Narayan argues that whilst the practice of dowry, like Bride Price, emerges in the cultural sphere the connection to religion is less apparent:

> While the institution of dowry can certainly be meaningfully connected to 'Indian culture' it is not, I think, given satisfactory 'explanations' by references to religion.

(Narayan, 1997, p. 113)

Narayan (1997) argues that in relation to dowry, Western liberal feminists essentially reduce dowry in India to an issue of culture. Under the same vein, she also questions or challenges the importance of 'culture':

> This picture tends to reinforce powerfully what I think of as the 'Idea of Vulnerability', making people susceptible to the suggestion that practices and institutions are valuable merely by virtue of the fact that they are of long-standing.

(Narayan, 1997, p. 22)

Challenging of a culture as an outsider was an issue that was brought to the fore by Narayan. Here she is helpful again in that she highlights the limitations placed on people when challenging cultures that are different to their own:

> this belief is perhaps a feminist version of a mistaken but common place belief, and that a deeply critical stance against one's culture places one entirely outside its orbit and influence.

(Narayan, 1997, p. 55)

This position was instrumental in giving me the freedom to change gears as necessary without being accused of being influenced by Western culture:

> by arguing that feminist work addresses patriarchal practices in 'another culture' is often subject to accusations of imperialism, nationalism, racism, capitalism and any other 'ism' more important than that can pose as broader and genocidal patriarchal.

(Narayan, 1997, p. 55)

Third world feminists are able to change gears as insiders when it comes to condemning certain cultural practices without being accused of either feeling superior or racist unlike their Western counterparts who tread carefully when it comes to dealing with cultural practices that affect other societies.

The questioning of certain cultural practices (especially harmful ones) by feminists in the host country removes accusations of imposition of ideas unlike when the same issues were raised by a 'Western feminist'. These Third World feminists also believe that they are in a better position to challenge elements of their culture which they feel are not compatible with modern times or that contribute to gender-based violence. They are against any attempt by 'Western' feminists to challenge an element of their culture as they believe that the 'foreigners' are not qualified to comment about their culture. This was asserted by Narayan, who argued that:

> Many feminists from Third-world context confront voices that are eager to convert any feminist criticism they make of their culture into a mere symptom of their 'lack of respect for their culture' rooted in the 'Westernisation' that they seem to have might like a disease.

(Narayan, 1997, p. 6)

Bashai and Grossbard (2008) argue that Bride Price does not only lead to the purchase of women's' freedom but also translates into the husband's ownership of the wife's sexual rights. In their study of Bride Price in Uganda, they concluded that women who had Bride Price paid for them are less likely to engage in extra marital relations, although the same does not apply to men (Bishai & Grossbard, 2008). It is also argued that since in most communities Bride Price is supposed to be refunded in the event that the couple separates, many women are bound to stay in violent relationships if their parents cannot afford to repay the property they received. Although there are remedies, like petitioning court for divorce, it may be a complicated matter especially for less wealthy or illiterate women with no money for legal representation or even knowledge of the existence of court. Secondly, securing a divorce in Zimbabwe has been almost impossible for women until 2009 when some sections in the Marriage and Divorce Act were annulled by the constitutional court; women had to prove both adultery and cruelty while men only needed to prove adultery in order to secure a divorce (Luyirika, 2010). Such laws result from the state and social structures that glorify male dominance while treating women like second class citizens.

Bride Price in some ways reduces the exit options available to wives (especially those who are poor) if the marriage becomes unpleasant. But even where the parents have the means to refund Bride Price, the process of refunding itself creates embarrassment and stigma and this may further compel wives to stay in unpleasant relationships (Strube, 1988).

4.3 The Social Ecology Model

As stated earlier in this book, there are few documented studies that provide reasons for the continuation of the practice or that seek to understand wider shifts in marriage patterns and gendered expectations. My decision to focus on Bride Price is because it represents a vehicle into understanding and exploring changes in patterns of gender relations within family structures and more widely across society. This involves looking at the shifting make up of families across the settings of this study as well as probing the ways in which Bride Price is observed. The diagram below shows how Bride Price is linked to other forms of violence.

Heise (1998) proposed a framework for analysing determinants of domestic violence as the interplay of personal, situational and socio-cultural factors as depicted in *Figure3*. From this model, violence results from interaction of factors at different levels of the social environment, ranging from biological and personal factors, relationship factors and formal and informal institutions in which the relationship occurs. Bride Price payment is one of the factors that apply in this ecological model. Factors that influence a culture of violence were classified by Heise (1998) into originating, promoting and facilitating factors. Accordingly, violence originates from breakdown of social integration mechanisms, followed by weakening of the family's role in socializing individuals and finally promoted by absence of mechanisms for peaceful resolution of conflict.

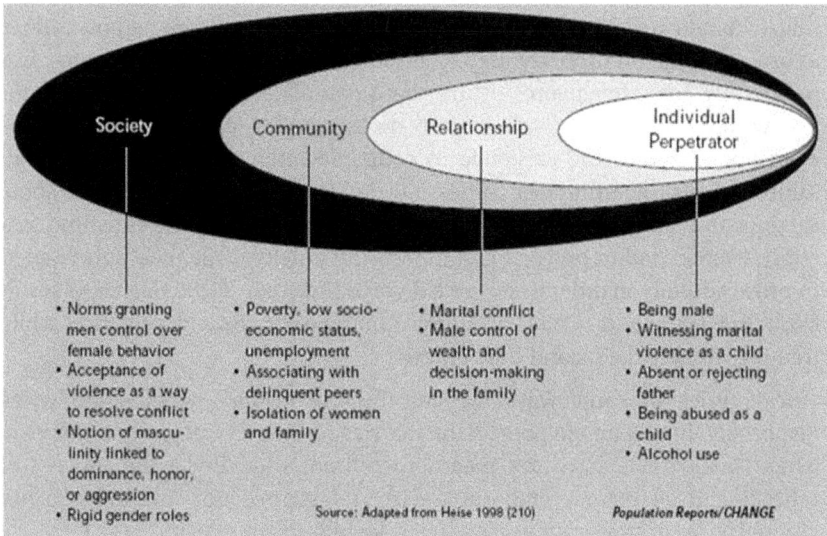

Society	Community	Relationship	Individual Perpetrator
• Norms granting men control over female behavior • Acceptance of violence as a way to resolve conflict • Notion of masculinity linked to dominance, honor, or aggression • Rigid gender roles	• Poverty, low socio-economic status, unemployment • Associating with delinquent peers • Isolation of women and family	• Marital conflict • Male control of wealth and decision-making in the family	• Being male • Witnessing marital violence as a child • Absent or rejecting father • Being abused as a child • Alcohol use

Source: Adapted from Heise 1998 (210)   *Population Reports/CHANGE*

Figure 4.1. The Social Ecology Model by Lori Heise (1998).

Furthermore, according to Silberschmidt (1999), Bride Price payment has implications on gender relations, values, expectations and roles. In her ethnographic work in Kenya, she conceptualized violence as a problem of transition from traditional to modern society. She found that men seemed to have lost identity and their position was weakened by altered gender relations following modernization, resulting in gender antagonism regarding perceived roles.

According to Cornell (1999) and Cleaver (2002), gender identity refers to activities, traits, and values that are socially, contextually and historically dependent and form a basis for identifying the roles of men and women. Scott (1986) agrees that the structure of the economy and the gender relations in production overlap to culminate into historically shaped experiences that frame the social reality of women. Accordingly, gender is based on social reality and is not biologically determined. In summary, Scott (1986) presents four elements of gender construction that operate simultaneously to reinforce gender roles, and which have been useful in my analysis. These include cultural symbols that elicit symbolic and conflicting representations and myths about men and women (for example 'Eve and Mary as symbols of woman', especially among Christians, represent goodness, innocence, purity and tenderness while men are symbolised as rough, dark, corrupt and other associated characterisations). The second element relates to the 'normative concepts' that tend to reinforce the above representations by defining what is perceived to be an 'ideal' male or female and that are used in social interaction over a period of time. The third element is the composition and structure of social institutions and organisations that are gendered or reproduce processes of gender construction. These include the family and household, the labour market, educational institutions, the economy and the state. The last element consists of the construction of subjective identities resulting from activities, representations, and collective treatments that lead a person to assume a particular identity. All four elements act upon each other to reinforce gender construction in particular contexts (Scott 1986, pp. 1067-1068).

Gender construction and learning starts at birth with the assignment of a sex category to a baby based on the genital organs. These result in the identification of the baby as a girl or a boy, followed by the allocation of feminine or masculine names and clothing and other gender markers (McClintock, 2013). This translates into treatment and training of the children based on sex differences, to which children also respond and behave differently in order to answer and conform to their assigned gender category. The process continues through parenting and, by adulthood, the children have adopted the particular behaviours considered 'normal' in that specific society. These behaviours are reproduced in the way the adults behave, the type of roles they undertake and how they relate with the opposite 'gender'. Scholars have described this as 'doing gender', which is the process of reinforcing, conditioning or disapproving of certain behaviours and gender markers on the basis that they are reserved for males or females (McClintock, 2013).

Due to the gendered institutions like the state, the family and religion, gender is implicitly and sometimes explicitly a present discourse for purposes of national identity, but it is also as a way to establish and maintain particular forms of social order, status, and recognition and to sustain power (Turmursukh, 2001). With the increase in other forms of family arrangements like same-sex couples, single mothers, single fathers, and the increased role of women in political and economic spheres, such perceptions and institutional arrangements are unsurprisingly scrutinised.

4.4 Masculinity & Femininity

Masculinity does not exist except in contrast with femininity, thus it involves the socially constructed characteristics of men or what is expected of men, especially in relation to women. These characteristics are socially constructed and differ from community to community and are not static as they evolve as society undergoes change. In several African societies characterized by patriarchal arrangements, men are expected to be strong, intelligent, and dominant (especially over women) and those who fall below these standards and behaviours may be labelled as not 'man enough'. These beliefs influence how society is organized and how different activities and practices are performed.

According to Connell (1999), masculinities is a relational concept to gender, and though all societies have clear perceptions about gender, some do not necessarily have the concept of masculinities. Notions of masculinities thus determine the type of behaviour one is expected to exhibit in society if he is to be considered masculine or feminine. Expectations about masculinity include being violent or dominant, having a high interest in sexual pleasure and in sports, for example. On the contrary, those who do not exhibit such behaviours or show the opposite are considered to be less masculine or more feminine (Connell, 1999). It should be noted, however, that there are quite a number of people who do not follow this binary classification of boy or girl, or male versus female - for example, intersex, transgender and others – meaning that identifying people based on binary classification is itself problematic.

Due to the effect of modernization and social change, the social structure is evolving in favour of an improved role of women in society which continues to challenge the dominance of masculine identity. For example, women are increasingly participating in formal education and attaining higher qualifications, are employed in formal paid jobs and earning incomes which are sometimes higher than men. The loss of jobs by some men results in the forfeiture of breadwinner status, along with reduced attainment of education by boys compared to girls and an increase in female-headed households is linked to the reduced role of the 'traditional' family. These developments have put the dominant masculinities under threat (Cleaver, 2002; Nicholson, 1997a).

Gender is a useful category of analysis as it allows us to examine and understand how and why certain perceptions and actions held against men and women are incorporated not only in social but also in political and economic relations of society. It is these socialized relationships, beliefs and roles that are referred to as gender. This results from institutions, beliefs, practices, knowledge, relations and cultures that promote gender as a major basis of identity, that is, a "social category imposed on a sexed body or a social organization of sexual differences" (Scott, 1986, p. 1054). In other words, these are social characteristics that are being mistakenly viewed as 'natural' and biologically determined, and they are then translated into roles that hinge on beliefs of 'dominant man' and 'subordinate woman' – i.e., hegemonic masculinities (Butler, 1993).

4.5 Linking Bride Price and Social Class

Class refers to the different social stratifications of people in society organized in a hierarchical order, though in some cases it is difficult to draw a dividing line between two distinct classes. The classes may be categorized into the upper-class, middle-class and lower-class. Class (like gender) is a relational concept which signifies vertical differences or hierarchies among people, groups, individuals, tribes, races, castes and position in the production systems. Talcott Parsons, theorizing under the influence of Weberian ideas, investigated the class system and social stratifications and argued that social stratification systems are influenced by the level of wealth, prestige, influence, education and lifestyle (Parsons, 1940). However, the Marxist approach to class analysis looks at the social relations of production, that is, the relations between the owners of the means of productions (capitalists and employers) and those who sell their labour to the capitalist for a living (the workers). In addition, it looks at the class-specific form of relations, the differences in class relations and how one's location in a particular class affects her or his political, economic and social standings, views and chances (Wright. 1999).

Breen and Rottman (1995) argue that people or groups of people undertake particular actions based on the level of social power and status they have, and this implies that individuals in a particular class are faced with similar resources or constraints on their behaviour. These resources or constraints may be held consciously or unconsciously. Thus, people under a similar social position or class have a high probability of sharing actions and beliefs in relation to a particular phenomenon, and hence they are likely to act in the same way. This was confirmed by Goldthorpe (1996) using what is referred to as the rational action theory.

Theorising on family and class, Goldthorpe (1983) argued that an individual's class is based on the family, and thus the family forms the basic unit of stratification and not the individual. Following this line, he argues that the class or the position of the family in the class system will be determined by the position of the male head of the family who is always a breadwinner. However, this line of argument by Goldthorpe is challenged by Stanworth (1984) who contended that using the family as the basis for categorizing the class of individuals is questionable as the class experience of wives differs from that of their husbands, meaning that a family-based categorisation ignores the vast inequalities that exist between men and women or wives and husbands and also overlooks the fact that some of the inequalities that exist between men and women are caused by the class systems. Further, Goldthorpe's assumptions do not acknowledge that some of the arrangements or unions that he calls family have changed and, as such, many individuals do not fall within any form of what is referred to as the 'normal' family (Nicholson, 1997b).

Many hypotheses have been put forward to explain the occurrence of Bride Price. One theory links marriage payment to the economic value of women. Brides command a positive worth - a Bride Price - in areas where women make valuable contributions to agricultural work or other economic activity. Another hypobook argues that marriage payments are "prices" that clear the marriage market, that is, these prices balance the demand for and supply of brides and grooms. Therefore, when brides are scarce grooms offer a higher Bride Price. Other theories link the existence of different types of marriage payments to the laws governing marital and social ties (kinship structures). For example, Bride Price has been observed very often in societies with general polygyny (polygyny practised by the general populace and not just the rich), whereas dowry almost always occurs in monogamous societies. Marriage payments have also been linked to norms of hypergamy, whereby brides are expected to marry into a higher caste or social group, and hypogamy, whereby brides are expected to marry into a lower caste or social group (Goody & Tambiah, 1973).

According to Pahl (1993), class and education attainment have a high degree of correlation and the level of education does not only determine life chances like getting employment but also determines values. In the same vein, Wright (2000) suggests that people in the same class category have a high likelihood of deciding between or attaching similar values to particular phenomena. On the subject of Bride Price, Caplan (1984) while studying perceptions on dowry in urban India, observed that there is a high association between class status and dowry and that those in the upper hierarchy have a higher preference for dowry system while those in the lower status prefer Bride Price. He observed that those with high education attainment and professionals, especially Christians belonging to the lower-middle-class, tended to have low preference for Bride Price and dowry while the poor and those based in the caste system had a preference for both, albeit in small amounts. Therefore, this means that there is a correlation between class and preference for Bride Price including the amount paid, and this helped me to analyse the situation in the Zimbabwean context.

In a study of marriages and property in Palestine, Conley et al. (2009) emphasises the role played by class and social status in determining the perceptions and values attached to marital gifts. Whereas during the first "*antifada*," less attention was attached to dowry and gifts and people would just marry even with "no ring, no gold," the situation later changed altogether causing difficulties for poor young men who could not afford the exorbitant costs. Although in some cases only a symbolic fee, like JD 1 (One Jordanian Dinar), is charged; this especially the case among upper-middle-class families or where the families know and trust each other. In many cases, though, expensive marriage gifts make the brides feel a sense of 'specialness', and those from the upper-class may feel embarrassed or humiliated among family members in cases where the prospective husbands fail to bring classy and stylish gifts (Johnson, 2009).

These observations relate to my study and help me to analyse how issues of class and social status influence the motivations for high, low, or no Bride Price in the Zimbabwean context. My study uses the Weberian (Talcot) approach since most of the class divisions in the study area are based on differences in wealth and education and not necessarily labour relations. The distinguishing characteristics between classes include economic status, level of education and to some extent, religious power. Thus, I considered the rich, the middle-income earners and the poor, then the highly educated (professionals above degree level), the moderately educated and the illiterate, and I also compared the rich but not educated, or the educated but poor. In addition, I considered those with political power, religious leaders and those with traditional power like clan leaders (sometimes referred to as local elders) as a distinct group. Issues investigated and analysed here include how different classes perceive and experience Bride Price, whether Bride Price is a class issue, how they have seen it evolve and why and how different classes approach the ceremony, as well as how issues of gender and masculinity interact with class and modernisation.

4.6 The Ecology Model and Intersectionality

Heise's (1998) model maps out how violence happens because of a number of different factors that all come together; there will be different factors in different contexts, so religion and culture can be more or less significant. At a societal level, religion is a key influencer and Heise (2002) states that its effect is also very strong at community level. As my data confirms, pastors are crucial in shaping gendered attitudes (see next chapter) as they require Bride Price in order to carry out marriages, this shows how embedded the practice is in the fabric of society which in turn shapes the community and individual levels of the ecology.

I am placing the individual women interviewed at the centre of my analytical framework and map from their experiences and the specific views around them. This also involves reflecting on the reality of violence that happens within their relationships and the role of male dominance in sustaining unequal patterns of gender. Understanding what it is in the context of the ecology model that ultimately sanctions and legitimises violence is an important part of my analysis. I will come on to argue more strongly and through my data that religious messages linked to practices such as Bride Price and FGM rely on religious texts and so reproduce rigid concepts of gender that ultimately leave women vulnerable to male violence.

Middle-class women and also some from the lower-class, are attempting to demand and negotiate the terms of their relationships including control over sex, a thing that was rare in the traditional era (Tamale, 2009).The above analysis reveals that when modernisation interfaces with social class especially the educated middle-class, masculinities, femininities and gender roles associated with Bride Price payment tend to gradually dwindle, though the price itself may be increasing in amount. While comparing masculinities, modernisation and Bride Price, Kaye observes that with modernisation, men seem to have lost identity, power, weakening gender gaps and roles and has somehow led to gender antagonism regarding the hither to perceived gender roles (Kaye, 2002; Schnidt, 1991).

4.7 Applying the Ecology Model to Bride Price in Zimbabwe

In this section, I apply the ecology model to the Zimbabwean situation in order to examine the interdependence between family with the other environments that it interacts. Attention is also given to the function of family as an energy transformation system, with particular emphasis on its role in the production of human capital through the building of family and individual competences. These competences are essential for families and individuals to cope with crises and problems on many levels including the individual, the family, the community and society. The use of this model can enhance the understanding of the relationship of behaviour to environmental conditions and the effects on families of the institutions and the organisations with which they interact. Additionally, this approach can also provide a framework for design and implementation of imaginative intervention programs and support systems based on knowledge of family-environment interactions.

At the individual level, men can be seen to be asserting their power over women in order to reinforce their personal feelings of total manhood. Sadly, this is acceptable in most communities in Zimbabwe and has been established as a cultural norm. This is further reinforced by Bride Price: once a man pays Bride Price at the point of marriage, then there is a feeling that 'he paid for the woman' and this usually results in mistreatment of the wife. On the other hand, girls are socialised from childhood to grow up as 'good' girls and become 'good' women and brides for the marriage. In the same vein, women are encouraged to be 'strong' regardless of the abuse they may encounter at the hands of their husbands. This is also regarded as being a 'good' wife or bride.

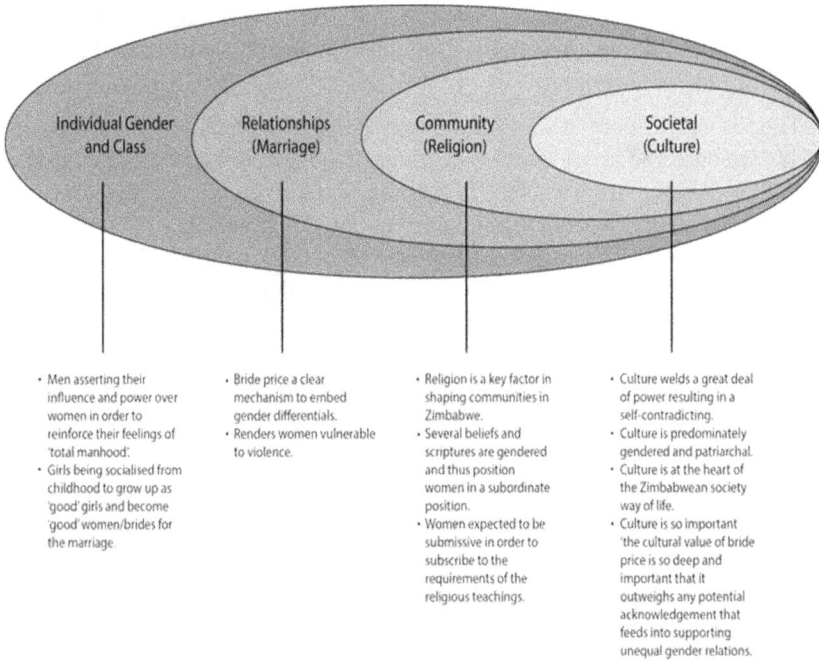

Individual Gender and Class	Relationships (Marriage)	Community (Religion)	Societal (Culture)
• Men asserting their influence and power over women in order to reinforce their feelings of 'total manhood'. • Girls being socialised from childhood to grow up as 'good' girls and become 'good' women/brides for the marriage.	• Bride price a clear mechanism to embed gender differentials. • Renders women vulnerable to violence.	• Religion is a key factor in shaping communities in Zimbabwe. • Several beliefs and scriptures are gendered and thus position women in a subordinate position. • Women expected to be submissive in order to subscribe to the requirements of the religious teachings.	• Culture welds a great deal of power resulting in a self-contradicting. • Culture is predominately gendered and patriarchal. • Culture is at the heart of the Zimbabwean society way of life. • Culture is so important 'the cultural value of bride price is so deep and important that it outweighs any potential acknowledgement that feeds into supporting unequal gender relations.

Figure 4.2. The Zimbabwe Ecology model.

The role of the Church on the issue of Bride Price is also quite important due to the fact that Zimbabwe is a religious country (Kuperus, 1999). The main denomination, Roman Catholic, recognises the importance of Bride Price but acknowledges that greedy parents are seeking to get rich by marrying off their daughters, thereby threatening the institution of marriage. The Church noted the abuse of the practice of paying Bride Price, which it said was becoming commercialised. There is a belief in the Church that there was a time when handing over *lobola* was meant to tie the two families together and deepen their friendship (Chireshe & Chireshe, 2010), but that it has now become a commercial transaction whereby the father-in-law hopes that his son-in-law will save him from poverty.

Additionally, the Church believes that if the son-in-law is poor himself (unemployed or underpaid), then the couple may decide to live in an informal union without any social sanction, let alone a church marriage. There is an anecdotal Christian belief that this type of union is highly unstable; that it may easily break up and that the woman will end up as a single mother, leaving the children without a father. The Church's position is used by Catholic priests to give guidance to married people, as well as those yet to be married and those whose marriages are facing difficulties (Kuperus,1999). The Zimbabwean Catholic leadership believes that the abuse of Bride Price is a major threat to marriages.

The Church respects culture and some of the traditional practices, but also acknowledges the abuse of this otherwise good practice that brings families together, beyond the couple. The Church equally condemns the abuse of Bride Price for self-enrichment in place of its original purpose of establishing a relationship. There is a belief amongst young members of the Church that some men were hard on their wives after paying high Bride Prices and having been pressured into funding lavish wedding ceremonies and receptions. They further argue that Bride Price is now being used by in-laws as a tool to take themselves out of poverty, as a status symbol to demonstrate that the son-in-law is rich, and to show that their child is valuable because she is learned. In marriage, this creates a sense of ownership on the man's part rather than pure love, no strings attached: if one pays more, one expects more (Dery, 2015).

4.8 Conclusion

In conclusion, many of the participants were of the view that Bride Price indirectly leads to the marginalisation of Zimbabwean women in most spheres of life and they are also compromised in their personal and professional development by being undervalued, underemployed and under-rewarded. In using Narayan's work, I explored the extent to which my data resonates with her critique on the impact of 'essentialist cultural narratives'. Narayan asserts that there is a tendency when talking about the lives of women in the developing countries to state that their culture is responsible for their inferiority and their vulnerability.

The post-colonial feminist theory confirms that Bride Price, which renders women inferior to their husbands, is also a clear mechanism to embed gender differentials. Once Bride Price is paid, a woman is expected to act and behave in a certain way. Gender roles are also defined at the point of marriage, and from then the man and woman are not equal because a payment has been made. The payer 'feels' that he can do as he pleases with his 'purchase'.

Additionally, the role of religion in cementing Bride Price is also significant because community pressure and expectation results in women behaving in certain ways and, should they go against community norms, they are likely to be disowned by their family or face domestic violence from their husband. Husbands in most communities can 'discipline' their wives should they feel they need to. Additionally, with Zimbabwe being a Christian country, religion is a key factor in shaping communities. Several scriptures and beliefs are gendered and place women in a subordinate position: they are expected to be submissive in order to subscribe to the requirements of religious teachings. As much as Zimbabwean society is changing in many other social aspects, when it comes to religious and biblical teachings, there tends to be stiff resistance to change. This can be partly attributed to the 'modernisation' forces from evangelical movements, especially from the USA, who have intensified their activities in Zimbabwe in the past three decades with heavy funding and conservative teachings particularly on matters of women, subordination and sexuality (Machinga, 2011a).

> Religious fundamentalist groups have forcibly linked their practice to restoration of a woman's' supposedly more authentic 'traditional' role when in fact there is little historical precedent for the unquestioned performance of such a role
>
> (Scott, 1986, p. 17)

Such gendered teachings promote unequal gender relations and women's subordination contribute to discouraging women from challenging religious teachings.

Chapter 5

Cultural, Religious and Gendered Dimensions of Bride Price

The previous chapter highlighted the theoretical frameworks I have selected to support the analysis of my data. In this chapter I will present my data using these frameworks that enable me to fill some of the gaps in knowledge identified at the start of this book. Additionally, this chapter acknowledges the power of culture and its relationship with religion, which together serve to support and legitimise Bride Price. Culture and religion are highly gendered and embed structural inequalities in society. This chapter explores through my data how these two dimensions are interwoven with the practice of Bride Price and embed unequal gender relationships. In emphasising the dominance of culture and religion I am diverging from the feminist post-colonial theorists whose work I reviewed in the previous chapter. They argue that culture and religion should not be overemphasised when explaining of violence against women. However, my data shows something different in that culture and religion come out strongly.

The current chapter starts by providing the participants' perceptions and views on Bride Price, and how and why Bride Price is observed today across my three sites. The second section of the chapter further interrogates the motivation to observe Bride Price and explores why people still regard it as important and whether they see it as a positive part of their identity. This section reveals how intrinsic Bride Price is to culture and religion and subsequently in shaping marriage. This relationship appears in many ways unchanged, despite major shifts in the global structures of the world and patterns of migration. The third section considers peoples' views in light of the feminist frameworks presented in Chapter two and reveals a slight departure from their standpoints.

5.1 Participants' Perceptions and Views on Bride Price

My research highlights that culture is important to my participants, specifically in having a cultural identity. My data reveals that the cultural value of Bride Price is so deep and important that it outweighs any negatives. Even though there is acknowledgement that Bride Price feeds into and supports unequal gender relations my participants did not advocate an end to it. The cultural value is so very strong that even with women and men that acknowledge violence in their lives, they are not equating it with the practice and will not accept this interpretation, analysis or narrative because the cultural value to them is that important.

Bride Price is a deeply rooted practice and almost an emotional need. My argument, which my data supports, is that the link between people and culture is so powerful that it dominates even when somebody knows that a practice is not a good thing. Whilst I do acknowledge that gender inequalities are embedded through a complex web of factors, I believe we do need to talk about culture. Culture is in fact the start and end point. Narayan's critique of how dowry is understood through a static cultural lens needs to be heard, but in my research, I have sought to understand how change has affected how and why Bride Price happens. Across my three contexts there is evidence of change in why it is practised and shifts in how it is practised, but Bride Price remains at the heart of Zimbabwean family and marriage life, and the symbolic meaning around it remains strong.

In seeking to understand why my participants feel Bride Price is still important I found that all but two were in support of Bride Price payment and exchange of other marriage gifts. Although they differed in age, class and level of education and other social variables, almost all the reasons given in favour of Bride Price were identical. This importance was summed up by a 53-year-old married male participant (Ndebele tribe) in Harare:

> Actually, let's not even accuse tradition. In its strict sense, traditionally, *lobola* was an appreciation. A man could give even one jacket to his father-in-law and that was it. If he couldn't afford, even helping to farm in his in-law's farm for a season sufficed. It was simply a way of a man connecting to his wife's family and feeling welcomed and be part and parcel of it. Nobody left with ill feelings or feeling reaped off. *Lobola* was celebrated when a man pays, and the wife would be highly respected. *Lobola* is not the same as buying a person it's not about making money. It's a gesture of goodwill and gratuity from one family to the other.

Further justifying the perpetuation of *lobola*, a number of participants described it as a unifying force, binding and cementing the relationship between two families; a sentiment expressed by Bourdillon (1990) as he describes Bride Price as a chain that links two families. Bride Price then brings families together; this position is further endorsed by another interviewee who said that, "It is our tradition; somehow it brings two families together another family appreciating the other". Furthermore, it is seen as a mark of respect from the bridegroom to his in-laws:

for the man to actually pay Bride Price will mean that his in-laws will actually respect him he worked towards that he actually paid unlike staying with someone's child and ignore the practice.

(Married female, 28, Shona tribe, in Harare)

Across my field sites, Bride Price was seen as a token of appreciation as evidenced by a married male participant (25, Shona tribe) in Birmingham; "I think it's a token of appreciation to my in-laws for raising a wife that I am marrying". The same message came out of the interviews in Zimbabwe:

I also think it should continue because if it is cut off, we will have a problem because it is a token of appreciation. The husband should pay a Bride Price to appreciate the wife he will be getting from the parents so it should continue.

(Married female, 20, Shona tribe, in Harare)

Differences in perceptions regarding why Bride Price continues can be seen in the second-generation Zimbabweans who are based in the UK. Some of my participants felt that Bride Price has become driven by money and greed and so has lost its original cultural value of bringing families together. One married male interviewee (28, Shona tribe) in Birmingham asserted that:

Yaah I think the Bride Price is a token of appreciation. The basis of it was the creation of a relationship between the in-laws from both families just to exchange. I think the purpose of it is to exchange courtesy to one another and as a result creating that kind of family relationships between the two families of the bride and the bridegroom. I therefore, I think it is quite important as a parent it is very important because it attach a value to the child. It shows that someone appreciates your child, from the parental point of view. It is more of an appreciation. Bringing up children is not an easy job so it's a way of appreciating saying we appreciate the effort of bringing up a wife for me. I think, in my own opinion it's a worthy kind of exchange.

The wife (26, Shona tribe) was also of the same view regarding the continuation of Bride Price that, "To me it is very important, culturally important, because it shows commitment and its shows that you are honouring where you are going to get your wife." A 72-year-old married male participant (Shona tribe) in Birmingham brought in a new dimension of 'identity' to the argument:

It bothers me when my own people try to move away from these things in preference to Western inspired ones. Of course, we have to move with the times and leave out some bad practices but *lobola* does not harm anyone. Having travelled the world a bit I have come across all races that populate this world. Indians, Chinese, Pacific Islanders, South American Indians keep their traditions. Come to Africans they want to be like hip hop stars and feel ashamed of their tradition and languages. When these people start looking down upon us, we make noise. It is because we have no identity. As for me, *lobola* is right for me and it is not for financial gains on my parents' part because that said cash will be used for whatever ceremonies that will take part be it wedding or whatever. And if someone cannot afford to pay the amount, I am here to help him. *Lobola* stays!

Paying US$40, 0000 for *lobola* is, according to some of my participants, ridiculous, unreasonable and unjustifiable. They argue that they would never advocate for such, and that there should be a set amount people should pay for *lobola*. My participants further argued that some people were not against the idea but did not support the exorbitant prices. The change in the practice from a traditional to a commercial one is summed up by one a 50-year-old male primary school teacher (Shona tribe) in Harare:

If I may also come in? it is unfortunate here that we notice quite a big number of men have not been able to understand the real value of *lobola*, and its suppose nature, they have taken it and equated it to a payment, to a charge, so because of that he who has paid has always paid that he has done something so the one who has not done something must bow must listen to the one who has paid, this is an unfortunate situation which has been created by a misconception in the first place. Otherwise, lack of education or knowledge of what *lobola* really is and what really it should be

Another 50-year-old married male participant (Shona tribe) in Harare who stated that:

When they try to reconciliate what marriage is thought of by Zimbabweans those of other nations, we have noticed that some people become opportunistic especially when they deal with someone new. They look at it as an opportunity to milk so the way they charge become exaggerated. And those who were witnesses how they pray to have a similar chance in their own families, they would also do the same. So, to some extent families, have influenced each other more easily because of the life that we live today, we're now a global village where we are mixing up, we are playing together, and our kids have chances to marry, so because of that the ceremonies have changed.

The justification of *lobola* on the ground that the wife extends the husband's clan through male offspring was clearly articulated by a 47-year-old married female participant (Shona tribe) in Harare who put it thus: "If you don't want to pay *lobola* but you want to have sons then you are mad", implying the absurdity of having one's clan extended without one having paid anything to one's in-laws.

5.2 A Sign of Honour

The giving of Bride Price can be seen as an act of honouring a new relationship and family union.

So, it's like you are placing a value to your wife. It was not only you the husband but your family that was involved in this process. It actually represents the name of that family. And the bride's family will respect the groom's family because there has been an interchange were, they have valued their relationship by actually putting a note to say the relationship of the two families is very important.

This married male interviewee (27, Shona tribe) in rural Zimbabwe goes further to justify *lobola* as, "A token of announcing the relationship and making your in-laws happy [...] when I was paying my *lobola*, I felt so proud of myself, it was a great landmark in my life". Some participants claimed it was about showing appreciation:

because the payment of the Bride Price is not that you are buying a slave. It was just to say, I appreciate you raised this woman and this woman is now my wife. What she was taught. You are protecting her name.

(Married male, 50, Shona tribe, in Harare)

This idea of Bride Price as a token of respect can also be seen in this response:

Bride Price is like you as I have said before its sort of a token of appreciation, as in I want this woman you have raised for me so that's sort of an appreciation according to our culture.

(Married male, 50, Shona tribe, in Harare)

The gendered dimension of Bride Price came through very clearly in my discussions. A 27-year-old married female participant (Shona tribe) in rural Zimbabwe who asserted that:

> Man was born with responsibilities and paying Bride Price is part of the core responsibilities. And even a woman is born with her responsibilities like waving mats, producing children and providing care to the children and the family and for that reason when she married away, she should be paid for. In fact, in the past a woman was not even supposed to own money since she received all care and support from the husband.

Another participant, a married male participant (53, Ndebele tribe) in Harare, asserted that a 'real man' must bring property and beer for men to feast if he marries in order to attain 'full' recognition.

The above statements from participants reveal how perceptions are rooted in beliefs of an all-powerful man and a subordinate woman who has to take instructions or risk being owned by the husband. It also reveals beliefs in the so-called traditional family where a male is the head and breadwinner and a wife is relegated to reproductive work. The implication here is that if the bride or wife is stronger either economically or professionally than the husband, the husband's hegemonic masculinities feel threatened and he may feel insecure or resort to weak masculinities, become suspicious and in some cases, husbands have forced their wives to withdraw from paid work or personal business in order to 'control' them. Magezi (2007) describes this as 'pulling her down'.

For some participants, the custom of *lobola* ought to be maintained because it attaches some value to the wife. A woman for whom *lobola* has not been paid is, according to Shona culture, not a legitimate wife but one of 'whiling up time with', a kind of toy. *Lobola* was cited as an indicator that the man values his wife. It was also pointed out that since the wife is an asset and she ensures the perpetuation of the other family, *lobola* ought to be paid for her to show her value. Thus, *lobola* was depicted as a custom that shows that the wife is valued and respected by both her parents and her husband. *Lobola* was also depicted as a custom that gives a woman a sense of self-worth. These findings concur with Gelfand's (1981) conviction that *lobola* payment gives the woman value in the eyes of all, especially the man. Furthermore, participants who registered support for *lobola* indicated that payment of *lobola* shows the husband's complete acceptance of his wife and his total commitment to her.

In defence of the perpetuation of *lobola* some participants argued that if *lobola* is abolished, women would be abused at a very alarming rate. A married female participant (43, Shona tribe) in rural Zimbabwe put it thus:

"Without *lobola* the man would take it as a simple thing to marry and divorce, abusing and violating women, causing gender inequality problems." A number of participants, echoing similar sentiments, noted that *lobola* preserves marriages, thereby reducing divorce rates, a finding in keeping with Hamisu's (2000) assertion that Bride Price is a socially stabilizing factor.

While a majority of participants showed support for the custom of *lobola*, they were quick to point out that abuse of the custom has detrimental effects on marriage. They noted that *lobola* should not be overcharged because '*mukwasha muonde haaperi kudyiwa*' (meaning even if a son-in-law has paid his bride wealth, he is still expected to help his father-in-law). The implication of this response is that if *lobola* is overcharged, the son-in-law will no longer feel indebted to his in-laws and will not be willing to offer them any economic assistance. Thus, while a large Bride Price gives status to the wife and to the marriage, in some areas *lobola* payments have "inflated to a degree that disturbs many" (Bourdillon, 1998, p. 45). This position was supported by one 54-year-old married women interviewee (Shona tribe, in rural Zimbabwe) who argued that a woman is likely to respect her husband if *lobola* has been paid:

Yes, even when Bride Price is paid, the man gets more respect from the wife more than when he hasn't paid Bride Price. There is a pay anything to my parents. But at times you just fear that this man struggled so much to pay *lobola* for me. There is a time when you just say ha, who am I to him because he didn't pay anything for me. He didn't.

Participants who argued for Bride Price to be abolished viewed the custom as a facilitator of the oppression and abuse of women in marriages. They perceived it as a dehumanising practice that equates women to property. This perception concurs with Wagner's (1999) assertion that in countries where Bride Price is still common, women are seen as property owned by their husbands.

Yes, at times those people as you were saying that I bought you, you are my asset. Anyone can abuse his asset because he wasted a lot of money for it. So many women are suffering because of that Bride Price. At times you shout to the men that even my parents can give you back your *lobola*. Because of abuse. Some people will say, I paid a lot of money to your parents. And you can even respond by saying go to my parents and get back your *lobola*.

(Married female, 38, Shona tribe,-in Harare)

This was further endorsed by a married man (61, Shona tribe) in rural Zimbabwe who highlighted that:

Some say I bought you. I will have that complex that I bought you from your family especially when you are not biblically minded. He will ill-treat the woman. Saying I bought you, not I paid *lobola*. I gave out all my expenses, so you are mine.

The perception is also consistent with Kambarami's (2006) argument that *lobola*, which is part of the patriarchal nature of the Zimbabwean society, breeds inequality and widens the gap between men and women thereby placing women in a subordinate position. The fact that most of the interviewees agreed that men made most of the decisions in the household because they paid *lobola* was quite disturbing.

But I think if I have paid that kind of money which I do think is a lot of money in terms of what is going on in my circles as a Zimbabwean, I say a lot really. It's a lot which I have known. I think, yes if it came down to who actually decides what we are doing with the money in the house it's gonna be the man, it's gonna be the one who controls what essentially what I have classed as the factors of production.

(Married male, 59, Ndebele tribe, in Birmingham)

The study revealed that due to *lobola* some men see their wives as objects who are always reminded 'mind you I paid *lobola* for you' or '*ndakakutenga*' (I bought you). It was also noted that some husbands insist that their wives obey their commandments because they paid *lobola*. This finding is consistent with Tsanga's (1999) view that *lobola* gives men unfettered rights and control over women. Thus, *lobola* renders women vulnerable to abuse by their husbands.

Yah, I think in some situations. Again, it boils down to the person who has paid the Bride Price, do they really understand the concept of Bride Price. Because if they think they have actually bought someone they think it's an object which you can just toss around because you own that like a cup which you can put in the sink if its dirty or whatever, So the abuse, I think it boils down to the person who paid because sometimes as Zimbabweans or as Africans it's something which is there you don't really understand why it is there for. You take it in your own way to a point where some cultural concept and things we don't really research more on them to understand why they are for. So, I again it just boils down to the husband if he understand what *lobola* all is about.

(Married female, 54, Ndebele tribe, in Birmingham)

That women are abused as a result of *Lobola* is also expressed by Kethusegile, Kwaramba and Lopi (2000) who argue that some husbands claim that they can do whatever they want with their wives because they paid *lobola* for them. The man acquires the status of a demigod that has a right to mete out punishment if the subject fails to remain subordinate (McFadden, 1999; Tsanga, 1999).

> Maybe that person thinks that beating a wife is a way to be a husband or that's the way to be the head of the house, but it's just depends on individuals, sometimes you hear cases were people end up saying she is being beaten up because of *lobola* amount that was paid for her. In a way it causes some form of abuse because there are cases that we hear.

> (Married female, 26, Ndebele tribe, in Harare)

Similar sentiments are also shared by Tichagwa (1998), Burn (2000), and Hamisu (2000). Men who abuse their wives on the grounds that they have paid *lobola* for them show lack of understanding of the essence of this cultural practice (Mapara, 2007). Mapara (2007) implies that *lobola* is a noble practice which is meant to promote harmony within the society rather than domestic violence. This belief came out of most interviews supporting the view that people who abused their wives did not understand the practice,

> In a way, the *lobola* caused abuse in some marriages, some would say they paid for a wife. Like she says she grew up in the UK, probably she won't understand what *lobola* is. She gets a man form the UK and the parents are in Zimbabwe. That's why she can say he doesn't need to pay money. She doesn't understand. I will say I only paid money for you so. It's like you bought a book or a dress.

> (Single female, 46, Ndebele tribe, in Birmingham)

The general sentiment expressed by those who advocated for abolition of the custom of *lobola* was that the custom had outlived its usefulness, thereby becoming a social anachronism. As one participant put it, the practice *(lobola)* is one of antiquity, yet insignificant in the contemporary sense. The payment of *lobola* was viewed as being at odds with the current wave of feminism and calls for gender equity. Some participants noted that while it is a reality that contemporary women are fighting for a voice, they are hacked down by the custom of *lobola* which relegates them to a secondary position in relation to men.

And also, from the bride's side, the parents if they don't know the importance of the Bride Price, they may be charge even exorbitantly, so that to the extent that it frustrate even the husband so now when they are living together, they are now married. The husband will now, vent the anger to the wife, there becomes an abuse "*wakandidhura*", you were expensive for me. "*Ini ndakabhadhara mari yakawanda*" it becomes a frustration and that marriage will start on an un level ground. Things will not be rose. But if things are done the way it should be done, like appreciating the bride's parents as well accepting the Bride Price as a token of appreciating then things will be well.

(Married female, 87, Shona tribe, in rural Zimbabwe)

In view of this the hope of women's liberation from patriarchal oppression, the search for 'a land flowing with milk and honey'; a land where women can enjoy equality with men (Russel & Wendel, 1995 cited in Mukonyora, 2001) is thwarted by the custom of *lobola*. Implicitly, if gender equality is an epitome of the feminist 'paradise' then the custom of *lobola* is one of the roadblocks on the highway to this 'paradise'. The abuse in the name of *lobola* is quite disturbing, as asserted by a 28-year-old married woman (Shona tribe) in Harare:

I think most fights definably are because of that Bride Price. Men usually say because I paid Bride Price for you. He can even wake you up at 2am and ask you to go and warm up his food whilst he was out drinking. Maybe "*kana kubasa chaiko anenge asipo*" he might not even be coming from work, he was just out. When you say please, I want to sleep, I want to rest, "*chibhakera ipapo*", you are beaten up because he paid *lobola* for you. It is regarded as disrespect. I paid *lobola* for you to do everything for me. Anytime I want to wake you up you have got to wake up. That is what is really going on.

Thus, although a number of legislative measures to address gender inequality have been put in place, their practical application is impeded by customary practices such as *lobola* payment (Gopal & Salim, 1988; Hellum & Stewart, 1999). Partly because of the custom of *lobola* the principle of shared power, enshrined in the United Nations' Convention on the Elimination of all Forms of Discrimination Against Women (CEDAW, 1979), cannot be fully applied in the home. Viewed as an impediment to gender equality, *lobola* is an aspect of malignant sexism (Mazrui, 1993, p. 45).

look I paid Bride Price for you, you have to do your job as a wife, I am not doing anything otherwise I will get my money back or something serious like that then you are in trouble. But if you are with some who is agreeable then you have a shared partnership.

(Female, 22, Ndebele tribe, in rural Zimbabwe)

Mazrui (1993) further contends that since bride wealth often gives the husband more power after the payment is made, the practice is stripped of all pretences of benevolence. From the views of those participants who opposed the custom of *lobola* it can be extrapolated that the voice of those advocating for gender equality is like the voice of one crying in the wilderness with no one listening. The custom seems to place women in the position of the colonized; silent and castrated in their ability to exercise their right to self-determination.

Ya but you see that's where the problem is but back home a woman is supposed to cook for the family, which when you come here it might be difficult for some men to understand that we are in a different environment, the woman has been to work, and I need to take over the kids. So becomes abusive to the woman because I have paid *lobola* for you. So, you need to perform all these duties in the terms of marriage

(Married female, 34, Ndebele tribe, in Birmingham)

The study also revealed that the abuse of *lobola* is also perpetrated by fathers who see their daughters as money-spinning projects. Such fathers tend to overcharge *lobola*. Overcharging *lobola* in turn leads to abuse of women by both their husbands and their in-laws. *Lobola* often gives the husband or his family members the feeling that they have rights over the wife and even own her (Kethusegile, Kwaramba & Lopi, 2000). A 24-year-old married female participant (Shona tribe) in rural Zimbabwe succinctly remarked "*Lobola* should be abolished because at times when the in-laws charge exorbitant amounts of money women tend to be seen as property or objects." In a similar vein another a 54-year-old married female participant (Shona tribe) in rural Zimbabwe stated, "The practice is now abused by men to get rich through their daughters whom they watch with a greedy eye from birth." In this context, daughters have become a high-priced commodity in Zimbabwe, where *lobola* has become a means of escaping poverty in a rapidly declining economy. *Lobola* nowadays has thus tended to become the epitome of the commodification of daughters wherein daughters are seen as a pension fund.

And I can assure you most of the people if you hear couples fighting in our Shona society, they usually say that I paid *mari kumba kenyu*, I paid the Bride Price to your house so I am the head. You have to listen to what

I say, I am the last word. This fact of saying I am bearing children because we men usually say no it's our children not my children.

(Married male, 34, Shona tribe, in Birmingham)

This was supported by another 28-year-old married male participant (Ndebele tribe) in Harare, who argued that:

I agree with you but being submissive is one part of the whole setup. Because abuse comes because someone feels he has been hard done by the-in-laws that's when abuse comes in.

5.3 The Commercialisation of Bride Price

The Zimbabwe Women Lawyers Association (ZWLA) director, Mrs Emilia Muchawa (Chireshe & Chireshe, 2010), condemned the demand for exorbitant *lobola*. She indicated that this was a violation of the essence of the custom. This demand for large amounts of *lobola*, she argued, has led to a scenario in which some parents refuse to bury their dead daughters as surety for *lobola* payment. Culturally, a woman's parents will usually take on part of the role (and cost) of burying their daughter, but at times have refused to do so when *lobola* has not been settled. The then Minister of Women's Affairs and Community Development, Oppah Muchinguri, also described this scenario as extortion (Chireshe & Chireshe, 2010). Like all traditional customs, *lobola* is open to abuse and distortion in the modern world, a sentiment expressed by May (1983) and supported by a married female interviewee (57, Shona tribe) in Harare,

the woman will not have any say in the marriage where the Bride Price has been paid which is very high because the she would feel that if I do this this man would not be happy leading to being submissive because of the Bride Price which is very high. So, even if the woman is being abused, she will just stay in that marriage even though there are difficulties and she won't even say anything? She will just keep quiet because of the Bride Price.

It became clear from the study that *lobola* has lost its traditional and cultural meaning of uniting two families and has become a money-making endeavour; and that *lobola* has more negative than positive effects on women as highlighted by one married male participant (78, Ndebele tribe) in Harare:

I think as much as Bride Price is important, we are not supposed to abuse that Bride Price when marrying off our daughters. We are not supposed to abuse the Bride Price because it creates problems for our daughters even in their future it creates problems because in the first place, the first impression that the groom's family gets from your family is that you are greed for money even if it's not you and it's your uncles who are charging and all but they just think you are greedy for money and already that's a foundation that is not good. It's just supposed to be an appreciation where, I think it's not even supposed to be charged maybe the groom is just supposed to give what he can afford, offer what he can afford. Although he can also come up with disadvantage that some grooms may end up abusing that as well. But it's just supposed to be something to show that you are valuing your bride but valuing in terms of what you can afford.

Some women argued that they were happy with the idea of *lobola* because it confers a certain status on them in society and among their kin. However, others are not happy with the current situation, and argue that the commercialisation of *lobola* has resulted in many family problems, including domestic violence. Essentially, the study showed that the payment of *lobola* brings about explicit and implicit obligations. Failing - or merely the perception of having failed - to meet these obligations may result in serious problems. Indeed, most women complained that their husbands abuse them out of bitterness for the huge amounts of money that they paid to their in-laws for *lobola*.

I think some men tend to think that way and end up saying I paid for you. I paid your parents. I paid a lot of money so you should do everything that I say. Yes, I agree that the man is the head of the house the woman is the neck but as I am the neck make your head to tilt so we should work together. We can think let's do this, but you just don't go and do it. We should communicate. Yes, a Bride Price is paid but you have to appreciate my position. You were saying thank you to my parents for raising this woman that I am now taking to be my wife. That I am going to take care of.

(Married male, 89, Shona tribe, in rural Zimbabwe)

Conjugal rights are central to all marriages. My interviewees concurred that men's understanding is that conjugal rights are purchased through the payment of *lobola* and as such, they should not be denied from them at any point. However, women feel that sexual rights should be negotiated and not controlled by one person. But some men insisted that they had paid large sums of *lobola* and this gives them the right to take all decisions to do with sex - even to the extent of forcing their wives to have sex when they are not willing. These findings reinforce Bergen's (1999, p. 4) postulation that men "are often portrayed as jealous, domineering individuals who feel a sense of entitlement to have sex with their 'property'".

The situation is made worse by the fact that women still find it extremely difficult to report cases of marital rape, even though the Sexual Offences Act has been in place in Zimbabwe since 2002. Bergen (1999) and the African Population Research and Health Center (2010, p. 1) found that "marital rape is one of the under-reported violent crimes because it is socially tolerated. Women feel that this is not only a betrayal to the husband, but also a disgrace for her family". In addition, women admit that it is harder to press charges when the husband has paid a large sum of money to their family as *lobola*.

Married men's control over sex does not only infringe women's rights, it also exposes them to HIV infection. In addition, men who have paid *lobola* sometimes resort to violence to 'discipline' their wives since they believe that the payment of *lobola* gives them a license to abuse their wives, who they consider to be part of their property. This situation has been worsened by the commercialisation of *lobola*. Gustafsson and Worku (2006, p. 5) noted that the payment of *lobola* is "as if the husband buys his wife". Most women interviewed agreed that *lobola* creates an uneven ground in a relationship in that it requires women to be submissive to their husbands this is evident from the women's focus group in which a 36-year-old participant (Ndebele tribe) in Birmingham asserted that:

> I think there are also misconceptions about that as well should be submissive to men. I think when a man pays Bride Price it doesn't mean that they have paid for you as a human being or for you to be a possession in that household. They should be some equality somewhere. For example, if you are both working, and you are contributing to the household even though the man is the head but there should be some communication and there shouldn't be one part that is submissive to the other. Does it make sense what I am saying?

While discussing *lobola*, it was critical to note the major role played by paternal aunts in arranging marriages and in the lead up to the payment of *lobola*. And the aunts continue to intervene after the payment of the *lobola* to resolve any conflicts. The aunts ensure that marriages are safeguarded at all costs, even if it sometimes means sacrificing the rights of the women. Where *lobola* has been paid, it is very difficult to get a divorce because the aunts will always encourage the woman to endure. One participant indicated that it is very common to hear the aunts saying "*Chingotsungirira mwana wehanzvadzi yangu, yeuka kuti murume wako akabvisa pfuma. Kana ukamuramba tinoiwanepi mari yekumudzorera?"* (You just have to endure my niece, remember your husband paid *lobola*. If you divorce him, where will we get money to reimburse his *lobola*?).

The above position was further supported by a 28-year-old married participant (Shona tribe) from the women's focus group in Birmingham who agreed with the notion that *lobola* creates gender inequality which can lead to abuse or violence:

> And I agree as well because knowing people who are from slightly different culture, the ones where huge amounts are paid for Bride Price there is that attitude that I paid for you, so you are going to do what I want you to do and it is very difficult for the woman to for example get a divorce. Your family will have to pay back the money and it's not given the woman but their family who would have probably spent it. You can imagine a debt that is over this woman's head because you have to comply in this marriage because you have been paid for. That is what happens in many parts of our country. Yes, I think depending on how much you pay for her in Bride Price then they can be a big problem.

The study also found that charging exorbitant *lobola* fees can result in animosity between two families. A lady who participated (20, Shona tribe, in Harare) in the study said that her husband normally speaks harshly every time they have an argument. She said that her husband says, "*Vabereki vako vakandidhurisira ende vakatopfuma neni.*" (Your parents overcharged me, and they are now rich because of me). The traditional purpose of *lobola* - to bring two families together as postulated by Bourdillon (1976, pp. 40-49) - is therefore sacrificed for the love of money. In contemporary Zimbabwe, some bitter husbands no longer treat their in-laws with respect as in the past since their relationship has been poisoned by the commercialised nature of the *lobola* process.

> I think it does because after marriage especially for the men depending how they handle the whole paying for the Bride Price it affects the way the in-laws treat them then or the relatives. It might not be the mother and father in -law but the rest of the relatives the way they treat the man depending on whether he paid the full Bride Price or not. And for the woman it also affects the relationship with the in-laws as well as depending on how much the woman's family charged and if they feel like they were overcharged, they might have a negative effect on the relationship between the woman and the in-laws, that's my opinion.

> (Married male, 90, Shona tribe, in rural Zimbabwe)

However, some women said that they were happy with the current situation despite the many alleged side-effects of the commercialisation of *lobola*. As noted by Nyambedha (2004) the payment of *lobola* guarantees women and their children the right to resources within the kin group, and a place within the kinship structure. Married women also told me that *lobola* gives them status because "if a large sum of money is paid for you, it shows that you have value". Some of the women interviewed said that if the woman is loved and has value then 'real' money has to be paid. They argued that the payment of a higher fee can denote true love.

An example was given of a police officer who earns approximately US$600 per month but managed to pay US$4500 cash. It was agreed that this kind of commitment bestows value on the woman who is being paid for. A married woman from the focus group (36, Ndebele tribe) in Birmingham claimed that, "if he loves you, he should pay a meaningful sum for you." Another married woman in the same focus group (34, Ndebele tribe) reasoned that "*Kana uchibva kuvanhu unofanira kuva munhu anokosha. Kubhadharirwa mari shoma kushandiswa.*" (If you are a person with a cultured family background, then you ought to be of great value. You are being used if nothing meaningful is paid for you.) These results concur with the sentiments shared by Thorpe (1991) and by Chireshe and Chireshe (2010), who argue that the majority of people believe that the payment of *lobola* reflects that the groom and his family are committed to the marriage. Bourdillon (1976, p. 50) in his study among the Shona people found that the payment of a high Bride Price conferred a higher status on the bride and reflected the value the husband places on the marriage. There was, however, an agreement that those things are changing from the old days where *lobola* was a token of payment.

> We don't know about nowadays but there in the past. On your part as a woman they would teach you how you are supposed to go and behave in your new family and that was that. That new family also, because you go there, they would come and visit the home and they would know you. There was just harmony. This is why they would get involved should you want to divorce that woman because they know you as an individual they know where you came from, they know your parents. So, there was that union. People were quite united.

> (Married female, 26, Shona tribe, in Birmingham)

5.4 Commodification of Women

The research participants identified the following issues in terms of the historical context of Bride Price. Importantly, all analyses of Bride Price or bride wealth must look at the practice in its historical perspective. In the recent era, Bride Price appears to have become a commercialised practice which is losing its former helpful role. My research revealed that this could be particularly the outcome in richer or professional class communities and in the cities.

> for me I think it has gone up as a sign of abuse usually by family members to continue to do their own projects and personal growth. Because once the Bride Price has been paid, you are expected to behave as a proper housewife, traditional wife. In a way it does, because once a man has paid Bride Price, is regarded as a father or head of the household so that places some superiority on the man.

> (Married female, 66, Shona tribe, in Birmingham focus group)

Thus, the traditional value of Bride Price is now less clear due to the impacts of modernisation and the resulting commercialisation of social customs in contemporary times.

> It has become so commercial now. It is like the girl's parents are selling off their daughters in order to become richer or to escape poverty. Every parent wants their daughter to get married so they can benefit from her... As if the woman becomes a commodity.

> (Married female, 32, Shona tribe, in Birmingham focus group)

> It is not right to put human beings on the commercial market, bargain for them and, when one is fed up with them, dump them, leaving the woman psychologically tortured. Women lose their dignity, have to do endless hard labour - and then failure to produce children becomes a big crime - once you have been paid for.

> (Married female, 26, Shona tribe, in Birmingham)

It was pointed out by interviewees that Bride Price tends to cement gender inequality into place in that women have little power in relation to the practice, but rather they are passed from family to family. Negotiations usually involve senior men in the two families who decide what the woman will do and how she will behave. Thus, Bride Price can be seen, in this instance, both as a symptom of male dominance and power in families and also as a cause of gender inequality.

Now because of the misconception, people are using *lobola* to abuse women, most people would even say, you can't do this because you never paid anything to my parents; I paid something to your parents therefore you are going to listen to me. I am calling the shots, you see, they are using muscles where they are not required. This is very wrong. The man is equal to his wife in terms of being equal players.

(Married male, 28, Ndebele tribe, in rural Zimbabwe)

One example of how it can be seen as a symptom of gender inequality is that it is a product of men being in a more powerful position in the family. It can then lead to men automatically expecting to control their family through its position. One example of how it can be seen as a cause is that women have little power to influence the custom but are bargained over and 'exchanged' from household to household by male family members so there are few opportunities for equal treatment of men and women. Rather, the subservient position of the wife is often made worse and greater inequality is therefore frequently caused by the payment of Bride Price.

Bride-wealth normalises men controlling everything and women's weak position as the one negotiated over, the object to be exchanged, so both ways the power difference is increased by bride-wealth - it gives men more and at the same time women less... So it changes the power both ways. No wonder men don't like it to be challenged.

(Single woman, 46, Ndebele tribe, Birmingham focus group)

Men and women should be equal in marriage according to Chapter 5:11 the Marriage Act of Zimbabwe. However, Bride Price makes the marriage unequal in that the woman is paid for by the man. Thus, the continued existence of Bride Price cements inequality between men and women. The woman can become an item of property in her own home. Bride Price can give the appearance of commodifying human relationships, "Selling a human being because the family want wealth, selling your daughter at a tender age" (married woman, 46, Shona tribe, in Birmingham).

5.5 Data and Theoretical Contradictions

My data is challenging to Uma Narayan's post-colonial feminist argument, which says that depicted in places like Africa cultures is painted as backward and it is blamed for the inferior position of women. What my data tells me is that the cultural aspect is important and highly complex. It is not useful to make that critique and view Bride Price as a matter of culture. This is because people are saying the reason they are holding on to it is because of the cultural significance that it has to them and because it is linked to their identity. At the same time, if Bride Price were removed, patriarchy would remain, and it is likely that some other forms of gender-based violence would persist. So, Bride Price is not the only thing that is holding all the other elements together: we cannot reduce everything to that practice but at the same time it is part of the web that is holding together the system in which women are more vulnerable than men.

Culture remains a central part of Bride Price. That said I concede that some depictions of women in Zimbabwe as inferior and victims are also unhelpful and inaccurate. However, the situation revealed in my data is complex, in part because both men and women are active in pursing Bride Price. So, it is not a practice that is done to women, as such. Rather, it is a part of marriage. I support the post-colonial critique insofar as women cannot be reduced to victims of Bride Price because they are not; they are also part of the process and even support it. The ways in which Bride Price is harmful comes out in my data in later chapters and requires a nuanced analysis.

Although my study reveals an overwhelming support for Bride Price, some of the individual interview participants reported some problematic outcomes that make Bride Price a 'sugar coated bitter pill'. They argued that as much as it is necessary and helps to solemnize the marriage, the actual payment and the haggling involved makes Bride Price appear like wife buying, yet there is no known amount of money that is enough to buy a human being. In some cases, husbands feel that after paying Bride Price, they have bought the freedom of the wife which leads to mistreatment and curtailing of women's agency.

> In some cases, I think it does appear like what we were saying that the man is superior. Some of the men use that and will be like well I paid for you, you know, so I can do anything I want.

> (Married man, 42, Shona tribe, in Harare)

The fact that this does not apply to men shows skewed gender relations where society condemns a woman's extra marital relations but treats it as normal for a man to engage in the same. In fact, one man in Harare argued that it is a sign of power and strength for a man to have many girlfriends or partners (part of masculinities). Conversely, a married woman interviewee (61, Shona tribe) in Harare believed that they had to submit to their husband as dictated by culture:

> As women, the bible says; we have to submit to our husbands, so submission is very important because that's what the bible says and

the man is the head of the family, you just as wife have to submit to the men to the husbands to here.

Similarly, Thiara et al. (2012) in the study of Bride Price and domestic violence in Zimbabwe assert that much as Bride Price has "an on-going cultural longevity" it is associated with many negative impacts on women and girls. Some of these negative impacts include physical violence and limited decision-making power by women.

Many women interviewed believed that as much as bride payment is not the major cause of wife mistreatment, it is a big contributing factor to violence against women since, after payment, a man feels that 'he is in charge', because 'he has bought the wife into his household' and therefore a wife is bound to follow his instructions without questioning (Ekstrom et al., 2005). This, in some way, contributes to reducing women's bargaining position for rights and other resources in the household.

You seem like an ornament really, a possession like. Because I paid so much you have to go. It's my way or no way.

(Married woman, 59, Shona tribe, in Birmingham)

Thus, Bride Price payment may be a cause and symptom of gender inequality in households. And such inequalities have to be addressed if sustainable development is to be achieved (Tripp, 2013). A male participant argued that if a wife was 'paid for' she will always 'think twice' before she leaves the marriage even when she is beaten, while another male interviewee lamented that a man who has not paid loses a voice in his own home and will always feel insecure that the wife can disappear any time. This leads to weak or subordinate masculinities for such men.

Until he finishes paying, he can't be superior, but men will always have that status in marriage. They are the head of the house.

(Married woman, 27, Shona tribe, Birmingham)

5.6 Is Culture a Force for Evil?

The above conceptions, in most cases, benefit men at the expense of women but can also at times put the men at a disadvantage according to my participants. Instances where men benefit include dominance in decision making, control of household finances and other associated privileges, both at household and society level. In other words, the social structure positions and allocates dividends to men (Cleaver, 2002). They may, however, suffer consequences in a bid to subscribe to such dominant expectations. For example, the need to prove their sexual prowess may expose them to HIV or, for those who feel that they are not at the standards required of a man in society, humiliation. My data acknowledges this through the interviews as echoed by a 61-year-old married male participant (Shona tribe, in Harare):

> It depends with the man, I think once there is *lobola*, the *lobola* is cultural. It means you are culturally married. You are married according to the culture so wherever you go even if you have not had the white wedding, you are automatically referred to as husband and wife. In so doing, it's just natural for a woman to then respect the man as her husband. So, in terms of that, that would make the man more superior. But there are two ways to look at superiority; there is the other way when the man would have control, ultimate control on his wife and his family and what he says is what goes. But then that's something that actually depends on an individual rather than the all the men would feel like that have paid Bride Price. Other men can pay Bride Price, he knows where he stands with his family, he knows he has the respect of his wife, and respect of his family. That already can give him confidence to feel superior with having a control or having to control his family in a bad, negative way.

The socialisation of roles and duties was asserted by a 51-year-old married female teacher (Ndebele tribe, in Birmingham) who argued that:

> But back home the woman is expected to perform all those duties. Not because of servitude. It's like their place in the kitchen. It's a matter of responsibilities, she looks after the kids and if man would bring a small portion of meat from the butchery, she would say what kind of man are you, you are taking up all the responsibilities from her of taking after the family. It is the lady who should go to the butchery, ok we have this type of menu this week, this is what my family is gonna eat. So, it's again the perceptive that you look at otherwise really when we get back home you won't see me in the kitchen. Not because I can't help, or I don't want to, but she takes all the responsibility because that's her place of influence and I will look after everything else.

This position was further echoed by a 57-year-old married female (Ndebele tribe, in Harare) teacher:

I think it makes the man superior, because the moment a man pays his *lobola* for you, you are expected to treat him with respect. Do things for him, wash for him, cook for him, and give him whatever pressures from a woman. Culturally, it's taken like when *lobola* is paid and you are joining that family to that who paid *lobola*. To please him mainly. So, in a way he will be superior to me that's what I can think. Like nowadays some would actually say that it's rare to find a man who comes to pay *lobola* for you. You have to treat him with care, handle him with both hands and all that because he has actually managed to raise funds *lobola* in this economic situation. It's tough so handle him with care that's why maybe it ends coming up with some sort of abuses taking place to woman because you just think that if one is paid for *lobola* for me I have to handle him with so much care. That can end up resulting in some form of abuses when you just want to save your marriage.

My data shows that Bride Price constitutes situations where men are trying to assert their influence and power over women in order to reinforce their feelings of 'total manhood'. It also reveals a process where most of the women are trying to fulfil the gendered roles and expectations as have been socialized by society over time. This was asserted by an 89-year-old married man (Shona tribe, in rural Zimbabwe):

It depends with the mentality of the person, when someone marries, they think they can just talk to the wife anyhow, they become abusive to the wife. Why because they think they have paid to get a wife whereas they were paying the *lobola* or *roora* as a sign of appreciating, so some they think by paying *lobola*, they are having a wife to abuse her. So, it depends with the mentality of the person, some they pay their *lobola*, they pay their *roora* and still respect their wives. So, it depends with the mentality of the person. Those less educated, yes some are being abused because some just take women as weapons they will just say I paid for you. One who is educated knows the value of a woman and life really there is no abuse.

As far as Bride Price payment and its gendered practices and perceptions are concerned, the different aspects discussed and issues analysed in these chapters shape experiences, especially in modern times. For example, in relation to Bride Price and the construction of femininities and masculinities, it was observed during the study that with increased modernisation, femininities and hegemonic masculinities have tended to reduce to a large extent, especially among the urban middle-class but also among the rural lower-class to some extent. One married female participant (49, Ndebele tribe, in Harare) summed this up by observing that:

> but these days you find that most men are not even formally employed. Most women are the ones who are formally employed these days. Maybe the woman is the one who is actually paying for the rent. Maybe paying for the school fees. Maybe the husband is trying here and there to find some income to add to whatever the woman is bringing.

In addition, middle-class women who want to appear 'modern' have contributed to the commercialisation of Bride Price by introducing modern and expensive items into the practice to the extent of sometimes outsourcing the services of the paternal aunties at a fee so as to conform to the socially expected feminine conduct, according to my data. It has also led to Bride Price functions going to the public realm, when it was regarded before as private matter witnessed by only close family members (Tamale, 2009). In short, with modernisation, Bride Price tends to gradually shift from an exercise that was performed to conform to the feelings and requirements of masculinities and femininities, to a class affair that has been commercialised among the middle-class, but at the same time has lost some ground among the poor. This has been attributed to the increased education and income among the middle-class women, which has affected and changed gender roles, plus the increasing poverty levels among the lower-class poor. This was echoed by a married male participant (28, Shona tribe, in Harare) who said:

> It has gone up over time, people these days they are now valuing the level of education of their child before getting married. Some have really gone up to getting like degrees, PhD, masters and all sort of education with an effort to improve their lives. So, before you even let your child to be a wife to someone you really value all those investments that you have done into your child then by the end of the day that can actually make some parents those who really feel they have invested a lot in their child to request for a higher Bride Price.

It is true that due to the social structure that glorifies male dominance, men are in most cases bound to control Bride Price property in the same way they control other household resources. But looking further, one concludes that there is male dominance even where it ought not to be. For example, during the negotiations for the price, mothers and women are not supposed to take part or even come near. It is only the duty of men (Baluku et al., 2012). When gifts are delivered, its men who take charge of the property and mothers remain with less or nothing, even when they are the ones who do a lot of child's upbringing.

Regardless, in our culture back home even when both parties are working, and a woman is earning $20,000 and the man is earning $5. The woman would bring the $20,000 and say to the man there is my $20,000 what are we doing with that. The man will decide. You will say we are doing a, b, c, d, but you both agree on the plan but submitting as the bible says.

(married female, 49, Ndebele tribe, in Harare)

In one of the discussions, I inquired as to why women do not have to come closer to the in-laws, one of the answers was that tradition had it that a mother-in-law might be more beautiful than her daughter (bride) and get sexually attracted to the son-in-law. Although I did not entirely agree with this, the claim reveals that some people in society are still obsessed with the stereotypical thinking that women are sexual objects who must always look attractive to men and that men are always looking for sexual favours from women.

What was fascinating about the interviews was that even those who acknowledged that Bride Price contributed to gender inequality still believed that the practice should continue, as asserted by a 46-year-old single mother (Ndebele tribe, in Birmingham):

To me, aah probably, specific to myself, irrelevant. In the sense that I haven't actually had it paid it per se. I like the sense that I haven't been paid for paid it. Actually, it didn't doesn't bother. In a selfish kind of way, I have ideas about it as I now am a mother to a daughter. I would like it paid.

One of the participants felt that the practice was irrelevant, she still felt that it was important that *lobola* was paid for her daughter. What was equally amazing was that the father is a second-generation migrant who grew up in the UK. However, there are some who believed that the practice was not right and equated it to buying a wife, as a 54-year-old married female participant (Ndebele tribe, in Birmingham) echoed:

Bride Price is like buying a woman. Yes, in some instances its going that way. This is caused by different factors; economic, migration and education.

Surprisingly, even though this participant had negative views about the practice, she still felt that *lobola* should continue, this is despite acknowledging that it was like buying a wife:

I think it's a bit of irrelevant to me like I said but as a tradition I think actually as a girl from Africa and being in England I'm conscious even though I am less positive. I actually hold the view that it is a bit more sentimental, I think I have to hold on to my culture because I want to keep the identity. Even though I wouldn't automatically want a Bride Price, I think the ceremony that comes with the Bride Price itself would be something that I would probably still want to keep because when I think about getting married that ceremony were it is paid it actually a ritual even though the Bride Price amount has changed I still want the ceremony itself to carry on. So, it will probably be more important to me here than back home. I don't want to lose the Africanism.

What came out of the women's focus group was also fascinating in that the female participants in their discussion agreed that *lobola* endorsed patriarchy, but they all agreed that even though the practice was harmful in that respect, it should continue:

Personally, I will never live with a man if he hasn't paid *lobola* no matter how emancipated that person might be or how educated. Even in my next life I want to be *lobola* to be paid. It's my DNA, culture, tradition. I am primitive like that.

(Married female, 36, Ndebele tribe, in Birmingham)

Another participant (female, married, 66, Shona tribe) in the focus group goes on to say:

I want Bride Price to be paid for my daughter but a reasonable Bride Price as a token of appreciation not exorbitant £25,000, no. And I would like my son to pay Bride Price for somebody's daughter as well.

There was an expectation that the women's focus group would yield different results, but the message seems to be the same in supporting the continuation of the practice:

For me Bride Price is important. To elaborate further, although I don't feel like it's necessary but culturally it's a sign that your spouse or whoever is marrying you values you and that your family values you, they are not just giving you away but it's not about how much it is the Bride Price. It's just the process.

(Married female, 32, Shona tribe, in Birmingham)

Most of the participants were of the opinion that *lobola* creates an uneven ground in that it treats the woman as inferior to her husband as dictated by culture. On the other hand, the interviewees still felt that the practice was important and that they would like it to continue. As much as law and education may exist, on the ground, a situation in which men are superior persists. A 36-year-old married female interviewee (Ndebele tribe) in Birmingham acknowledging male superiority argued:

> The feminists point of view here is that all people should be treated the same and that we are all equal and there is no one who is greater. No one should be superior. But then the Zimbabwean cultural context is very different. It says that the man should be the bread winner. The man should be the lord of the house and the women should be lord of the kitchen. But here it different it says throw all those practices in the bin and do as you please as long as there is no one killing anyone its fine. I think this is where a lot of people are confused. Even I am still confused as to if there should be clear division. It now differs from person to person and everyone have a different take on what they believe equality is. Who know now? Every household is different. You can't say that if you see your friends and think that they are identical even though we are from the same cultural background. There is no uniformity in our cultural understanding of our roles now. In one house the man is masculinity, in another house the man is femininity and in another house the women is the who is masculine and in another house, there is some sort of equality. This is what we are told to believe as the new norm. And from the Zimbabwe cultural point of view it's not, it's very hard to us as Zimbabweans to adjust as ideology. It's a difficult question really. I think it's something that plays on us as Zimbabweans in the diaspora as to how we view our gender roles.

Some men also believe that paying of Bride Price would put them at an advantage as evidenced by a 60-year-old married man (Shona tribe) in rural Zimbabwe:

> If I have to pay Bride Price, I definitely want that woman to come with a disclaimer that says that I won't have an argument with my husband. This one I think we argued minutes into the marriage about the flower girl.

Some people would question the possibility of a young man who is starting out life paying *lobola* to his in-laws and being able to look after his wife and treat her right. They reckon that there are millions of men on the planet taking care of their wives without paying *lobola*. Conversely, they believe that there are many men who paid *lobola* who are having difficult times taking care of their families right now.

According to my data, those who are against *lobola* believe that one can live without *lobola*; you can live with a partner (live in partnership) with or without paying *lobola*, and on top of that, a union of two people must never be prevented just because of some practice that is claimed to be theirs. Questioning *lobola* is not synonymous with being Westernised. They believe that it is backward, and should either be removed or modernised, and question the reason behind its existence in the first place. Men as well as women have questioned this tradition, and there was no clear answer as to why they had to pay *lobola*, an often popular response being that it is their culture or tradition. There is a feeling that the men of today are questioning this tradition in the hope of transforming the practice. The question, then, should be; why do they *not* want to follow this and not what is *right* about following it? Some have taken to following the Western way: buy rings, get married and have kids, and those that argue that *lobola* is no longer relevant believe that paying it has been all about wealth. Women were forced to marry wealthy men, this still has not changed.

Some people paid *lobola* simply because they loved their wives, but agreeing to pay *lobola* does not make it right, and yet disagreeing to pay *lobola* will only create problems especially if those around you are practising it. There are some who recognise that *lobola* itself is not a bad practice, but it is the commercialisation of it that makes it bad. However, my data argues that there are those who advocate for a change to our traditions which they believe does not harm anybody or infringe on other people's rights. Another argument is that they should lose their roots, tradition and culture. *Lobola* in their culture was a way of bonding the spirits of the children born from the marriage to the spirits of their father. Each time a child was born, a portion of the *lobola* was given to the parents of the woman. *Lobola* was in the form of cows, goats and sheep.

My participants revealed that the *lobola* process is quite complicated and involves intricate customs, for example, the young couple are usually forbidden from meeting until the actual wedding ceremony. The purpose of all this fuss and decorum is to create a feeling of trust and mutual understanding at a deeper level between the two families, and more importantly, a feeling of community. There is no sense of personal enrichment in *lobola*. Additionally, *lobola* is also a gesture of gratitude on the part of the groom's family for looking after and bringing up the young bride. The fact is that *lobola* used to be a means of spreading wealth among the community so that everyone had something; there was a philanthropic and social initiative behind it. This is also the reason why rich men could take more wives; it meant that they would be spreading more wealth in the immediate community. For the same reason, people were encouraged "*kuroora kumatongo*" (to marry within the neighbourhood) because it kept the wealth within the community.

What makes *lobola* so important for marriage is that it is a means of bringing two families together. Mutual respect and dignity are interwoven into the process, and the love between the man and woman is expanded to include the immediate and extended families. The reason for this is that the extended family is an important element in African culture and especially in the institution of marriage. They have a significant role to play, and that is why members of the extended family are the ones who actually conduct the negotiations and not the parents of the bride and the groom. But my participants also argued that *lobola* added weight to a relationship because it shows that the two people are committed to each other. For them, to go through the process shows the seriousness of their intentions. *Lobola* does for them what marriage vows in the Church do for people in other parts of the world. It is an unwritten contract which means that when things go wrong, both families can intervene and try to sort things out amicably.

Without *lobola* there is no reason for them to get involved in a shameful relationship. There is also a belief that paying *lobola* is a tradition which is as modern as marriage customs in Europe whereby the parents of the bride are expected to sponsor their daughter's wedding. In Zimbabwe *mukuwasha*, the son-in-law, has to prove he is man enough to be the head the of household by paying a *lobola* to his in-laws, an equivalent of a credit rating system. To supporters of *lobola*, it does not create greedy parents: there are greedy and corrupt people by nature. Whether it was *lobola* or anything else they would be greedy in any case, while any person who loves their daughter will not want to overprice her. The existence of a few greedy parents does not corrupt the institution, it only means there are a few greedy people in the institution. There is also a recognition that *lobola* has been a practice around the world for almost every race, and is just like buying a ring.

Nonetheless, they see *lobola* as an old and backward belief, and they also recognise that it creates gender inequality in that it makes a man superior to his wife.

> I think it is an individual perspective, in reality no one should feel superior to the other. In the true sense of a relationship. Though culturally, says that the man is the head of the house. This is why when they say "*avathwana vanjani*" how are the kids? They include the wife. So, if we take it from that point of view. How are the children? The wife

becomes part of the children. So, with that perspective it sort of gave the man an upper hand.

(Married male, 59, Ndebele tribe, in Birmingham)

This is further supported by another interviewee (married male pastor, 35, Shona tribe, in Harare), who asserted that:

Bride Price does not make a man superior to his wife, that's what I believe because by paying the Bride Price it's just a sign of appreciating. But what happens in marriage is that the husband is the head of the family, so the wife has to submit to the husband, by so doing that does not mean that the husband is superior to the woman. It's just a principle, wives should submit to their husbands. By paying your *lobola* it does not mean that husband is now superior to the wife.

Interpretation of the practice and some of the words of the bible was also called into question, and the way that the Church leaders interpret the texts does not help either. The idea that women cannot do anything without men, and they have to go through men demonstrates the misinterpretations of the Bible, and the Church leader's word is held in high regard within the communities that they serve. Being submissive creates a power imbalance, but the Church leader and the congregation think otherwise:

Ok when I am talking about the wife being submissive to the husband. I don't believe when one is submissive to someone, the person who is submissive there is a sign of potential, there is a lot of abilities in that person. It has to be the potential of that person but under someone. It has to be the abilities; it has to be power under control. Which means when the bible was saying that woman has to be submissive it was saying that the women, they have to have power, but that power have to be controlled by the husband who is the head of the family.

(Married male pastor, 35, Shona tribe, in Harare)

Furthermore, as much as the interviewees recognised that the practice was not ideal for the modern world and especially its commercialisation, which has thrown into question its relevance and its legitimacy in this day, they still want the cultural aspect of *lobola* to continue without the financial aspect. This is supported by an interviewee (married female, 24, Ndebele tribe, in Birmingham) who grew up in the UK and is a second-generation migrant:

But what I also want in addition to that is that even if the Bride Price falls on the way side and I think it is a good thing that there is something of cultural significant is done. Because I do think that has a place. You may say that you are paying money, but their family still needs to meet my family and have a talk about their children. I think that bit is important and its basically two families promising each other that this is what they are bringing to the table. And I think that part of the Bride Price is important without the money aspect.

I think the idea of belonging, a sense of identity, plays a role when it comes to practices as evidenced by one interviewee in the UK who accepted that Bride Price was important simply because it was important to her family. I suppose the thought of being dishonoured played a role in her response. Another participant (married female, 26, Shona tribe, in Birmingham) who grew up in the UK also summed this up by saying;

> I think it's not incredibly important to me because I grew up in the UK but it's important to me in the sense that it's important to my family and for my husband to be accepted by my family. I have to do it; in that respect it's important.

Conflicting views were also voiced in which women accepted that the practice can contribute to gender-based violence, and at the same time, some women were not accepting the progress made in terms of gender equality. This was highlighted by one interviewee who said:

> Yes, I would say so, it's not a negative but I think women like "*sekuru*", uncle, said when you get back home women are in the kitchen. It's the context. But it's not a negative thing it's nice. It's part of our culture and even as someone who grew up here those are some of the things that I am really proud of in the Zimbabwean culture.

> (Married female, 36, Shona tribe, in Birmingham)

However, there are some people who believe men should pay more *lobola* due to the fact that women are doing better these days, due to having more opportunities in life, they believe that the 'price' is not enough in line with the amount of *lobola* paid. This is also because the wife's earnings are administered by the husband. This only serves to confirm the uneven ground which *lobola* operates and creates.

I think on the basis of *lobola*, men should pay more than what they are paying because for example these days most women are working. Someone would have paid Bride Price for you. But will be earning less than you and at times you are the most supportive woman in the house so people should pay even more than what they do. Actually, in Zimbabwe, everybody is bringing cash in the house, so Bride Price should therefore be paid. Because at times for example I myself I would be working, and I will be the one who will be taking care of the parents. My-in-laws would be blaming me for not taking food to them whilst their son is doing nothing. So, Bride Price should go higher than it is now.

(Married woman, 74, Shona tribe, in Harare-Shona)

5.7 Religion, the Bible, and Bride Price

I have brought out religion as a key factor in shaping society but also shaping community and relationships. I needed to consider how and to what degree religion shapes gender and sanctions harmful acts against women. Research shows that there are very high levels of violence against women in Zimbabwe (Fidan & Bui, 2016). I know that gender inequality is a big problem and I was trying to understand why it is so embedded and so normalised in Zimbabwe. According to Wood (2009), biblical teachings that portray a woman as a helper have contributed to increasing women's role as caregivers and as the providers of reproductive labour in the family while the men are portrayed as breadwinners and rulers of the family. This viewpoint is seen in many of my transcripts. For example, a pastor I interviewed in rural Zimbabwe asserted that:

I personally think that our culture and I being christen, I think a woman should submit to a man. Not that a man should abuse a woman. But they say that I am the head of the house because culturally, I should be the head of the house and the woman becomes the neck. So as the man, I should be running the house and making decisions regardless of the status of the woman but aah it doesn't make me superior. I can't explain it properly but in a way, I think a woman should submit to me.

(Married male pastor, 79, Shona tribe, in rural Zimbabwe)

My data also reveal that community pressure and expectation acts to discipline women and ensure their compliance with the dominant norms. For example, women who do not conform to post marriage can be disowned by their family and/or face domestic violence from their husband. Husbands in most communities can legitimately 'discipline' their wives if they feel she has not conformed. With Zimbabwe being a Christian country, religion is a key factor in shaping communities and in particular religious leaders convey messages that are fundamentally gendered. Pastors across Zimbabwe teach of the need for women to be submissive.

This was echoed in the conversation I had with a married 35-year-old pastor and his 28-year-old wife (both of Shona tribe, in Harare) during my fieldwork. The following is an excerpt from our conversation.

Interviewer:
Does Bride Price make a man superior to his wife? I think I am at the right place because I am talking to a pastor here.

Pastor:
Bride piece does not make a man superior to his wife, that's what I believe because by paying the Bride Price it's just a sign of appreciating. But what happens in marriage is that the husband is the head of the family, so the wife has to submit to the husband, by so doing that does not mean that the husband is superior to the woman. It's just a principle, wives should submit to their husbands. By paying your *lobola* it does not mean that husband is now superior to the wife.

Interviewer (directed to Pastor's wife):
You have brought in an important word; 'submissive'. What exactly do you mean when you say submissive? When you say the wife has to be submissive? What's your take?

Pastor's wife:
As women, the bible says we have to submit to our husbands, so submission is very important because that's what the bible says and the man is the head of the family, you just as wife have to submit to the men, to the husbands.

Pastor:
As a wife, if you don't submit to your husband, it will be like two lions in the same house, so there will be always quarrels, there will always be fights. So, one has to submit, so that there would be that unit, that peace in the marriage and in the family.

Additionally, another religious leader (married male, 79, Shona tribe) I interviewed in rural Zimbabwe, stated that when a man gets a wife, he has got a precious gift from God, and he has to appreciate by paying something to the wife's parents first and then proceed to church for the wedding so that God can bless the union. But before any wedding is conducted the Church has to prove that the bride's parents have consented to their daughter's marriage, and this is proved by reading the consent letter that the parents write after receiving the Bride Price.

Pastors have an important role in determining or continuing the practice, as shown by the link between Bride Price, culture and religion reflected by my data. The conversation with the pastor and his wife continued as follows.

Interviewer:
So, if someone stays with a wife and they haven't paid Bride Price, would you recognise that as a marriage?

Pastor:
Yahh, of course it is not recognised as a marriage, why? Because you have not yet paid Bride Price. Marriage is something that was started by God, marriage is something that was ordained by God. For one to marry, you have to pay as my wife was saying as a sign that you are valuing the person. So, staying with a person that you have never paid Bride Price for in Africa as our culture its wrong. You have to pay Bride Price.

Furthermore, the pastor asserted that Bride Price is ordained by the Christian teachings and as such, the custom has to be followed.

Interviewer:
So, in Christian teachings; you encourage people to get married?

Pastor:
Yes, in the Christian teachings, when you are a grown-up man, when you are a mature man, there have to come a time when one has to pay that Bride Price, that *lobola*, marriage is something that was something that was started by God. When God created Adam and Eve, he did not create Adam and Steve. He created Adam and Eve, so which means God himself respect what we call marriage. So, marriage is very vital, in Christianity we encourage people to pay *lobola*, because it is something that is vital.

I was not expecting to hear people being strongly supportive still of Bride Price. In understanding why, I need to appreciate the links between the practice and religious values and beliefs about marriage and strict gender divisions.

In building my critique, I began to have a conversation with scholars whose theories I was sympathetic towards but did not always seem to really reflect what I could see in my data. One particular quotation from the pastor highlights my confusion in applying these critiques:

> Even the bible says women should be submissive to their husbands once they are married, it means the man is superior. This is according to God's design and cannot and should not be challenged.

5.8 Conclusion

My data highlights that culture seems to be such a powerful force in people's lives that it forces them to often contradict each other or even contradict themselves. In a number of examples, people were saying Bride Price is not good, but it is important. Narayan says that Bride Price should not be reduced to a matter of culture or religion, but to patriarchy. But actually, Bride Price is such as central part of all three elements that it is very hard to say it is not contributing to the structure of unequal gender relations.

In fact, my data shows the picture to be far more complex and highlights that culture is central to Bride Price. Marriage, family and kin are structures that are inherently unequal, but because they also come together to form cultural identity, people are not seeing them as such. My data shows that culture is interwoven with religion and also with globalisation. It also shows, as I will later present, that diaspora also heavily relies on culture as a mechanism to recreate bonds or maintain a sense of belonging even when people have migrated.

The scholar I focus on here, Narayan, argued that there is a tendency when talking about the lives of women in the developing world to claim that their culture is responsible for their inferiority and their vulnerability. Yet such an explanation is not afforded to white Western women who also suffer harm, abuse and inequalities. My data shows the picture to be really far more complex and highlights that for my participants culture is the critical factor in shaping their relationships with each other and, to a large extent, this is played out through the practice of Bride Price. As such, many cited culture when asked what is to blame for gender inequalities.

Culture wields a great influence, resulting in levels of contradiction in how my participants viewed the necessity of Bride Price. The female participants often claimed that Bride Price has harmful consequences, but on the other hand, they want the practice to continue. Culture is predominately gendered and patriarchal and women are disadvantaged in the name of it. Their space to challenge this is limited: culture seems to be untouchable. All my participants talked about the need to respect and maintain cultural heritage and saw Bride Price as a part of this.

Many people claimed that Bride Price is not good, but then said they will keep doing it. The cultural value that practices such as Bride Price bring far outweigh any negatives. In this respect, my data contradicts Narayan's argument that we should not be reducing the problem of patriarchy to culture. Additionally, religion is clearly influential in shaping unequal gender identities. Bride Price cements this inequality into everyday life through marriage and, as such, religion and culture emerge as key dimensions. The next chapter compares the practice in three contexts and seeks to ascertain if Bride Price is linked with harm and how perceptions of it vary depending on context.

Chapter 6

Comparing the Three Contexts: Bride Price and Harm

The previous chapter explored the role and importance of culture and religion in maintaining Bride Price. This chapter focuses on presenting a comparison between different contexts and questioning participants' perceptions of the importance of Bride Price. I also explore the different ways in which it is practised in rural and urban areas, and my findings do reveal that the differences between the rural and the two urban settings are significant. However, the differences are not so great between the two urban settings, despite one being among the diaspora in the UK and the other being in Harare, Zimbabwe.

The chapter also addresses my main objective through exploring the links between Bride Price and different forms of harm against women. Understanding the wider implications of Bride Price as a trigger for harm is important, given the high rates of violence against women and girls in the country. I also draw in the theory and the context that I set out at the start and discuss how this research fits within and adds to the wider field of research.

The chapter begins by presenting my findings on Bride Price by location: in the diaspora community in Birmingham, the urban setting of Harare and the rural setting in Zimbabwe. I then look at how Bride Price is practised, including the logistics, how much is given, what is given, and who receives it. I also address some of the ways in which the practice has changed over time. Following this, the link between Bride Price and other forms of harm is considered. The argument is that Bride Price is at the heart of marriage and is therefore also at the centre of setting patterns of gender relations that are unequal and can be problematic. My participants report that there is a lot of harassment connected with Bride Price. For example, husbands become resentful of the fact that they gave up so much to get married, leading them to feel a sense of ownership and entitlement over their wives. My data reveals contradictory views on the harm associated with Bride Price and its support.

The chapter goes on to discuss these contradictions and particularly how people position Bride Price in relation to gender inequalities and forms of harm and violence. Here, I also seek to understand how the practice has evolved over time. I explore the differences in the practice and suggest that different things may be given because family structures are now different. For example, men and women who want to marry in the diaspora often have to raise money between them to give to the bride's family, whilst in the rural setting, it is still traditional but varies from one family to another. I also captured data relating to the differences in what is now asked for. Finally, the chapter concludes by looking at regional variations and questions the extent to which this affects the amount given whilst noting that in all contexts Bride Price is seen as a token of payment.

6.1 The Diaspora and Urban and Rural Families in Zimbabwe

According to my participants, the relationship between the Zimbabweans in the diaspora and their counterparts back home is an interesting one. The people in the rural areas remain close knit, and are likely to accommodate the extended families, whereas this is a rare occurrence in the city and largely non-existent in the diaspora where families drift further apart. The rural areas remain the centre of culture, with elders who are seen as the custodians of cultural life. Thus, most traditions and cultural aspects continue to be observed in the rural areas. With Zimbabwe's dual legal system, chiefs and herdsmen are legally permitted to settle most civil matters that occur within their jurisdiction. However, even if couples meet in the diaspora or in the city, the *lobola* ceremony is still held in the rural areas. This arrangement is described by a 47-year-old married male participant (Shona tribe, in Birmingham) as follows:

> Not abroad, abroad the simply reason is that once Bride Price is paid that is the end of it. For me, I think it is more symbolism than actual culture and practice. Whereas in Zimbabwe, you find that most people will say it's a done deal so people must live up to the expectations. I think also in Zimbabwe, social and cultural aspects in that there are more 'eyes' watching. There is more expectation visible, whereas here (in England) once the ceremony is done, we all go our separate ways. Then people mainly interact through social media, occasional phone calls. It's not as tight knit as the Zimbabwean society where you will have people coming in and checking. In Zimbabwe it's not just the end of the process; people are going to make sure that the agreement is honoured. Whereas here it's different.

However, there is a recognition that those who move abroad may choose aspects of the culture that they want to follow, this is mainly because elders are not around. The same participant went on to add that:

> I think others still do it and I do appreciate it. I feel that when people migrate here others come here whilst they are still young, and I feel

that they start to capture the culture from this end and other people call it westernisation. So, they tend to forget or to enjoy how people do it like you said that there is so much freedom here. They can easily move in with their partners or they can stay without payment of the *lobola*. So that's my opinion.

This position was further supported by a single female participant (46, Ndebele tribe, in Birmingham) from a focus group:

I think this is also being affected by moving from your culture to another culture say in UK. The law in UK and the values in UK tend to affect the *lobola* part that probably. Here there is a lot of freedom; you are away from your relatives, as being away they take it as if no one sees them and no one will guide them. Being away will affect. Being away will make young people make their own decisions which affect the *lobola* and end up being scrapped.

A consensus emerged from the interviews that the relationship in the diaspora and towns is not as close-knit as those in the rural areas due to a number of factors, even those who grew up in the rural and moved to urban areas have noticed the changes:

Then the attachment becomes very small it's widening unlike the relationships in the rural areas. People have got a strong relationship even with the extended family. But when it comes to children even when they brought up, they won't even know how important it is to have that relationship with everyone in the family. So, you find that even the children are now regard the strong bond of relationship is only with their parents instead of looking at the other extended family members like in the rural areas where everyone. Me, I grew up in the rural areas where everyone was very important even those who we were not closely related to because we grew up as if we are one in the community. But my children grew up in an urban environment they lost that importance of the other family members. Even if you tell them that this one is my aunt and this one is my uncle, they won't even look at that. They don't think it's very important because they know they were brought up in the urban areas where they only saw their mother and father and that was it. And those ones will only come shortly and then they go back. So you find that is affecting the relationship with extended family.

(Female, 49, Ndebele tribe, in Harare)

And this was reiterated by a 51-year-old married female participant (Ndebele tribe) in rural Zimbabwe:

> In rural areas, we still have the extended families. And those ties are still very strong in the rural areas. The extended family ties. And when someone is getting married, she is getting married into a family. A big family, an extend family. Then when we come to the urban areas, the urban areas are controlled by the socio-economic situation. The families become smaller. Because one, the sizes of accommodation. The houses can accommodate a certain number of people. And when you look at the urban areas, they could be some local authority by laws about overcrowding, so the family unit becomes smaller from rural to urban areas. And the structure changes as well. Although we still have the extended family living in urban areas for most families you can find that it has become more of a nucleus family in the urban areas compared to the rural areas.

Furthermore, there was an acknowledgement that most of the problems with family structures were down to urbanisation and migration as asserted by a 52-year-old married male participant, (Shona tribe in Birmingham):

> I think the problem is to do with migration; there is not a lot of support in this country, cause back home there was really good support, aunties, uncles. Because the environment sometimes don't allow you because you don't practice your culture. There are certain limitations. Ya, the diaspora I think you do lack family as she says. If you have a problem in Zimbabwe you have an aunt, here there is none of that. You lack support, you need child minding, at home you have twenty people looking after your kids for you but here to get the money you will be luck really.

What was interesting was that most people agreed that *lobola* remained an integral part of the Zimbabwean culture regardless of their location.

> *Lobola* is the same; I don't see any difference whether you have moved from rural to urban areas, because it's the importance that is the objective of Bride Price. That is what is important than moving to here [UK] or internally [Zimbabwe].
>
>   (Married female, 48, Shona tribe, in Birmingham)

Equally important are the ceremonies associated with *lobola* which are still held in the rural areas regardless of the location of the couple involved.

Yes, I have witnessed so many marriages here whereby some people are married by the people back home that perform all the transactional part on behalf of this couple which is based in the UK. Especially when people are back home and normally do it at home that's confirming the couple as husband and wife.

(Married female, 34, Ndebele tribe, women's focus group in Birmingham)

On whether *lobola* was more important in the rural or urban areas of Zimbabwe or the diaspora, conflicting responses emerged from these discussions. Those in the diaspora believed that the practice loses its value once people migrate.

When people migrate, especially to Europe, it loses its importance because when we are back home in Zimbabwe, when Bride Price is paid especially in rural areas. It is meant to strengthen the relationship of the two families. And it is done properly; they use the proper procedure as everything is followed such as the use of the money. But, when it comes to this country, when people migrate you find that they don't follow all the procedures because what it is now being done are like it is a commercial thing, they want it commercialised and it has nothing to do with creating a relationship"

(Married male, 60, Shona tribe, in Birmingham)

This position was echoed by an 82-year-old married female participant (Shona tribe in rural Zimbabwe) who asserted:

I think as well as society becomes more Westernised in terms of importance, I think that importance is sort of wavering. It's no longer like how it was long ago. They used it as a value to the family and it was barter trade. There wasn't any amount put to it. But, now because of migration, it's becoming less important and at the same time it's becoming a business enterprise

This stance was supported by what came out of the women's focus group in Birmingham:

No not really, because through migration and urbanisation people don't seem to respect the purpose of *lobola* payment." Additionally, there was that idea of giving the children in the diaspora the choice to decide on whether to continue with this practice which seems irrelevant to them

I think I would say that because of our culture and background it was important for their father to pay the bridal price. But, because they are born in England, it's their choice really if they feel they want to do it they can.

(Married female, 36, Ndebele tribe, in Birmingham)

The same participant added to the discussion that the practice continues even after migration and that this has led to the commercialisation of the practice:

I think people still stick to it even with migration. I think with migration that's what has led to Bride Price going up because I am now in a First World country and they think people have money. So, they charge more, because they think everyone who is in the First World has money as compared to those back home.

The people of the second focus group believed that as much as the practice is not understood by many, it still continued as a form of maintaining identity once people migrated.

I think it becomes less important, although cultures even though we have migrated to a different country, I think a lot of people stick to it. So, I am in between really.

(Married female, 28, Shona tribe, women's focus group in Birmingham)

Those in the third focus group believed that regardless of location, the practice of *lobola* maintains its importance. This was highlighted by a 68-year-old married male participant (Shona tribe, in Harare) who argued that:

I think our culture doesn't really look at place or the issue of migration. I think it all depends with culture. In Shona culture, even if you are marrying someone from the rural areas or marrying someone from the urban areas, as long as they are following what is required by our culture, I think it will just be the same. Yahh it is requirement, it doesn't change whether people migrate or not. It is a requirement. *Lobola* is important both in rural areas and in urban areas, it doesn't matter where you are coming from, *lobola* is *lobola*.

Equally, this position was endorsed by a 59-year-old married male participant (Ndebele tribe, in rural Zimbabwe):

I think the value still remains the same and maybe in rural areas it might be a case of having more people cohabiting together without paying because normally people in the rural areas they don't have resources and they are under difficult circumstances. But in towns generally people have ways and means of raising funds. So, I think in towns there should more people who are prepared to pay *lobola* than in rural areas.

And also, by a 90-year-old married male participant (Shona tribe, in rural Zimbabwe):

To me the importance remains the same there is no change from whether you are still in the rural or in the urban areas the essence of *lobola* is still the same. I agree with him because it's all about culture wherever you are. Even if you migrate to town, that *lobola* is needed you have to go back to your roots. Culture has to be followed. Its importance is still the same.

This was in sharp contrast to the second focus group who believed the rural areas were regarded as the centre of culture.

I think in the rural areas the strictness is quite tough compared to the urban areas because for example here in Harare you can stay with someone for six months then you notify them after some few months that this is what happened. But, in the rural areas, I think it doesn't work that way. They are being guided by the laws.

(Married male, 28, Ndebele tribe, in Harare)

The other group were of the opinion that people in towns where more relaxed when it comes to issues to do with culture than their rural counterparts.

I think, cohabiting is mostly done in towns because we don't have those elders around, people who we are afraid of. Whereas in the rural areas you are reported to the chief very quickly and things are known very quickly but in towns, I might not know the person who is living next door, so I go and stay without the parents knowing that I am cohabiting.

(Married female, 72, Shona tribe, in Harare)

Another dimension was brought to the discussion by a 74-year-old married male participant (Shona tribe, in Harare) who argued that due to the cosmopolitanism of the population in the capital city, the culture was diluted.

> I would like also to agree with Grace because, in towns we are having like for instance in Harare we are having more like people from different areas even from abroad, they come here. So, in towns we are taking different cultures as well. But in rural that's where the elders are there. The custodian of the culture will be there so you cannot do things outside your culture because the custodians will be watching you. Unlike here in Harare you can do whatever you feel like doing.

This view was supported by the participant that was interviewed in rural Zimbabwe (Married male, 60, Shona tribe) who said:

> In towns people can just stay together without paying the Bride Price and they will just say will you marry me after having three or four children and they will start from there. But otherwise in the rural areas you are not allowed to go and see your parents if your Bride Price is not paid.

And those in the diaspora also believed that culture was more valued in the rural areas.

> I think its people in the rural areas, that's where culture is most valued and observed and you will see that even when you are marrying your daughter in the city, you will invite those people from the rural areas, maybe the grandfathers and the other family members from the rural areas, those are the people who are going to charge and or maybe prepare the list and all. It will only differ may on the amount that they are going to charge because they look at how the groom can afford.
>
> (Married male participant, 29, Shona tribe, in Birmingham)

However, some argued that it was easier for a couple to stay together in the diaspora without Bride Price being paid than in towns and rural areas in Zimbabwe due to lack of monitoring by elders.

> Within Zimbabwe, whether you are in town or in the rural areas it's just the same. When you meet your girlfriend in urban areas you would actually go to the rural areas to pay *lobola* there. Normally that is what happens. When you in the city and you agree to marry somebody you

actually go their rural areas. So, it's just the same within Zimbabwe. When people travel to abroad, I think there comes the problem, people just stay together.

(Married female, 55, Shona tribe, in rural Zimbabwe)

6.2 The Practice and Logistics of Lobola

The word *lobola* originated from the Ndebele, the second largest ethnic group in Zimbabwe. The Shona use the term *roora*. Originally, cows were given in exchange for a bride; in certain parts of Africa and India, cows were given to the groom's father. Cattle were the measure of wealth in Africa and milk from the cow was used for children's health sustenance.

There is a belief by some that the practice remains the same, as was asserted by an 83-year-old married female interviewee (Ndebele tribe, in rural Zimbabwe) who said:

It has never changed, it is just the same, because, African culture they believe when one is being married, they come and celebrate. It has never changed, what was happening long back it is still happening nowadays whereby people they come from may be rural areas, they relatives, they will come and enjoy and celebrate, with the person who is getting married or the person who is marrying. So, it has never changed. So extended families, aunt, uncles they will still come to witness the ceremony and to celebrate.

However, many people interviewed felt that the practice is changing, especially with the use of cash, and becoming commercialised. For example, one participant said:

To me to some extent it has changed because long ago they used to pay Bride Price like, they used to go with cattle and goats, and they didn't go with the monies but now they want both cash and cattle. This is true especially with the use of cash and moving away from the symbolic idea, Historically from the way we hear it, in the early 80s and stuff this Bride Price was actually in the form of grain some a hoe. The African type of hoe as a Bride Price and you could be given a wife formally saying that this is now your wife because we have seen this. But I can tell you nowadays it has to be about figures. And actually, depending on whom are you marrying and from what historically where is that wife of yours coming from. If she is coming from a rich family and I am from a poor family, I have to work for that to make sure that they are happy. Some they just accept the Bride Price as saying that's fine that is what our daughter has wanted but they won't be all that happy.

(Married male, 79, Shona tribe, in rural Zimbabwe)

The situation has been exacerbated by the turmoil facing the nation, as asserted by a 70-year-old married male interviewee (Shona tribe, in rural Zimbabwe) who added:

It was a bit different because before the economic hardship, you would actually get help even from your family members, your brothers, your sisters, your elder sisters, your parents if they are well up, they can chip in and help you so as to raise money for *lobola*.

Most of my participants believed that today money is used and that sometimes the money is squandered and not used to sustain the children. Historically, *lobola* really brought about unity and purpose among the man's family members. The extended family, such as uncles, also contributed to the *lobola* and then when the uncle's children married this favour of contributing to the *lobola* was reciprocated. And on the woman's side, it brought about a sense of pride and belonging in the woman and also unity among her family. It is only nowadays that you convert the number of cows into money and crucify the man to pay it alone. This is one of Africa's most beautiful practices according to those who support the practice.

The other aspect that came out was that the cultural *lobola* was paid in instalments

And this *lobola* is not paid as a one off payment, it can be paid in your lifetime. It's like a mortgage. Traditionally, that is what it was. Because you were not supposed to finish paying it. They will refuse that no... no... no... we don't want everything. So that in your relationship you keep on going there.

(Married male, 91, Ndebele tribe, in rural Zimbabwe)

The participants further asserted that the *lobola* system entailed that the man getting married was never meant to pay all of it alone. His parents, uncles and other relatives were supposed to contribute and participate in the *lobola* process. It had a formality and structure which has been forgotten, the whole process was supposed to introduce members of the two families and getting to know the family members, the aunties, the uncles and who the new couple could approach for advice should they encounter problems or difficulties in their marriage. In both Shona and Ndebele customs, women were trained by their aunts on how to 'treat' a man. Supporters of the practice argue that one should not give out one's daughter to another man without 'seating down' with the groom's family, and them showing appreciation by paying *lobola* because one's daughter is going to give birth to their grandchildren and grow their family tree and surname. This involvement of the extended family members was summed up by a 47-year-old married female interviewee (Shona tribe, in Harare).

> Yes, because during my ceremony, I remember that it was one person negotiating the Bride Price on behalf of my husband. But these days I am hearing of ridiculous cases whereby the father and the mother are the ones dictating or demanding directly how much they want for their daughter. So, there is a shift, it has changed. During my time, my aunt, my father's sister, was the one who was responsible for the negotiating. But these days because of strange relationships, the role of aunties doesn't exist anymore. Those involved also received a part of the cake, and they shared whatever was paid. They would share as a family. There will be something for the aunt, something for the grandmother, something for the mother, something for the sisters and the brothers. It was shared. But now it is for the two parents because the family unit have changed.

Some of the interviewees also highlighted the controversial issue of 'virginity' which was associated with Bride Price, in that a girl who was a virgin commanded a higher *lobola* than one who was not. Additionally, they argued that there was the whole tradition, which was laced with meaning; the question of whether a woman was a virgin or not was a recent development as that was never an issue originally.

In the same vein, some of my participants believed that there are still some culturally strict fathers who vowed that their daughters and granddaughters would not be married to uncircumcised men, and this they pass on to future generations for customary reasons. Additionally, they trusted that politics, the Church and social media have a role to play in this, as well as the grandfathers and grandmothers left who may have the right ancient oral wisdom.

During some informal discussions, people believed that *lobola* should be abolished and that there should be a debate about how this could happen. Supporters of the practice argued that asking for too much money, like a marriage contract, should be questioned but not that the *lobola* payment should be abolished. They believed that their ancestors had genuine reasons for asking for it. They therefore argued that a man is not obligated to pay the whole *lobola* upfront and that he could do so in instalments until it is fully paid for. They did not see a reason why the practice should stop. They did not see anything wrong with it, they just did not agree with some of the prices. They argued that 'if done properly, it's a good practice'. They also argued that those who want to pay should pay, but you should not feel obligated to do so. High Bride Price had led most men to struggle in raising *lobola*, which is what the practice was meant to be. A 42-year-old married male participant (Shona tribe, in Harare) who had struggled with paying summed this up by saying:

> Yahh it is quite common because when I married her, I did struggle because we wanted to raise the maximum amount. There is no price really. You can't put a price tag on a person. But you do try and put maximum effort so it's the dedication of the person. Because you can't go with £20 and say I am going to marry, you need sort of to be prepared. So, I think it is a struggle, it was a struggle.

The high Bride Price also creates social classes because those who are poor and cannot afford a higher price are expected to marry those who are of the same social status:

> And also, what I have seen if you marry a woman from the rich families, you won't even afford to. Because one maybe that lady would be very educated then you suffer that inferiority complex. You won't be in a position to marry that woman because they will charge very high. Like myself, I cannot even afford, marrying somebody from university who is educated, you see the gap between.

(Statement by the above participant)

The Shona, the largest ethnic group in Zimbabwe, have several forms of customary marriage. Most common are the regular proposal marriages, a traditional marriage with a lengthy and formalized prelude and the elopement marriages, a more popular form of marriages that ignores the prelude and makes for a prompt formalization of the relation (Holleman, 1952). In both types of marriage, the start of a formalized relation concerns the respective families and not only the individuals. This is illustrated by the fact that all males of the bride's family become "father-in -law" to all members of the groom's family who, in turn, become "son- in-law" to the bride's family (Bourdillon, 1987). A 74-year-old married woman (Ndebele tribe, in Harare) said that, "there were so many people, they were relatives, and the others who were related to my husband". However, some people believe that this position has now changed due to mistrust, and belief in other cultural practices, as was expressed by a 30-year-old married male (Shona tribe, in rural Zimbabwe) participant, "Yes not all. Those close to you. Those who you trust, a lot can be done, and some can end up casting the bad omen".

Most of my participants asserted that an important element in Shona marriage is the negotiation and payment of Bride Price. At the end of the preluding period, or after elopement, the groom chooses an intermediary who approaches the family of the intended bride. After the presentation of some gifts 'to open the mouth of the girl's father', representatives of the groom and the father of the bride negotiate the bride wealth or *roora* (Kileff & Kileff, 1970). Bride wealth is composed of at least two transfers. The first, called *rutsambo*, is usually a gift in cash and kind such as clothing, utensils, groceries, and goats. It is associated with sexual rights to the woman. The second, *danga*, involves a more substantial payment. It is associated with the rights of the groom's family over the children born to the woman. Although there are regional differences and variations according to family background, generally the value of *danga* depends on the number of (additional) children a wife is expected to bear (Holleman, 1952). For women who have had children before, a reduction in *danga* can be expected. But, the birth of one child prior to the current marriage may be appreciated as it confirms that the woman involved is not barren. *Danga* is expressed in cattle and is sometimes augmented with a demand for cash.

My participants argued that customarily the major part of *lobola* was *danga*, which is paid to the in-laws in the form of a head of cattle. In rural areas, the importance of cattle is also linked to subsistence farming where cattle is used for pulling ploughs. Hoogeveen (2001) shows that households with at least two beasts are able to realise a substantially larger agricultural production than those without any because they are able to plough. Kinsey et al. (1998) evidence that in times of drought cattle fulfil an important role as buffer stock; or as a source of nutrition (i.e., milk) and manure. The possession of cattle is also associated with status (Scoones, 1996) and the animals play an important role in cultural ceremonies (Parker, 1980; Holleman, 1952). This came out in one of the interviews in rural Zimbabwe when a 48-year-old married man (Shona tribe) said, "Although there was a cash element but it wasn't a lot but the main Bride Price was the cattle which is still the same, ten cows, which is normal".

The participants agreed that in addition to *rutsambo* and *danga*, Bride Price consisted of two additional head of cattle, the so-called 'cow of motherhood' and a bull for the bride's family. The 'cow of motherhood' is presented to the mother of the bride, to acknowledge that she carried the wife in her womb, and the transfer of this beast has a spiritual connotation. Delayed or non-payment is believed to displease ancestral spirits of the mother's family and may cause bad health or other misfortunes to children born from the union.

Payment of the 'cow of motherhood' generally takes place after the first child is born. The symbolic value of the bull for the family varies regionally in Zimbabwe. In the eastern parts of the country, payment is related to the virginity of the wife while in others, it serves to strengthen the relationship between the families involved. In either case, payment of the bull by the son-in-law is interpreted as a sign of respect to his parents-in-law and as appreciation for the upbringing of his wife. Upon transfer, the bull is slaughtered, and the meat divided between the father of the bride, the mother of the bride and the son-in-law, who will each take the meat and consume it with their respective relatives (Bourdillon, 1987). The extra-individual character of marriage is further illustrated by the fact that all males in the groom's lineage may be asked to contribute to the bride wealth of one of 'their sons', while bride wealth received for any of the daughters from the lineage is customarily reserved for the marriage of the sons (Bourdillon, 1987). Nevertheless, the prime responsibility for the payment of the bride wealth rests with the groom himself.

The amount of *rutsambo* and *danga,* according to the informal discussions I had with my participants, is assigned during the Bride Price negotiations. The timing of the payments and the kind of animals that have to be provided are a topic between the two families; a cash equivalent can be negotiated, though customarily a first instalment of the bride wealth is paid at the time of marriage. There is an argument that there are too many items on the lists these days; you buy something for your mother-in-law, brothers and sisters-in-law and even grandfathers and grandmothers-in-law. These gifts are very expensive considering the current economic situation in Zimbabwe. However, some people believe that all this has changed, as came out during one of my rural interviews when a Married female (43, Shona tribe) said:

> Yes, it has changed because now we can just throw a list, whereas long back there were so many stages even the groom didn't know what he was going to pay until the day. But now the list can be send before meeting it means you would know the amount because the list is already send to him.

Conversely, an interviewee in Harare (with a married man, 78, Ndebele tribe) believed that nothing has changed whether in rural or urban areas:

> Yes, Bride Price if looked at in term so its breakdown, was supposed to remain the same. It is made up of *danga* cattle payment for the father, *majazi ababa,* clothes for the father, *mombe yeumai,* cattle for the mother, *mauchiro, kupizwa mumusha,* and other numerous charges. All those are common characteristics of Bride Price. Why we are forced

to at this present moment to talk about Bride Price in town, Bride Price in rural areas, perhaps we are being influenced by the simple fact that most people today prefer to be in town where they seemed to be opportunities of finding jobs and better life.

A typical *lobola* list is shown below. This is a list given to the researcher by one of the interviewees in rural Zimbabwe (married male, 24, Shona tribe) which gives an example of charges of the *lobola* requests by his-in-laws, charged in US dollars.

Ndiro	$300	(charge for the wooden plate used during the ceremony)
Kupindamumusha	$300	(charge for setting foot into the-in-law's homestead)
Vhura muromo	$300	(a small fee is paid for the introductions)
Sunungura homwe	$300	(a fee charge for the process to start)
Danga		(the livestock that is given to the bride's father, traditionally the groom would bring cattle but nowadays part of it can be paid in cash)
Dhemeji	$5,000	(fee charged if the bride is no longer a virgin)
Makandinzwanani	$300	(charge for acknowledging the father-in-law)
Chiwuchiro	$300	
Mufukidza dumbu	$150	
Hotamiro	$150	
Kurera	$150	
Mbariro	$150	(miscellaneous charges payable to the mother-in-law)
Rusambo	$1600	(This is the main amount which is deemed to constitute the Bride Price)
Mombe 10	$700	(per beast: cattle paid to the father-in-law)
Mombe youmai		(cattle paid to the mother-in-law)
Majasi ababa		(clothes for father-in-law inc. black suit $500, white shirt $75, black Shoes $100, brown overcoat $350, tie $20, belt $20, socks $20)
Amai		(clothes for the mother-in-law in. Dress $300, handbag $300, perfume $95, shoes $125, pulling socks $30, necklace $300, umbrella $25, overcoat $350, handkerchief $20)
Masungiro Mudya	$400	
Mbudzi yaAmai	$100	
Mbudzi yemusha	$100	
Mbudzi yababa	$100	
Mombe yechishava	$700	
Mombe yemasungiro	$700	(miscellaneous charges payable to the father to the-in-law)

The payment of a first instalment, according to my interviewees, at the time of marriage leaves the son-in-law indebted to his wife's father, a practice that is referred to as *jeredzwa*, which literally means 'something outstanding'. The indebtedness is actively sought as is illustrated by the fact that even if the family of the son-in-law is in a position to pay the bride wealth in full at the date of marriage, one is not expected to do so. Full payment of *danga* (referring to the livestock that is given to the bride's father, traditionally brought by the groom but nowadays part of it can be paid in cash) is a sign of disrespect and is thought to deny the relationship that exists between the son-in-law and the family of his wife (Bourdillon, 1987). This was highlighted by one of my participants:

> So, you always owed the in-laws in a way, as a result you also like and respect them more. You give them their dues unlike saying I paid everything up. I don't owe anything, whatever it is becoming arrogant. Even the Ndebele culture has the same take, its culture, the Ndebele culture says it cannot be paid in one go. If you had everything, they would not accept it. What they would simply say is that aah you are just paying that? You seem like you just want to buy her out. So, what they used to say is that you can't pay it all in one go. Even if you had everything you will go back and bring the rest at a later stage

> (Married man, 53, Ndebele tribe, in Harare)

They are not interested in what one was bringing in, but instead are interested in seeing a relationship develop between the son-in-law and their daughter. You and your wife. That was the purpose of it.

There was a feeling among many participants that *lobola* should still be a part of their culture. It has always been practised and they felt the tradition should continue but not as a 'get rich scheme' whereby people ask for flat-screen televisions or Range Rovers. The difference in cultural practices especially in the diaspora is said to have contributed to the dilution of some of the cultural practices, and this was a recurring topic in most of my discussions.

> And some of the people are no longer marrying from the same culture. Let's say you are coming from Zimbabwe, you come here go into a relationship with someone from Ghana or someone from Nigeria so that means that will also contribute to some of those changes. Unless if you are from the same country.

This is was further endorsed by one participant who asserted that:

I think it has changed. I think currently because the world has become a global village. There is cross pollination of cultures in the marriage ceremonies. People are taking a few things they see from another culture and a few things from another culture and make up their own marriages.

(Married female, 68, Shona tribe, in Birmingham)

There was also an argument put forward by supporters of *lobola* that it should be 'nationalised', and everyone should pay a standard Bride Price.

And this effect of globalisation, where we know that Mutare are very cheap and people from Masvingo were very expensive, but now it's coming to the same level. So, maybe there should be a common Bride Price for everyone, but I don't think we will end up agreeing because, if you go to some regions like in Matebeleland, Bulawayo, say. I don't think they charge as much as what are other regions say Masvingo does, say Mrewa does.

(Married man, 53, Ndebele tribe, in Harare)

This also came out even in interviews in Birmingham when a 24-year-old married woman (Shona tribe) said:

So, it's better to have a common Bride Price for those regions so that you know if you are going to marry in Bulawayo, from Bulawayo then you know what to expect. If you are going to Masvingo you know what to expect.

Some interviewees in the rural areas also expressed a similar view:

I think *lobola* must always exist, but the only thing that I think can be done is to nationalise so that it becomes uniform, and when one is married the *lobola* paid on family X is the equal to the *lobola* paid on Y and Z.

This was further supported by women only focus group when one woman said:

Yes, I was thinking along the lines of putting across a law which actually protect and bless *lobola* in making it a well-defined thing which can never be misunderstood by anyone.

(Married female, 20, Shona tribe)

When one is based abroad and the parents are based in Zimbabwe, the ceremony is still held in Zimbabwe in the rural areas, even if the couple were not able to attend. The bride is encouraged to attend (and if not, she was represented by her sister or aunt), but she is not expected to formally participate in the actual ceremony. All the interviewees agreed that the ceremony was still to be held in the rural areas, regardless of where the couple were based.

> Because most of these rituals are not performed in the diaspora even though people are getting married in the diaspora. However, the actual ceremony is being performed in Zimbabwe.

> (Married woman, 21, Shona tribe, in rural Zimbabwe)

6.3 Changes in the Amount Given Over Time

Most of my participants agreed that a younger educated bride is preferred in the marriage market and will command a higher *lobola*. Conversely, *lobola* is likely to decrease with the bride's age and increase with more years in school. In Zimbabwe, my data revealed that the higher the education attainment of the girl child, the higher the social-economic strata from which she can choose a potential husband and consequently, the higher her Bride Price. In this case, the increase in *lobola* is caused by more education, which increases the value of the bride.

> Yes, it has changed to some extent. Aah in my own opinion, I think some families have made it an economic unit. They use a child as an economic unit. They will start saying I send my child to this schools and paid that and that. It's like when they charge this Bride Price, they want you to pay back whatever they spend on their daughters. But in my own opinion, personally, if as a parent, I won't see it that way. It is my responsibility to make sure that child is valuable. I will bring up my child so that she is of value. But, when someone wants to marry my child, I don't think it is fair to look at what I have spent on my child. I spend on my child because I wanted my child to be what she is. To be someone of value and if it's someone of value, that child will be someone of value to that man that she marries. I don't want the man to pay for what I did, but I want the man to appreciate my child.

> (Married male, 61, Shona tribe, in Harare)

This position was evident in all the field sites. In Harare, one participant remarked that:

> So, whether we want to actually be real about it or not in as far as that process is concerned it has been commercialised because there is a proportion somewhere along the lines that is attributed to the fact that actually you are no longer just marrying my daughter, she is now a doctor. So, you pay for it one way or the other. The more successful she has become, in terms of making good for herself academically and professionally the more it's becoming a problem for the guy intending to marry her.

(Married female, 20, Shona tribe)

The payments vary from place to place and include such preliminary payments as a token and a head of cattle. Other issues to be considered when determining the size of Bride Price include; the behaviour of the girl – the better the behaviour, the higher the bride price. The education status of the girl proposed for marriage in that in some areas parents indicated that they would send their girl children to school so as to demand higher *lobola* for them. Additionally, the affluence of the girl's family. In most cases, the *lobola* demanded by well to do families is on the higher side than that demanded by poor families. One other factor taken on board was in determining a Bride Price was whether the girl is a virgin or not. A virgin or a girl who has neither given birth nor married before attracts a high *lobola*.

Advocates of the continuation of *lobola* in this study believed that in its true sense *lobola* was meant to bring two families together as one through marriage unlike this idea of demanding exorbitant figures, reaching as much as US$40,000 but this could also be as low as US$500. Most of my participant reckoned that Bride Price has become excessive. My data also shows that what was meant to build a relationship between two families is now being used as a 'get rich scheme'. Some would argue that a token payment which is affordable would suffice. Many of my participants were of the view that it would be beneficial for the couple if both families put resources together to give the couple a head start as well as share wisdom with them to ensure they have a happy and healthy marriage. The participants further argued that this would bring the two families together and would also show gratitude from both sides for producing and raising someone worth marrying. This should apply to both rich and poor and would ensure happy and successful marriages, and functional families that are the base of any nation. There is also the argument put forward by participants that people should pay what they can afford.

I think men should raise what is within the means. Not to have a price tag dictated to them. If I am earning £10 if I can pay £3 that's what I can afford so when you say raise it's like putting a price tag on it.

(Married male, 61, Shona tribe, in Harare)

This commercialisation has contributed to the practice losing its value as asserted by a 55-year-old married male participant (Shona tribe) in rural Zimbabwe:

Yahh, I think it has or it is losing its value because as they are all saying parents end up comparing that this one has gone at so much amount and mine should also go on a higher fee. So really the actual reason why we pay *lobola* is end up not being appreciated. It's not noticeable any more. In our culture, *lobola* was a token, even in the bible people used to pay camels and stuff. Yahh it does make it lose its value because people are losing focus looking at money more than the practice itself.

The love for the latest range of assets has contributed to the commercialisation and greediness of the practice:

It has gone up for example, in the late 80s to early 90s, you would find that people were influenced by new assets such as new cars Peugeots, Cressidas, 504… at home some people will simply say eeh you buy me a Peugeot for marrying my child. So, this is evidence that marriage was becoming a commercialised thing. The initial purpose of that Bride Price was losing its value. Because of that, I do believe that problems started emanating because of that kind of the commercialisation. It gave the man an idea that he is buying a woman and made the woman's position subservient. So, the woman become indebted to the man because the man says in his mind, I bought you. I paid so much. Your parents demanded so much, therefore, you are my property. But the initial purpose of that token was for a mutual relationship where it was based on mutual respect and understanding of each other. And as a result, you find that if the woman did anything wrong, it was her family who would put pressure on her because what they valued is not what they were paid but the relationship with their in-laws. Rather than what they were paid.

(Married male, 48, Shona tribe, in rural Zimbabwe)

Most of my participants agreed that some greedy parents have taken it to a new level, they still believe that even though the man knew what was expected of him, paying *lobola* should not give him the green light to objectify and abuse his wife. Many argue that *lobola* is good a practice in that it demonstrates that the man is ready and willing to start and take care of his family and acts as a token of appreciation to the bride's family. However, those against the practice feel that *lobola* is being used by most brides' families to extract and make money out of poor men. Among the Shonas in Zimbabwe, some people are made to pay amounts ranging from US$10,000 to US$100,000 for *lobola*. There is a belief among many that this is wrong. There is a suggestion that it should be an average of US$100 to US$1000 for *lobola*, irrespective of whether the bride is a doctor or an engineer. This *lobola* money should not be linked to status. It should just be what a man has to pay as a show of appreciation. The risk of not paying *lobola* leads to what is regarded as 'illegal' marriages. A marriage is considered to not only be for the bride and groom, but rather it is for the two families. The families are fused together, and this is the main aim according to my participants. Pressure to conform to certain norms is affecting other people, as echoed by a 30-year-old married female participant (Shona tribe) in Birmingham:

> But I still think there is a general feeling it's not only one person who is married. People will still ask what the going rate of at that time. So, there is a tendency of checking the market if you want to get the best value.

Most of my participants believed that the whole concept of *lobola* needs a review in view of the contemporary social dynamics. Marriages hardly last any more, they argued, and there is a lot of interference from the extended families of a married couple which makes the *lobola* issues an unnecessary nuisance. There is also an argument that the younger generation do not really care about this aspect of culture, especially those children born or raised in the diaspora; they know nothing about the cultural requirement of Bride Price. To them, it is just something they have to do to please parents. There are those who believe that the commercialisation of *lobola* has not helped as it is now competing with foreign borrowed celebrations such as Valentine's Day and Christmas Day. This lack of understanding of the practice has led to its misuse and overcharging.

> It depends who you ask, it's gone up, but it depends on the family on how they calculate what the Bride Price is or whether it's through greed or general culture. Ya, I think it's gone up because people don't understand the actual concept of *lobola* so to say. Putting monetary value on people.

(Married male, 52, Shona tribe, in Birmingham)

There was also a belief that this can lead to young couples being forced into a marriage when they are not ready financially, as alleged by another married male participant (29, Shona tribe) in Birmingham:

> Very common, in terms of the amount being charge is too high, very unaffordable. Not only that, the other thing is at times you are forced into a marriage before you even save for paying *lobola*. In a way it will put a strain on the relationship because for the man especially here in the diaspora to raise the amount of money required or to pay of the whole Bride Price before he is able to live with the wife it means the men has to work harder thereby spending most of his time at work. Say your wife is in Zimbabwe, and he is here, there cannot have a reunion because he cannot invite his wife without the wedding. That will tend to take longer. In some cases, the relationship can even fizzle out.

My data reveals that cases of men being dragged to traditional courts for failing to pay *lobola* are on the increase due to the economic challenges the country currently faces. In most cases, a 'deposit' is paid to ensure the marriage goes ahead with the balance often paid over many years, but some in-laws are now demanding immediate full payment as economic hardships continue. The hyperinflation of the last decade and the subsequent multi-currency regime has also been blamed for the commercialisation of *lobola*, with parents cashing in on their daughters by charging exorbitant prices. A 61-year-old married female participant (Shona tribe) in Birmingham remarked that the financial plans of the bride' parents have an effect on the *lobola* charge:

> Ok, I will put this example; a cousin of mine wanted to get married but the parents wanted to build, and they had projects that they wanted but they didn't have enough financial. They didn't have enough money to do the projects that they intended. So, conveniently it was the time their daughter was getting married and they raised the Bride Price so that they could gain from it.

In the same vein, a 48-year-old married female participant (Shona tribe) in Birmingham believed that other factors could contribute to a high Bride Price:

> And also some of the people who are increasing *lobola* maybe they are some push factors that will lead them to increase or charge exorbitantly their Bride Price because like the situation in Zimbabwe right now because of the economic meltdown, one would think to

revive himself economically by charging exorbitant Bride Price especially if the parents sees that the bridegroom is from an economically stable family, they would want to take advantage of that and then try to charge exorbitantly so that they are in a better position because they are facing economic hardships.

If we consider a young graduate who begins his first job and is receiving US$650 per month, then deduct travel expenses, rent, and utility bills, saving to pay an exorbitant Bride Price could take an extraordinary amount of time. There is an indication from the interviews that a young educated 'ready–to-marry' Zimbabwean man might be afraid of getting married, not because they do not value the practice but because *lobola* has become very expensive.

> I think the monetary value; the pressure that put in the younger generation is much. How much did you pay and how much were you charged. Say you compare family siblings and you find out that one got $10,000 and then that's put pressure on the other siblings. The husband must now pay more for me etc. I think it put unwarranted pressure on other women in the family. This is only the younger generation, I think. Like Martin said, I think it is beginning to lose its value but other than it be this is what I am paying or thanking my-in-laws for the woman that they raised. It's now a question of price. In the younger generation it's now a question of prices, the more you pay, the better is for you because your husband is more successful, and your family is more successful. If that makes sense.

> (Married male, 61, Shona tribe, in rural Zimbabwe)

There is also a belief that the economic crisis in the country has contributed to many families wanting to cash in on their daughters.

> It has gone up because of the economic situation, the hardship are forcing people to bargain from Bride Price. So, when a family gets a chance to marry their daughter, they take advantage of that and try to make money out of it.

> (Married female, 61, Shona tribe, in Harare)

In the rural areas, there is a belief that *lobola* has not gone up in real terms but because of inflation and the use of multi-currency.

It's difficult because we are using a multi-currency system which artificially holds the local currency to the US dollar at par whereas the reality at the black market is that these currencies have a different going rate. This makes *roora* more expensive should you be quote in US dollars and having to pay in the local bond notes.

(Married male, 42, Shona tribe, in Harare)

Supporters of *lobola*, according to my data, believed that it is meant to bring together the two families as well as symbolising the stage at which the woman leaves her family to be welcomed into her husband's family. Most people in Zimbabwe are of the opinion that *lobola* is their culture and that it is a tradition that should be upheld, and quite rightly so. In the Zimbabwean culture, it is regarded as an abomination to have a wife when you have not paid *lobola*. One has to pay *lobola* first before living together with a woman. However, the salaries are not enough to cover all the *lobola* requirements, according to most of my participants.

The participants believed that even though parents help their sons to pay *lobola*, this is still not enough to cover all the requirements. So, most families have resorted to taking out loans, especially from family members and also from banks. They do not feel that there is anything wrong with taking a loan to pay *lobola* for one's wife if there is love. However, some of the participants argued that it should not be a bank loan and advised that one should get a family loan which has no interest rate and can be written off if one struggles to repay. Alternatively, *lobola* should only be paid on your savings, or if one has a rich father or generous brothers who are willing to offer a 'soft loan' of some sort.

My data revealed that some parents are known to be taking their sons-in-law to court asking for rulings that will force their son-in-law to at least pay something. Unfortunately, some men also end up abusing their wives because of these court rulings. However, it was reported that some men were using the economic hardships as an excuse, even when they could afford to pay.

6.4 Women's Contribution to Lobola

Part of the reason for the increase in Bride Price is that women are now better educated, which is seen as an investment in the value of her as a wife.

It has gone up over time, people these days they are now valuing the level of education of their child before getting married. Some have really gone up to getting like degrees, PhD, masters and all sort of education with an effort to improve their lives. So, before you even let your child to be a wife to someone you really value all those investments that you have done into your child then by the end of the day that can actually make some parents those who really feel they have invested a lot in their child to request for a higher Bride Price.

(Married male, 59, Ndebele tribe, in Birmingham)

Supporters of the practice believe that the amount of *lobola* is determined by the wealth and status (i.e., the perceived ability to pay) of the family of the groom. There is anecdotal evidence that people are paying as much as US$40,000. For example, if one is marrying a girl from a wealthy family and she is a doctor or a University professor and the groom is from a wealthy family then it is not an issue, because the woman comes endowed with a lot of cultural, economic, and social capital. Her earnings, too, will contribute a lot to the wellbeing of her family. These advocates believe that one cannot dispute the fact that if the woman is a huge earner her husband will benefit a lot more in the long run and US$40,000 will be nothing compared to the returns. By virtue of marrying into that family, they argued the groom immediately has all the advantages that marrying into a family that is well-off in society will bring: he gains a lot of social contacts in the right place.

The participants remarked that the groom and his family agreed to pay that money through negotiation and mutual agreement. However, there have been occasions when people have been known to walk out because the price was too high, although those stories are very rare. Most of my participants did not know of anyone who had ever walked out of a negotiation. If a family agrees to pay US$40,000, it probably means they can afford it and that it would not affect them financially.

Some would argue that if *lobola* was for the display of wealth, the families would give the option to the poor to provide labour in return. Additionally, they did not subscribe to the spiritual argument about *lobola*, as put forward by supporters of *lobola*. However, both sides agreed that *lobola* was a bonding mechanism and a sign of commitment. Once Bride Price was paid, the groom could then ask for permission to marry in a civil ceremony. The-in-laws were expected to help financially in preparation for the wedding so the groom would end up with more money than their *lobola* payment. There is then this argument that the son-in-law should therefore not pay less in terms of *lobola*. In fact, the participants argued that the groom and the bride stand to benefit in the long run in terms of start-up funds and furniture for their new home.

However, those against the practice argue that paying will just put the new marriage under strain both financially and emotionally. Therefore, they believe that the parents of the bride should be mindful of this and that their daughter is not a slave to be sold to the highest bidder. They advocate for the girls' parents to be supportive if a man wants to do things properly. Additionally, they believe that there should not be a price tag on *lobola* due to different earning capacities, and they want men to pay what they can afford. This would ensure that the new couple are comfortable after all the proceedings are done. Some men also forget that their wives will have contributed a lot towards the marriage. In such instances, women also contribute towards the outstanding *lobola* balance. There is an assumption that if the woman is also based in the diaspora or has an earning capacity, then she will contribute towards her *lobola*. This is then taken into account when *lobola* is charged.

> On the other side of it as well, if both the individuals are here you tend to find if the girl is educated and is here, she can control the situation. It does put a strain on the relationship, but she can say look you got to be realistic. Because most people are under no illusion that both people are working. People are not living under a rock, they know that there are two earners there. They know there are two sets of money and unfortunately nobody cares who is paying what at the end of the day. Nobody says the money comes completely from the man. As the man presents the money. That is what matters. I think that is one of the things that people in Zimbabwe take into account. That listen, if they are earning this money together, they should be able to make it. Why should they strain their relationship if both people are working? They should both work harder. In most cases that is what happens, people will just decide to work together, get some more shifts, get the money together so that these people can get on with it.

> (Married female, 59, Shona tribe, in Birmingham)

Though it is often regarded as taboo for a woman to contribute towards her *lobola*, it is feared that this is the case, especially in the diaspora where a woman can contribute directly or can meet other financial obligations whilst the man saves money for *lobola*.

> But that was never allowed. Before this diaspora thing, it was forbidden for a woman to contribute towards her Bride Price. Because people will end up saying you married yourself. You paid the Bride Price which you are not supposed to do. Your husband is the one who is supposed to pay. If you as a woman you contribute paying that then you are paying it yourself which is a taboo. Because he is the one who will have paid all the Bride Price. It's not the woman who pays the Bride Price

> (Married female, 28, Shona tribe, women's focus group in Birmingham)

The pressure to fit in, the pressure from families to be seen to be outbidding one another, the pressure to be better than the rest has led to a situation whereby women contribute towards their Bride Price, which is not acceptable culturally.

> Generally, when you go to marry, you know it's an uphill task. It's a daunting task you are sort of afraid whether you going to meet their expectations and you always work hand in hand with your spouse. And she often assists you with the cash so that at least you present a good image to the-in-laws.

> (Married female, 47, Shona tribe, in Harare)

However, some people feel that the money paid by the groom is paid back by the father-in-law in the form of hosting the wedding ceremony, which is separate from the Bride Price ceremony. So, in the end, the son-in-law does not spend as much as the father of the bride.

> But if we go deep down to where it started that is how it is. That money goes back, it is not worth it. They even gave back more. And the other thing was, when this *lobola* is being paid, that money still goes back, because when they are getting married in our tradition you have got to provide, you have got to give them the gift which is even more than what they have paid. Because when they are getting married maybe, if he paid £800 on their wedding you might even give them £2000.

> (Married male, 90, Shona tribe, in rural Zimbabwe)

Additionally, in the diaspora, couples are likely to live together before Bride Price is paid, thereby enabling the couple to contribute jointly towards the Bride Price.

> I agree that it can be quite difficult and most of the times is what Neo pointed out that when you pay *lobola* it's now the two of you raising that money. It's not just the one person 'cause you will be living together at that time, so it is.

> (Married female, 34, Ndebele tribe, women's focus group in Birmingham)

6.5 Some Reasons for the Increase in Lobola

According to my participants, practising *lobola* is becoming more prevalent over time. Furthermore, the practice of lobola plays a significant role in marriage. It is at the centre of marriage and without it, the union would not be recognised. We see that there exists strong regional variations in the practice of marriage transactions, demonstrating diverse cultural heritage surrounding marriages in Zimbabwe. The practice is highly prevalent in the whole of Zimbabwe, but in the south-eastern province of Masvingo, the *lobola* prices are the highest in the country. An 87-year-old married female participant (Shona tribe) in rural Zimbabwe argued that:

> Yes certainly, I tend to disagree on the diaspora aspect. I think the value of Bride Price in Zimbabwe is determined regionally. Some regions charge more Bride Price regardless of educational background. Some regions just charge Bride Price as a custom, as a tradition, they don't commercialise it. So, I don't think it's determined by whether the women is in diaspora or not. I think it is to do with different traditions within the culture of Zimbabwe.

Meanwhile, in the South West of the country, in Matabeleland has the lowest charges of *lobola* in the country. There has been no explanation to date as to the causes of these regional disparities in charges. District level sex ratio of females to males is also highly significant, confirming the demographic claim that as women become relatively scarce, men will compete for them by paying higher *lobola*. The results here show that the scarcity of females in the marriage market results in larger *lobola*. Another factor that came out frequently as the cause of a high Bride Price was educational attainment of the bride.

> Not only that but they are considering that, given for example like our mothers the level of education attained and the level of education that's being attained nowadays, I think it also comes into effect because nowadays most parents are sending their daughters to school maybe up to A-level or university level so after sending those people to school they begin to value more of these girls as per the level of education that one has attained. If she has gone through like to university it means when you want to pay Bride Price for that girl, it means you have got to fork a bit more than somebody who hasn't really been to school that much.

> (Married female, 38, Shona tribe, in Harare)

Supporters of *lobola* argue that women do not want to discard their fathers' surnames and take another man's surname and grow that man's family by bearing him children for free. They feel that the issue of *lobola* should not be debated due to its importance. Furthermore, the more conservative participants believe that it is hypocritical to advocate for abolishing *lobola* whilst at the same time advocating for the de-criminalisation of prostitution. Additionally, they believe that this has been caused by a lack of understanding of the practice.

> Really to say that it has increased or not would be getting lost otherwise we must accept that there are people who are mishandling; they are abusing the whole idea of *lobola*. They take it as an opportunity perhaps to make something or to milk the other person who is new in the scenario. So, actually these are the people who make the whole thing very unfortunate, but otherwise Bride Price was not supposed though in terms of increasing or decreasing because it is simply like a prayer.
>
> (Married male, 42, Shona tribe, in Harare)

The participants agreed that the groom's residential status/passport also played a role in the amount of *lobola* a woman commands, with those in the UK commanding a very high Bride Price.

> I think people moving to the UK has changed a lot of prices, because some parents are actually charging that my daughter is in the UK. And they tend to charge more just like when one is educated.
>
> (Married male, 60, Shona tribe, in Birmingham)

A 27-year-old married female participant (Shona tribe) in Birmingham supported this whole notion of UK based grooms commanding high Bride Prices:

> No, even if the parents are back home. The daughter has migrated from Zimbabwe to UK and you pay for their daughter from here they will say that my daughter is in the UK and I am this and I am that, so they tend to charge more.

My data revealed that *lobola* differs by region due to cultural differences. The tribal affiliation is added as a control variable since *lobola* practice is expected to be highly influenced by tribal background. Statistically, there has been a significant rise in the practice of *lobola*, showing no support for the anthropological argument of a that the practice is declining. The probability of *lobola* payment suggests that the regional diversity is deeply rooted and that the variables included in the analysis are not sufficient to explain these effects away. The social impact of Bride Price on a culture varies depending on the culture, the frequency of its practice, and the amount paid to the father of the bride. However, regardless of region or tribe, in real terms, there was an agreement that *lobola* has gone up. For example, one participant said:

> Generally, it has gone up. Because… even in the diaspora it has gone up. It has gone up and it's also influenced by the upbringing whether the child is send to high school and also different regions looks like have different set prices for *lobola.*

> (Married female, 27, Shona tribe, in Birmingham)

6.6 Bride Price & Different Forms of Harm

Results of past studies point to the fact that the practice of Bride Price sanctions gender inequality: husbands see their wives as inferior. Additionally, Bride Price validates marriages and if unpaid, society, in general, does not recognise the marriage. Culturally, it was an expression of gratitude to the bride's family. Whilst Bride Price accorded status to both husband and wife in traditional marriage ceremonies, the practice is abused to suggest that a husband and his family 'own' the wife. Added to the other patriarchal practices, Bride Price has become the foundation of oppression of women by men (Chireshe & Chireshe, 2010). Previous research by Townsend (2008) also testifies to this. For example, an interviewee from Townsend's study stated that:

> My husband does not consider my opinion in most cases. When I try to reason with him that we need to discuss issues and arrive at decisions together, he would not have anything of that, citing his payment of *roora* as having given him the right to make decisions on my behalf.

> (Townsend, 2008, p. 35)

In a similar vein, another interviewee said:

> When we were still dating, we had such an understanding that I believed my marriage to this man was going to be enjoyable. Our relationship changed the moment he paid Bride Price to my father

> (Townsend, 2008, p. 37)

Paying Bride Price gave him a sense of possession (Bourdillon, 1993; Kethusegile, Kwaramba & Lopi, 2000). Spousal abuse has become commonplace. Women are forced to be silent by the token of Bride Price. It seems to give men the power to exercise authority over their wives and it relegates women to the status of servitude. It should be highlighted that it is not Bride Price per se which the problem, but its abusive nature. Furthermore, the practice renders women vulnerable to economic, physical, sexual and emotional abuse. This problem is brought by the silence or lack of voice which is associated with Bride Price. Since Bride Price results in the subjection and exposure of women to many forms of abuse, it is, in Mazrui's (1993, p. 45) view, "an aspect of malevolent sexism".

My data reveals that men mistreating their wives often points to a culture in which Bride Price plays a huge role in objectifying their wives. Men forget that culturally, a husband is expected to treat his wife and family with honour and dignity. My participants argued that what was worrying was that a man who abuses his wife tends to apply elements of the culture selectively. It was said by my participants that some people misquote elements that they feel justify their behaviour whilst ignoring the other elements that disapprove of their behaviour. It was with this in mind that Bride Price can be used to facilitate abuse of women as documented by many studies (Armstrong, 1998; Chireshe & Chireshe, 2010; Gwazane & Hove, 2011; Kambarami, 2006; Maluleke & Nadar, 2002; Mesatywa, 2009; Townsend, 2008; Tsanga, 2003). The literature points to the fact that the practice of Bride Price is a huge contributor to women's vulnerability to domestic violence.

A study by Tsanga (2003, p. 61) asserts that:

> The payment of Bride Price is indicative of the reality that women are largely regarded as property that exchanges hands. When a man views his wife as a piece of property, it is unlikely that he would give her a voice in the marriage. Rather than promoting the dignity and welfare of women, Bride Price can become a dehumanizing custom.

Thus, high Bride Price has serious implications for marital instability. This is reflected in high rates of divorce, domestic violence, poverty among the newly married, and violation of women's rights.

6.7 Connection between Bride Price and Gender Inequality

This section responds to the guiding research question of this book that seeks to capture change in Bride Price and the implications that it has on the lives of men and women in Zimbabwe and the Zimbabwean diaspora in Birmingham. Matters investigated in this research included why people think Bride Price is good or problematic, how gender roles and stereotypes play out in the process of Bride Price payment and why resources and gifts are given to the father and not the mother. My objective was not only to get responses to these questions but also to understand how the responses are influenced by gender. I assess for example whether the social institutions themselves are gendered, the lived experiences of women and men in relation to Bride Price, the guiding definitions and ideologies about Bride Price, and the respective roles of men and women. It further examined how perceptions about Bride Price and its processes are gender-neutral, and gender-biased elements of inequality and the role of class and modernisation.

> Yes, I support him. Because once you have paid that Bride Price it means that the bride is going to change even her surname to your surname. You are going to change your family to the groom's family. So, you are supposed to join the family and live up to the expectations of that family and you expected to be submissive to your husband mainly because he has paid that Bride Price. Because, let's say it had been the other way round that the women were supposed to pay for the husband it means husbands were supposed to be submissive to their women.

> (Married female, 54, Ndebele tribe, in Birmingham)

My participants revealed that in most cases, many men felt they have a right to beat up their wives or have two or more wives (polygamy), because they paid *lobola*. Additionally, they revealed that if a woman goes to report to her family about the cruelty of her husband, her family would tell her to be strong and to go back to her abusive husband. This appears to be the only course of action because a bride's family have already spent the *lobola* and therefore cannot refund it. Additionally, a bride's family often does not want to be associated with the stigma of having their daughter return from her husband. However, in my discussions, most people did not link any forms of domestic violence to the practice of *lobola*. Some acknowledged that the practice has outlived its usefulness due to its disadvantage on women, but they still wanted the practice to continue as a marker of cultural identity (see Chapter Four). This position was shared across all the fieldwork sites; in particular, the acknowledgement that it puts a lot of pressure on women

> Eeh I really agree with that as well. Honestly, it has changed overtime because I have heard so many people saying that 'I paid a lot of money for you' So, at the end the husband will be expecting the wife to do everything, work and everything because of the amount of money which was paid. I mean when I was back home not here. So, they will say because of the money which was paid for the Bride Price. So, they will be expecting so much from the wife to do everything

> (Married male, 34, Shona tribe, in Birmingham)

The participants argued that this is more so due to a lack of understanding of the practice, men end up abusing women. They believed that it was important to teach most men, especially the young ones, about the importance of Bride Price and why it happens. This is especially true for children who were either born or grew up in the diaspora. The practice is imposed on them without ample knowledge of its cultural significance.

> I think it depends, because of evolution and the like. For example, children who grew up in this country their parents still expect them to pay Bride Price. They don't understand that which would potentially lead to abuse because they don't understand it. They have been forced to do it which is not part of the belief of the practice, like going to church. I was going to church as a kid when I was growing up, I never understood what church was, but I did once I was grown up. So, my parents say to me you have got a woman and you should pay Bride Price, I might not understand it. But if I understand the concept and the principle of it. I don't think it amounts to buying or abusing a woman. A woman is not an object. The value is for the parents not me in that case.

> (Married male, 25, Ndebele tribe, in Birmingham)

My interviewees acknowledged the gender inequality existed as a result of expected roles between men and women and that there were some expectations which women had to fulfil with none whatsoever for the men. This is summed up by a 53-year-old married female participant (Shona tribe) in rural Zimbabwe who said:

> In my opinion it depends upon the cultures, different cultures. I think if you look at it from the cultural perspectives. When a woman is married into family, the family tend to expect certain things from the woman. Let's take the old system, everybody wants to be cooked for. Everybody wants their clothes washed by the woman. The new *muroora* daughter-in-law should be able to clean the homestead. From that perspective, it used to be what they expected of the *muroora* daughter-in-law. I don't think they were doing it to punish but they wanted to see whether she is someone who is valuable. They wanted to see the value.

These participants acknowledged that a higher Bride Price could lead to a woman being by abused her by husband, but they also felt that this was not a reason for the practice to end.

Yes, I do agree that it can. There is evidence that women get abused because of the Bride Price. And to some people the higher the Bride Price, the higher the rate of abuse or the greater the intensity of abuse.

(Male participant, 27, Shona tribe, in rural Zimbabwe)

The informal discussions I had also revealed that when a woman is working, and earning more than the husband, the man can be abusive due to feeling inferior and gender-based violence can emerge. The man feels that because he paid *lobola*, the woman should not be better, or do better than him.

But that leads to a lot of domestic violence. Back home it wasn't recorded and the inferiority the man felt when a woman working and earning that much.

(Married female, 46, Shona tribe, in Birmingham)

These participants also believed that often husbands do not object to *lobola* and the amount at the point of marriage but instead vent their anger towards their wife after marriage.

And I think it's the one that invokes other vibes or attitudes out of men especially about ok fine now if you want x amount I will give you x amount but I am going to feel like I own her somehow which means to a certain extent I am going to feel like not just be the man in the house but maybe even the one that walks around with the chest out because you paid first of all.

(28-year-old married man, Shona tribe, in Birmingham)

What came out of the women focus group in Birmingham was that there is an uneven ground in terms of relationship and what goes on in families, as well as constantly being reminded that you were paid for. It also emerged that Bride Price means women are indebted to their husbands. For example, a 46-year-old single female (Ndebele tribe) in Birmingham argued:

I think how I see it is that when a man has paid Bride Price for you; there are expectations that you have to be a very submissive wife, very homely housewife so it's what your husband says or nothing at all really. So, I think it's very difficult you are always reminded, 'ooh I paid for you'.

Feminist scholars such as Jone Johnson Lewis (2009) and Buchi Emechta (1989) have argued that *lobola* has never been for the good of both families, but it was a form of displaying one's wealth and power, through which women were somehow forced into marrying the richest men. From this perspective, the whole idea of *lobola* was to generate as much wealth as possible from the rich man, and it is argued that this is evident in the non-uniformity of the Bride Price culture itself. Furthermore, they suggest that this culture from the onset has never been about anything good, only gloating.

Even the former president of Zimbabwe, Robert Mugabe, waded into the debate whilst addressing war veterans and service chiefs in 2014 when he said, "I tell the women, as long as the man pays *lobola*, you cannot have equality with him" (Muzulu, 2014). Most of my interviewees agreed that those who fight for the abolishing of the practice would agree with the statement by the former president that Bride Price creates inequality. A 26-year-old married female (Ndebele tribe) in Harare remarked:

Women's groups must now fight against *lobola* if they are genuine. The problem is that while women support *lobola* (naively I must say) it's also the men who demand and get it. Additionally, it is disheartening to know how the president thinks of *lobola* as a commercial exchange for women. Anyway, he confirmed that is what it is, and our struggle should be modernising or doing away with the practice. It might not necessarily be a commercial exchange but listening to what the president says is a discourse that he questions, that the gender activists should also question as to its relevance in discourses fighting for gender equality.

She went on to say:

Personally, I fail to understand the significance of *lobola*. What purpose does it serve besides perpetuating the oppression of women on whatever way, shape or form as some men thus feel as though they own the women since they paid something for her hand in marriage. Aren't we objectifying women who, on addition to being groomed to make good wives from a young age, are then handed over to a man after money has exchanged hands? And why does a woman's value increase or decrease depending on her accomplishments or whether or not she has preserved herself for the husband as reflected by the different amounts of *lobola* charged depending on her status. What does that say about a woman's worth and how society values or perceives her, especially on comparison to men.

Some of my participants argued that the practice of Bride Price is not applicable in today's context. The questions that were posed by the participants who were against the practice included; why is it that *lobola* has to be paid for a man to show his commitment? How does a woman show her commitment?

> Because you are superior, because the groom is superior it mean that they take advantage of that and at times there are no equal rights, they are not observed. At times you are being oppressed. Just because you are supposed to be submissive at times you just need to close it in and suffer maybe emotionally.

(Married female, 32, Shona tribe, women's focus group in Birmingham)

The participants who were against the Bride Price argued that *lobola* creates a lot of harm. They believed that a young family starting out needs all the resources to make a strong foundation and that paying *lobola* takes away those resources. They further asserted that a young man getting married starts off his married life with a burden because of saving money for *lobola* and might have to incur a debt to his in-laws for what he was not able to pay upfront. In addition, they believe that the practice objectifies women, as in reality, the man is buying her. In some instances, men get discounts if the woman is not a virgin. This mindset does not, according to some of my participants, promote a healthy relationship between people. It makes the man feel that the woman he marries is his object and can to do what he likes with her. My participants further argued that this practice also creates greedy parents who seek to marry off their daughters to rich men just so that they can get paid. My participants claimed that the practice does not promote mutual respect between a couple because one is a buyer and the other is a commodity; even though this may not be shared verbally, it is silently understood by both. There are some parents who acknowledge that high Bride Price can lead to their daughters being abused, as asserted by a 72-year-old married female participant (Shona tribe) in Harare:

> As for me I think we just want is relationship to build relationships between me and my-in-laws. Even between my child and her husband. So if we charge a lot maybe it will result with my daughter being abused by my son-in-law who would be unhappy with the amount charged for Bride Price. So, I think it must be reduced to serve its purpose of building a relationship. It must be paid but needs to be reduced.

Additionally, due to paying *lobola*, the men would regard their wives as objects as echoed by another interviewee in rural Zimbabwe:

The reason being that they paid Bride Price. So, you have to do what they want. And you must not do wrong. Because they claim to have bought you.

(Married female, 23, Shona tribe)

The participants against the practice also questioned what justified paying for a wife in a marriage. Since it causes various societal issues, why do we not come up with another system that serves the same purpose without the flaws? How does a man paying *lobola* show that he is committed to his wife or that his wife is committed to him? Have we not had men who paid *lobola* but are cheating on their wives? Do we not have societies where men do not pay *lobola*, but are committed to their wives and vice versa? *Lobola* is not a magic wand to fix relationships. What guarantee does *lobola* give that a man can or cannot provide for his family? We have many men who paid *lobola*, but due to the economic hardships are now unable to provide for their families. And in other cases, because of the burden put on their finances due to *lobola*, a man who could have provided for his family is now struggling because he sent part of his wealth to his in-laws. This can lead to emotional, financial and physical abuse as highlighted by one participant in Harare:

But you know that there are some instances where like the groom will not even allow the bride to go back to her parent's family occasionally to visit them just because you have joined their family. Some brides will only visit their family maybe once in a blue moon because you now belong to that family which is not fair. Yes, in some instances.

(Married male, 74, Shona tribe)

The participants believed that equating the ability to pay *lobola* with ability to fend for a family was just an illusion. A 20-year-old married female participant (Shona tribe) in Harare asked:

If the man robbed a bank to pay for his wife, what guarantee is there that he will be able to keep providing for his family?

The problem with paying *lobola* as a show of appreciation or commitment, my participants further argued, is that it is an illusion and makes the woman an object that anyone with money can buy, meaning love has little or nothing to do with it. Those who are against *lobola* believe that only a woman who is naive will take a man paying *lobola* as a sign of his commitment. They further asserted that *lobola* is a wrong practice whether it is men buying wives or women buying husbands. The problem is the payment, which then produces many other issues. Another anti *lobola* participant summed this up as follows:

> I think it does, because I think it comes from the traditions of the old where women were seen as a property and that's where Bride Price comes from. Of course, now it's not going to be the same, obviously things have changed, and women are no longer seen as a property and in most traditions anyway. Basically, you are asked to pay that you can put anything on top if you want to, but you don't need to, and I think when you do that then it takes away from buying somebody because you are just giving something to make your intentions known. It is a value and a sign of my seriousness. It takes away from that how you are treated property or just belonging to somebody.

(Married female, 21, Shona tribe, in Birmingham)

The participants who were against the practice believe *lobola* is an unnecessary added burden. It does not produce any of its intended benefits in reality. The *lobola* system is based on money, some believed that there is a need for a system void of money exchanges, and this will curtail the evils that *lobola* has produced in our societies. Below is an example of a typical response I got when I put forward the question of whether *lobola* can lead to women being abused:

> In most instances yes especially when they struggle to raise that money and you will be abused for that reason. In some cases, this Bride Price now stands, men take you as their commodity because they have paid for you. They bought you and, in most cases, if they are insulting each other that's the statement that they bring out, that I paid for you, so you have to take my orders.

(Married female, 28, Shona tribe, in Harare)

Even though there was an acknowledgement from these participants that *lobola* contributed to gender-based violence, most of the interviewees still want the practice to continue. Supporters of it argue that domestic violence is found everywhere not just because *lobola* was paid. As mentioned earlier, the men that will treat women like a commodity are generally called 'abusers' and you will find them everywhere whether *lobola* was paid or not. They believe that the practice does not need any modification because the practice is not at fault but there is a need to tackle men who abuse the practice by mistreating their wives. It is men who have not understood the system of *lobola* that are the problem, they argue. One supporter of *lobola* in Harare had this to say:

> That question, I think Bride Price doesn't lead to abuse because let's say you are raised in a Christian family and you haven't seen a person being abused, you haven't been in an environment where people have been abused, you don't go and abuse your woman because you paid Bride Price. But if you are raised in a family where people were being abused you would automatically become an abuser also. Because of your upbringing. Bride Price doesn't lead to a person to be an abuse but it's a background of a person that leads him to be an abuser.

(Married female, 49, Ndebele tribe)

My data reveals that critics of *lobola* believed that no amount will make a non-submissive woman submissive. They believe that submission is when one surrenders their authority over themselves to another in order to put themselves in harmony with the will of the one they are submitting to. However, submission (or the expectation of it) renders women vulnerable to violence. This is different from merely yielding, because several factors can lead to yielding, like, coercion and fear. Some of the interviewees believe that *lobola* is not the magic wand to make a wife submit to her husband. However, it is deemed to be a very critical element of women being submissive to their husbands. The whole *lobola* system has so many loopholes that it creates more issues than the benefits it is meant to provide. However, some still acknowledged the effect that the practice has on couples. For example:

> Of course it does, because earlier on she mentioned that once Bride Price is paid, it means automatically the lady is expected to change not only her surname but even the totem. So, once somebody changes the surname or the totem for my surname and my totem then automatically, I think I become superior.

(Married male, 89, Shona tribe, in rural Zimbabwe)

Supporters of *lobola* believe that the problem is not with the practice but with men. They argue that if we are talking about changing the attitudes of men, then we need to approach the debate from that angle. Additionally, they have a belief that there is nothing wrong with *lobola* the problem, they believe, is with those who have no respect for women and abuse them. Masculinity is clearly linked to a sense of being superior and this is the problem. For example, returning to the issue of income, one participant said:

Provided the woman should demean me, because once they work, they suffer that superiority complex. You will be very inferior as a man such that you will always be afraid to be at the house because you think I can't look after myself, yet she is the woman. I am man enough. I feel Bride Price should be fair. So that we don't charge exorbitant. So that it doesn't end up stressing the families, the newly wed families.

(Married male, 59, Ndebele tribe, in rural Zimbabwe)

This superiority then extends to a sense of ownership.

I agree, I think it's because there is a power difference once he thinks he paid for a woman. So yah, I think if you are of that mentality that I have paid for her and she belongs to me, then it does affect how you treat her, and abuse may or may not be part. Like George said it may not actually be physical but just emotional. A lot of the times in some cultures anywhere you hear things like what are you going to do because I paid you Bride Price and your parents are not going to want you back... I paid Bride Price. There is this thing to the woman that money has exchanged hands and she has no way to go and if she is not happy and she wants out then you have this thing over her. So potentially yes.

(Married female, 51, Ndebele tribe, in rural Zimbabwe)

However, supporters of *lobola* do not agree, they believe that the practise does not objectify women. Questions that were asked during the focus groups included; Why is it that when dowry is paid, and it is the other way around people do not complain that it objectifies men? Why is it that you have nothing to say about women paying money for men? Why is it that only when men pay money, there is this thing about 'objectifying anyone'? Most women dream of having a wedding that will cost them so much money for a few hours. In comparison, according to my participants, one only needs to pay a deposit for Bride Price. The rest can be paid off over the person's lifetime. In most cases, interest never used to be considered, but since the change of the currency, people have been reconsidering.

The participants who supported the practice believed that if a man is not able to provide for his wife, then he must not get married. A man should only marry if he can afford it. Otherwise, he must work and make his money first. There is no greater preparation for a young man to show his responsibility that he can take care of his wife by showing that he can raise the money. This shows his commitment and the fact that he is responsible and reliable. Not paying lobola represents a loss of respect for your own culture, traditions, values and belief systems, and is to accept that one has diluted or lost their very identity.

Supporters also argue that *lobola* has long since been part of our culture. Even foreigners marrying into our families have adopted it. According to my participants, many countries have it in their cultures, hence the English name 'Bride Price'. The term Bride Price denotes a charge, which some of my participants were not happy with as it is seen as a misunderstanding of the word *lobola* that is unacceptable. This is in sharp contrast with the anti-*lobola* rhetoric, which questions the logic of paying and what purpose the payment serves besides the man buying his wife. Why would both families gathering together for a ceremony be an insufficient practice? Nothing changes the facts stated above as far as the flaws in this system are concerned. And it is unclear how the system might be improved to make sure that it is not corrupted or exploited. It is a fact that in these capitalist times the system is now being used as a get-rich-quick scheme, and it is impossible to ignore the flaws in the system and dismiss it as the result of only a few greedy and corrupt people: greed and corruption has become the norm. Even if a tradition has been practised for trillions of years that does not mean it must continue to be practised or observed, when facts on the ground show that the system is in need of improvement or a complete change. The notion of it being a get-rich-quick scheme is a common perception among those who do not want the practice to continue.

The critics argued that if the payment is not buying to own, what is its purpose and what makes that right? If people say somebody receiving US$1,000 or US$10,000 for their daughter getting married is not a get-rich-quick scheme, then we are on different wavelengths. How does one define 'rich' anyway because the fact is somebody is getting money and resources in exchange for their daughter getting married and that process can easily be corrupted or exploited just as car salesmen attempts to make as much as possible out of the transaction? These thoughts obviously come into the minds of those coming up with the price for the *lobola*; they charge as much as they can so that the bride's family has as much money as possible to spend on what they like.

Some statements from the interviews were riddled with inconsistencies, especially regarding Bride Price and different forms of violence and the idea of harm. They did not see Bride Price as directly harmful, but quite a few of them did talk about it. Additionally, some people did not justify what makes *lobola* right, but they also did not mention alternative practices or make any recommendations. Some of the participants believed that *lobola* did not produce a union, trust, or mutual respect between families. These aspects cannot be bought, they said, they have to be earned through deeds. One participant in Harare (married woman, 49, Ndebele tribe) added that:

> One has to be out of their mind to develop trust or respect for someone just because they paid a certain amount to marry their daughter. Thieves make a lot of money from scams and robberies, so do they earn my trust and respect if they come and pay 1 million dollars for my daughter, and then go and abuse her? In other words, what people are saying is the benefit of *lobola* is an illusion. They cannot prove that with facts. People in the west who got married in Las Vegas develop extended families too, and what makes their relationship work is based on the awareness of the parties involved. *Lobola* is not a magic wand that when it is paid it will guarantee the families to have mutual respect for neither each other, nor does is it guaranteed to produce trust, love or respect between those involved.

Some of my participants held the view that the practice of Bride Price, which is used to govern them, needed some improvement or a complete overhaul. They believed that this included liberating most people from this practice and from the flaws of yesterday. Some of the participants were offering an alternative which would provide the benefits that the *lobola* is supposed to provide as well as address the holes that the current system is riddled with. Those against the practice argued that *lobola* creates an unhealthy class system which promotes the big "I" little "you" syndrome, which is fuelling disunity amongst people. My data reveal many situations where a woman from a rich family falls in love with a noble but poor man and their relationship is affected because of the class system promoted by the *lobola*. It is situations such as these that invalidate the *lobola* system. As discussed elsewhere in this analysis, some participants believed that *lobola* needs to be improved or changed completely for it to be right and so that it serves everyone equally regardless of social status or gender norms. A participant in Birmingham (Married man, 47, Shona tribe) summed this up: "We are not to settle for mediocrity if we are to advance as a people".

Earlier in this book, I stated the factors that determine the Bride Price and that there are some of my participants who argued the practice was justified. As one male participant (married man, 72, Shona tribe, in Birmingham) asserted:

> Not every woman has the same qualities so they can't all have the same price paid. If a man is marrying a woman who is a high earner, then he can't really complain because he will reap the benefits of having a wife who is a high earner and if he is out of work, she can maintain their standard of life. That differs from a woman who would expect to be his

helper, raise his children, cook him food, wash his clothes, and act like his domestic servant.

6.8 Linking Bride Price with Violence

The vast majority of participants in all the data-sets in the study believed that there is a connection between Bride Price and domestic violence. The connection, however, was acknowledged to be a complex one in that domestic violence is a much broader social problem, and Bride Price can be seen as a contributing factor. They suggested that it would be inadvisable to attribute abuse to a cultural practice which is so widely observed and accepted, stating that the causes of domestic violence are much wider than Bride Price and that, in some cases, the practice may actually be of help in that the wife is accorded more worth. Many different examples of domestic violence resulting from Bride Price payment were raised by research participants during the study. However, the principal ways in which Bride Price cause domestic violence were identified by interviewees as follows.

Domestic violence occurs because the man often feels that he 'owns' the woman and she is therefore his servant.

> Ya, sometimes the abuse may come from the husband's family, especially the mother. It can be emotional abuse. Because they would be considering the amount paid and then a lot of expectations like highlighted earlier from the daughter-in-law.

> (Married male, 72, Shona tribe, in Birmingham)

Thus, if the wife does not do as the husband wishes, he may feel entitled to punish or chastise her.

> Yes, because when you pay Bride Price to my parents, they expect me to do the best to you because you paid Bride Price. Just because he has paid a lot of money then he expects that I will never do wrong because he bought me.

> (Married female, 28, Shona tribe, in Harare)

Further, he may lack any feelings of respect for his wife due to the payment made, so that he may engage in domestic violence as a matter of course.

> There has been abused but it's, but it's not abuse because culturally it was the way we lived. But things have changed now. When you are

looking at the real traditional African perspective, when we pay something for a woman that a woman should follow the word of what the husband says.

(Married male, 53, Ndebele tribe, in Harare)

If a wife leaves due to domestic violence or marriage problems, her family often cannot repay the Bride Price and therefore cannot take her back. The woman is frequently forced to stay in or to return to the violent marriage.

This happened because he paid Bride Price. Many times he would say 'after all I have paid for you...'

(Married female, 26, Ndebele tribe, in Harare)

However, my participants who were professionals made it clear, as noted above, that domestic violence may be the real problem and Bride Price is one symptom of this. While domestic abuse is widespread and endemic in some communities, Bride Price itself appears to increase the types of abuse that wives experience and the reasons why violence occurs. It cements women's inequality and the likelihood of their husbands feeling that they have a right to dominate and control them, using violence if they wish.

It really places superiority, because being submissive to someone it means he will have the final say to whatever will be taking place in a home and truly speaking if you want to be open here Mr Tembo, it is what is happening in our family, because you don't want me to make decisions.

(Married female, 57, Shona tribe, in Harare)

Bride Price is one part of an enormous and wide problem, there are many other causes of domestic violence, of course. You will not get rid of domestic violence by getting rid of bride-wealth, but it would certainly help. This indicates that combating domestic violence requires a multi-pronged approach.

That is not reality; you are not saying something from a real point. Reality says I am submissive to you, whatever, you say I must follow it. Because by virtue of you being the head of the family, you have the final say on everything even if I see that your suggestion is not so sound.

(Married female, 57, Shona tribe, in Harare)

6.9 Linking Bride Price with Class

Critics of *lobola*, according to my study, also believed that even if you have the money nothing justifies paying vast amounts for Bride Price as doing so gives the husband a reason to ill-treat his wife later, with the excuse that he paid US$40,000. Later on, it can be used against the woman and it can create a very unhealthy relationship. But, the problem is not with the Bride Price. Many men have never paid that kind of money, but they abuse their wives nonetheless. The problem is with the individual, not the practise. In Zimbabwe, according to my data, most men did not and still do not allow their women to go to work or into tertiary education. Women are supposed to act like the domestic property of men. *Lobola* does not give men the right to abuse their women. An 82-year-old married female participant (Shona tribe) in rural Zimbabwe stated that:

> The thing is, even in societies where people don't pay *lobola* women are still involved in abusive relationships. How do they justify that?

One of my participants said he has heard of two people who fell in love and wanted to get married but were from different economic backgrounds. People describe experiences of relatives that reflect this when the stories of *lobola* start surfacing. Abusive relationships will always be there, regardless of *lobola*, that is a fact.

The participants also highlighted that *lobola* is not related to class. You have that in every society. In England and in the USA, you have it, but they do not pay *lobola*. In England, working-class people struggle to marry into nobility or the aristocracy. In India, they have a caste system and they do not permit people to marry above their class. And if you remove *lobola*, how is that going to solve the problem of abusive men? If they did not pay *lobola*, we could call it 'taking the woman for granted', and if they paid *lobola* the abuse is 'justified'.

Lobola is not an excuse according to my participants. It does not justify a man abusing his wife. Zimbabwean men have made a mockery of the institution and they are the ones who really need help and to change. Many of the interviewees I spoke to about this issue also admitted that it is men who do not understand what *lobola* stands for. They did not believe that a man is justified in abusing his wife simply because he has paid *lobola*. The flaws in the system that I outlined still exist and no one has offered solutions around them. Some of the participants proposed a better system which would require an identical amount charged for all, and that produces tangible benefits that the *lobola* system claims to offer without the flaws. Some of the participants shared the issue of 'damage' which objectifies women. It is a view most people obviously support and which they believe justifies the price tag of a woman. And yet no amount of *lobola* ensures a healthy relationship; it is an illusion. Trust, harmony and respect between families and couples cannot be attributed to the *lobola* system.

My participants believed that they do have facts, mathematical proof to show the social ills that the *lobola* system promotes, like corruption, disrespect between couples, class systems within society, unhealthy marriages and traumatised partners and young families. Problems in families exist because of a lack of knowledge among the parties involved, just as healthy relationships and functional families exist because of people applying the knowledge effectively. This happens in all societies, those who practise *lobola* and those who do not. No amount of *lobola* will correct that, only knowledge and the application of it will produce the harmony in families and relationships that the *lobola* system is supposed to produce. However, as I pointed out in this analysis, the *lobola* system is in fact part of the problem, by producing its own social scenarios that need to be corrected. Are we saying as a people that there is no way of officiating marriages and bringing the two families together without making some form of payment?

Some of the participants admitted that there are flaws with how some people are going about it, but entirely disagree on what the intention of the institution is, or why the original man put it into his culture and tradition: why was it deemed necessary and befitting? People's awareness has expanded, and the times and the circumstances we find ourselves in have also changed, demanding a new system to govern ourselves with. Even if the flaws in the *lobola* system affected only one percent, that is still an issue because it is far too many people suffering unnecessarily due to a system we can do something about. As most participants said, the biggest issue with *lobola* is the part where somebody has to pay another person who is not in the relationship a certain amount of money or resources. The recipient can then do what they want, while the married people go off to start their family with that much less resources available to them.

Some of the participants believe that they are all intelligent enough to come up with a better system which accomplishes many positive benefits for both the couple and their families without payment being made. They recommended an alternative system, which still needs to be debated. Who said a wife has to be paid for and what purpose does that practice serve? What happens to people in love who cannot afford *roora* or *lobola*? We still have quite a significant number of people marrying off their daughters to wealthy men, especially in times of economic hardship. Even if it was just one girl sold to a wealthy man, that alone makes the whole system unacceptable to intelligent human beings.

Some of the participants questioned if there was another intelligent way to unite two families without involving payment and/or wife buying. They considered whether the practice has always been part of our culture or if someone came up with it to suit a certain time and awareness. Are they to perpetuate out-dated and detrimental practices just because they are part of a culture they inherited? The *lobola* system is a result of someone's thoughts, and a man is not separate from his thoughts. People have not shared factually what makes *lobola* right, besides expressing their beliefs and allegiance to an out-dated tradition because they are Africans. They have nothing else to say to justify it besides pride, which I understand. As far as what produces healthy relationships, I already explained that knowledge and the application of it will produce healthy relationships. Like I said before, even if I do not know anything about *lobola*, that does not change the fact that the system is flawed and needs to be improved or completely replaced with something that is right. Perpetuating an out-dated practice in order to maintain a tradition is unwise.

6.10 Conclusion

This chapter focused on culture and religion. Post-colonial feminists argue that forms of violence or harmful practices cannot be reduced to culture and religion because violence will happen anyway. However, the chapter reveals that the way in which Bride Price maps onto violence is not straight forward, but clearly religion and culture are at the heart of what is perpetuating the practice and that practice is at the heart of reinforcing certain gender relations. So, one cannot separate culture and religion from Bride Price, or Bride Price from violence.

What my data suggests is that violence against women in Zimbabwe happens for many reasons. Bride Price is clearly an essential part of holding together marriages and ultimately supports gender inequality. If we magically removed it, we would not necessarily transform Zimbabwe into a place where gender equality is embraced, but to remove it would require a reconfiguring of gender. On the other hand, what my data also says is that culture is really powerful as a mechanism for sustaining Bride Price even if people know it is not a good thing. And that does challenge elements of Narayan's critique. So, I can argue the relationship between culture and religion, and the way in which they together influence all of the different spheres of the ecology model, needs to be further investigated in order to achieve gender equality. The web needs to be unravelled in order to explore how embedded this practice is. The next chapter concludes the book by considering the questions that I set out to explore and discussing the extent to which they have been answered.

Chapter 7

Conclusion:

The dynamics of Bride Price

7.1 Summary of Findings

As claimed by anthropological studies, I found evidence that the real value of Bride Price has changed over time. My research has demonstrated that Bride Price is harmful, though the harm might not be direct. This was reflected through my data, which showed that Bride Price had indirect consequences to the lives of both men and women. One of the most significant findings to emerge was the fact that my participants do not see it as being as harmful. This observation is in line with the work of Dery (2015), who asserted that there is a likelihood that the older generation will support customs more than younger people do. This study makes an important contribution by highlighting the role of the older generation as custodians of culture as indicated by many of my case studies (Mbiba, 2012; McGregor, 2011; Mesatywa, 2009; Moore 2013; Moraga & Anzaldua, 2015; Musisi, 2002). This conclusion presents an outline of the main findings of the study with some recommendations and gaps for further research. I also discuss how the findings fit into the questions and hypobook that I set out at the start. First, I summarise how Bride Price is practised across the three contexts, following which I explore the extent to which it can be seen as harmful. This provides insights into how gender relations and family structures are shifting in Zimbabwe and among the diaspora in the UK. These observations form a foundation from which to explore the decisions being made around gender relations at the household level. The latter part of this conclusion considers whether Bride Price is changing due to migration and modernisation and ends with a number of recommendations and considerations for policymakers, as well as highlighting some potential areas for future study.

7.2 Shifting Gender Relations and Family Structures

This book has sought to understand whether Bride Price should be reformed in contemporary times. In answering this question, I found that my participants advocated for the abolishment of the practice as much as they respected other people's diverse cultures and traditions including practices like Bride Price. They believe that it is yet another cultural anachronism from the past that needs to be reviewed, critically, and then probably discarded. This supports studies by Ncube and Stewart (1995) and Nyambedha (2002) and Mvududu (2002) who argued that there is a need for Bride Price to be reformed and to be aligned to present times.

There is a belief among those who are in support of Bride Price that the desire for respect, wealth, and popularity can only be fulfilled if people follow their culture properly as a society. Those against the practice argued that in the West, women are valued both as life givers and wealth makers, though their priorities are different. Those who supported the practice also argued that in some societies, the ratio of women to men is higher and this attributed to the ability of men to pay *lobola*. Additionally, they believed that in African societies, the women provide labour to plant crops and so the man is paying for productive rights.

My interviews revealed that in societies where there is no *lobola*, the families want to be strong. They hope to have enough income to support setting up and raising a family with education and resources to thrive, they needed all their income to help raise the new family, including a gift to the bride and the groom. Conversely, those against the practice, asserted that cultures and traditions are meant to evolve; this happens by doing away with some habits or rituals or by incorporating other habits in a kind of synbook. *Lobola*, according to my data and those against the practice, was paid in kind before money was introduced to Africa. The age of emancipation and women being equal to men should be a big enough change to eradicate Bride Price. My data questioned how those in support of the practice could have the nerve to 'charge'. My data further suggested that the only *lobola* one can accept is when a young man offers gifts of his own accord and his own free will. My participants in towns believed that charging makes *lobola* a sale. One young man in Harare complained during the interviews that his in-laws are putting him under pressure to pay the remaining *lobola*. This supported wider critiques of the practice, including those made by Mbiba (2012), that the notion that Bride Price leaves the young couple broke, which can create resentment on the part of the son-in-law.

The participants who were against the practice believed that *lobola* is nothing but daylight robbery. They saw absolutely no reason why one human being should pay for another. They went on to say that there are things one should ask to be paid for, and raising your own child is not one of them. They should be ashamed of themselves. A business of selling women is passed off as culture, they argued. Those recommending reform of the practice regarded *lobola* as human trafficking. They believed that it is high time women's pressure groups began advocating for the banning of this *lobola* practice.

They questioned why older people would want a young man, less than half their age, to give them cattle or money.

Those who wanted reform believed that some parents do not charge *lobola* because it is culture; it is because they really need the money. They asserted that it should be up to the man to thank his in-laws, from his heart, and he should not be obliged to pay anything at all. Furthermore, those who were against the practice believe that in-laws see a cash machine in their son-in-law. They also argued that the buying and selling of women must come to an end. Both the buyer and seller are guilty. Traditions were started by people; people must put them to bed. At the time it was created, maybe it was relevant, but now it contributes to poverty and abuse of women. Why not give the couple money to start up instead? It is way too primitive, and extortion at its worst. The government should act quickly and ban this out-dated practice. Hopefully, ten to twenty years down the line, this *lobola* issue will be a thing of the past, they said, supporting Muzulu's (2014, p.14) observation that "Bride Price is a payment and therefore creates unequal gender relations".

The then deputy and current president of Zimbabwe, Emmerson Mnangagwa suggested the abolition of Bride Price but was attacked by most Zimbabweans on social media, including women. There has been a suggestion in some quarters that some women support *lobola* because they get to make money for their parents without having to lift a finger. Some are argued that a ban is long overdue, or alternatively people should come up with a national Bride Price list, which represents a token of payment. This also supports wider critiques that Bride Price should be a token of payment, as advocated by Kurebwa (2015), Matembe (2004) and May (1983). Some of my participants believed that one cannot talk about empowering women when we still 'buy them' using livestock, with the highest bidder taking the commodities. Maybe there is a need to petition the government to set standard payment after a full inclusive consultation with all stakeholders. Parental selfishness should never come between loving partners. Some of my participants argued that reforming of the practice was important, and they believed that the Church elders are not condoning fornication, but customarily it is cheaper not to follow this practice. They noted it was simpler to pay US$15 at the courts to formalise a marriage than to pay US$8,000 for *lobola*.

Some of my participants also questioned how the practice comes into play when with regard to promoting, protecting, supporting and strengthening marriage and family values as compared to a civil wedding. In their understanding, when one pays *lobola*, one is establishing a relationship with the family. However, they also believed that this has become a money-making scheme and that it was destroying the importance of a family. Most of the participants in towns believed that people have discovered that the marriage process is easier for those who impregnate future wives than it is for those who want to pay *lobola* the right way.

The participants, who were Christians, believed that sometimes the system complicates things because they lack an understanding due to having a lot of borrowed cultural practices. There is also therefore an argument that Christians should strive to create the right platforms which help establish proper relationships. For example, if their bride wants an engagement ring and *lobola*, it is a very high price, and men pay for almost everything at the wedding. They have kept the *lobola* tradition and also adopted the 'Western wedding' culture. So, my participants believed that if they want to follow these two cultures, a man should pay the *lobola* and the bride should pay for the wedding or the amount payable as *lobola* should be reduced. Bearing in mind that the essence of *lobola* is to strengthen family ties, there is no standard on the price. Thus, the participants supported the view that what you have been charged by the father-in-law is what you must pay.

Moving forward, some of my participants believe that *lobola* must be de-commercialised and returned to its original purpose of being a token of appreciation. Marriage, according to them, is about creating relationships between families, not just individuals. They believe that if one goes back to the original intention of *lobola*, this would lead to good moral behaviour and respect from the two sides. My study argues, however, that respect was brought by the token of appreciation (Mazrui 1993; McFadden 1999; Moore 2013) and henceforth unity of families. Commercialising *lobola* is not helping because relationships between in-laws become strained. Another argument is that the practice of *lobola* should not be abolished, but as more people become enlightened it is naturally going to die off, like most ideas that have seen the light of day and then have quietly slipped into oblivion.

7.3 Bride Price Across Contexts

I found that while consideration was given to the important role Bride Price plays in cementing relationships and bringing families together as well as the enactment of cultural traditions, participants from the three sites differed significantly in their views on the importance of Bride Price. Most of the participants across the three sites very clearly spelled out the items and quantities that were deemed acceptable. Some of the participants in Harare said Bride Price is 'catered for' both 'culturally and biblically', and it was also acknowledged that the Bride Price items and quantities differ depending on the tribe and its 'customs', of which the Shona tribe was often mentioned as an example.

However, many factors appear to affect the decisions made during negotiations. Those in the rural areas believed that education and the 'background' of the girl were deciding factors, with 'background' referring to the financial status of the girls' family or their position in the community. This is supported by Anyebe (1985) and Asante (2007) who both saw Bride Price as a 'class affair'. Participants in Birmingham suggested that a girl's education should not be considered as a factor in the decision of Bride Price and added that the practice is unfair because the boy's education is not considered. However, Bride Price as a solution to the problem of a lack of support among families for girls' education came up among some of the participants in the rural area. The practice was essentially seen as a bargaining process whereby the bride's family had the last word about how much should be paid. Terms such as 'negotiation and agreement' between the two sets of relatives were often used to describe the process.

According to the participants in Birmingham and Harare, Bride Price items were separated into cultural items, such as cows, and additional items that have been added in more recent times. An increase in the value of cows was often mentioned as a particular problem that adds to men's inability to meet the economic demands of Bride Price. In addition, it was noted that Bride Price is increasingly becoming a commercialized process. This is supported by Chireshe and Chireshe (2010, p. 35), who asserted that, "Bride Price is business in many communities." The increased financial status of women in Zimbabwe and its conflict with Bride Price was also mentioned by some of the participants. They said that women who make enough money could refund the Bride Price, but it was also said that this could lead to domestic violence as women no longer show any dependence because they can manage their own affairs.

The research showed that Bride Price remains a deeply embedded cultural practice in the study sites. Many participants said that it was considered 'necessary', and participants in the rural areas also explained it as a form of cultural symbolism, representing the acceptance of the woman and man into each other's families. This was supported by Dery who observed that:

> Bride Price symbolizes that he or she is officially married and known to the parents on the lady's side. Through Bride Price a man is recognized as a member to the family of the lady and respect is given to that man.

> (Dery, 2015, p. 51)

Additionally, participants mentioned that for all marriages to be solemnized and recognized a Bride Price had to be paid first. Many of my participants reported that people are getting married (i.e., in civil ceremonies) before Bride

Price is paid. Many of the young participants did not agree on the Bride Price culture and said, 'Today things are changing'.

The term 'appreciation' was commonly used in describing Bride Price in all three contexts. Its purpose was explained as a "sign of gratefulness to the side of the lady's parents because it gave confidence to parents of the woman". This study supports the wider discourse in which Bride Price is regarded as a token of payment (Davis 2008; Dekker & Hoogeveen, 2002; Dore, 1970; Gay, 1982). Bride Price was important for some of the young women interviewed since they perceived that the status of a wife was bestowed through this process. The participants in the rural areas also believed that one would not be deemed as married unless *lobola* has been paid as dictated by the culture. *Lobola* has to be paid whether people were greedy or not, they argued. It is their culture and they wanted it respected as such. Furthermore, they asserted that *lobola* was meant to cement the relationship between the two families whilst marking the beginning of new ties and relationships. These participants in the rural area who supported the practice were against people who were commercialising what they described as a 'beautiful custom'. Their other argument was that there is nothing wrong with *lobola*, but only that greed has crept in. They were also of the belief that *lobola* is a good custom and it was designed to cement the relationship because one holds dearly anything that they pay for: they value it since they paid for it. They agreed that it was wrong to commercialise the practice but they were also against abolishing it.

This supports the discourse in which it is argued by Janhi (1970), Jeater (1993) and Ekstrom et al. (2005) that the rural areas are the places in which elders reside and these elders are the custodians of culture. The concept of *lobola*, they believed, was in itself was a noble and respectful practice, but that some people were using it as a 'money-making scheme' and focussing only on how much was paid. In such instances, the participants in Harare who support the practice believed the amount of pressure put on the couples to outdo each other can be quite hilarious. They thought that it was sad when women compared how much was paid or when they talked about how much they are 'worth'. The people who are in support of the practice asserted that the discussion is still important, especially for women and girls in Zimbabwe. The participants in Harare who supported Bride Price agreed that this was still an important discussion (see also, Kambarami, 2006 & Ekstrom et al., 2005).

Supporters of the practice in the rural areas believed that there is nothing wrong with *lobola*, as long as it is done the way it was meant to be. They said that *lobola* to an educated man in the city and *lobola* to an ordinary man in the rural areas had a completely different meanings and contexts. Those who supported the practice were of the opinion that there was a need look past the suggestion of completely abolishing the practice, though they believe that the token should be respectful and appropriate to the circumstances of the families involved. Advocates of the practice in the rural areas believed that some families are happy to continue the practice: the husband and his family happily paid *lobola* to their in-laws who were happy to receive it, and the woman was happy about the process as she was part of the 'beautiful custom'.

Conversely, the participants who were against the practice in Birmingham believed that Bride Price was an out-dated practice and that it had the potential to leave the man bitter in his heart with no appreciation of what is before him. They saw *lobola* as a senseless and meaningless practice, deeply rooted in greed, selfishness and sexism. They classed it as a business of selling women that is being passed off as culture, and asserted that *lobola* is charged, negotiated and paid there and then as a business transaction. They also added that sometimes the negotiations break down because the father and uncles refused to lower the Bride Price. Thus, those against the practice concluded that *lobola* commodifies women. They also argued that *lobola* is a practice that was started by their forefathers who used to take women as possessions: in simple terms, *lobola* is wrong. They added that it was wrong for men to gather around and negotiate the price of a woman as if she was a commodity for at a market place. More so, it was wrong for a human being to pay for another. Those against the practice in Birmingham also believed that it was wrong for adults to extort money from a young man who is often less than half their age, which usually left him worse off at a time when he needed the money most. They believed that this out-dated practice led to many young couples entering into marriage penniless and debt-ridden. This argument that Bride Price commodifies women supports Goody (1973) and Davies (2008) who argue that the commodification of women through Bride Price contributes to creating unequal gender relations.

The participants in Birmingham who were against the practice also believed that the world has changed and so has a woman's place in society. To them, marriage is no longer a master-slave relationship; it is an equal partnership. They added that the feeling should be mutual with equal benefits, so there was absolutely no reason why one should pay for the other. The participants who were not in favour of *lobola* argued that women's empowerment was therefore only a dream if they were not prepared to challenge their customs and traditions. However, there was an acknowledgement that their culture was rich, "though there are some ridiculous charges that make a circus of the whole practice". Finally, they also supported the feminist argument that *lobola* commodifies women. Those against the practice were of the view that *lobola* was about paying a woman, with her going from her fathers' ownership to her husband's ownership. Though it is meant to be a token, in the present day, it is a commercial transaction.

Many elderly participants in the rural areas explained the process as a series of events starting with courting followed by families from both parties deciding together on the Bride Price and ending with a religious ceremony in a church or mosque. Participants in the rural areas believed that amongst the Shona culture Bride Price payment is a continuous process and therefore does not come to an end. The example was given of how men continued to pay a cow to the in-laws whenever a child was born, or a man would be asked to contribute to his brother-in-law's Bride Price by donating a cow. A recently married young man in rural Zimbabwe related his experience, which illustrated how closely linked Bride Price is to the process of marriage. He explained how he could not afford what was asked. This position was echoed by another recently married participant in Harare who also highlighted that the bride is not involved in the process. She can attend but does not contribute. Additionally, the bride was worried during the negotiation because the money that was requested by her family was a huge sum and that she was concerned that the groom might not meet those expectations. A young married man in Harare explained the minimal role he and his wife played in the negotiation process and the lack of power they had in the agreement of the Bride Price. Parents and other older family members were in complete control of the decisions. Some of my participants in Harare believed that people must stop treating *lobola* like a business; otherwise, they would never grow to understand what it really means and its importance. Those who supported *lobola* in Harare argued that it is relevant and affordable as long as it is done in good faith. They believed that many people will never understand the merits of *lobola* if they allow outsiders to remove the best parts of their African customs. *Lobola* is not a business transaction, they argued.

However, my participants who were against the practice in Birmingham questioned how *lobola* had turned out to be corrupt. In ancient times, they believed, that it was about two families coming together, but now it was more of one family getting richer at the expense of the other family. They argued that it was necessary to question the importance of embracing their culture and the way their forefathers conducted this custom. Some of my participants in Harare also argued that when a family genuinely paid *lobola* out of love and a family accepted *lobola* out of genuine love they never failed to unite their children when they faced difficulties in marriage.

Those who supported Bride Price in rural Zimbabwe believe that those against the custom are influenced by Western beliefs. They were pained to hear Africans debating something that is one-hundred percent African, and they questioned how the West has influenced African beliefs. They were concerned that Africans have allowed their traditions and thoughts to be diluted by those who are influenced by the West. There is also a belief that what makes many people think negatively about *lobola* is that they no longer have what their forefathers had. This supports the view by Hamisu (2000), who stated that Bride Price is our culture and that this undiluted part of the culture ought to be respected.

The findings of this study highlighted that disrespecting women emerges in marriages where Bride Price was not paid because such women were considered to be living 'in prostitution'. Similarly, the husband was not considered a part of the family or as a son-in-law. Young men also spoke about feeling humiliated when they were not able to pay Bride Price. A young man in Birmingham said his wife used his non-payment to humiliate him when she reminded him that he had not paid Bride Price. The study also showed how non-paying of Bride Price had a significant impact in the event of the death of a woman. If payment was not made, the woman was not considered married and the Bride Price had to be paid fully before burial could take place. This has led to many disputes between families. It was explained by most of the participants across the three field sites that in the Shona culture, if one does not pay Bride Price and should the woman die before officially marrying, one would pay double: it acts as a way of disciplining the man.

The research identified that young couples were starting a marriage while in heavy debt and this was highlighted as leading to much conflict between the husband and wife. Recent literature has highlighted the perception that young men have been 'overcharged' (Machinga, 2011b; McGregor, 2011; Moore, 2013) and that this could lead to numerous conflicts with the wife and eventually the husband abandoning the marriage because he feels cheated. Impudence thus emerged on both sides, with the girl's family being disrespected by their son-in-law if the Bride Price was not paid, and the man's family being offended if the price was considered too high. The book demonstrated, in agreement with the research conducted by Mapara (2007) that the continuous conflict between the man and his wife can emerge due to his non-payment of Bride Price, which can lead to divorce. Women were said to feel 'insecure' in their relationships if Bride Price had not been paid.

The study also argues that Bride Price has an effect on the lives of women. This exploitation was also mentioned by most of my female participants in Harare who believed that Bride Price turned a woman into the property of the man after paying and she is exploited and deprived her of her rights. A significant finding was that the economic burden for men was a common theme reported by most participants. The economic impact on the couple and the couple often starting their marriage in poverty was also frequently mentioned. Some male participants in Harare argued that the practice has resulted in poverty, and sometimes couples are left broke after payment of Bride Price. They suffer after marriage because all the money would have been diverted to the Bride Price payment. Contrary to wider literature that recognises Bride Price as a way of stabilising marriages (Chigwere, 1982; Musisi, 2002) the study found that Bride Price affects the men financially as they may have to borrow substantially and go into debt and impoverishment in order to pay Bride Price, even though they may have no income.

Another notable finding of the study was the increasing demand for a higher price for more educated girls. The imitation of other marriage norms from neighbouring tribes and cultures was also noted. Many referred to the commercialization of the Bride Price process and mentioned that low-income men are particularly affected by the rising costs. Some men are 'overcharged', thus leading to many financial hardships at the start of the marriage. Pregnancies outside of marriage and elopement were mentioned as problems related to Bride Price expenses. This is because there are extra charges that accrue to the man should the bride fall pregnant before Bride Price was settled. This is as a result of the cost involved in the payment of Bride Price (especially with commercial tendencies attached to the traditional concept). The study also found that a loss of respect was commonly mentioned as a consequence of inability to pay Bride Price. A man was reported to be respected less if he was not able to pay and he may also lose respect for the girl's parents if they make huge economic demands. Another way in which a man could not earn the respect of the woman's family is when he is considered poor.

My study also revealed that those against the practice talk of similarities between paying *lobola* and the slave trade, where people were bought at a price after negotiations were held to discuss their abilities, health and what they could do for their master. They further argue that the practice of paying *lobola* is immoral and should end immediately. Most of my participants believed that daughters should not be considered the property of their fathers to be sold to a potential husband. This practice, my participants argued, should be abolished as it is completely out of date in modern Zimbabwe. To them, it is demeaning to women to be bought like slaves. The love of money, they further argued, is what is perpetuating these old out-dated practices. It is all done under the cover of keeping our traditions and culture, but beneath it lies the love of profit, benefits and cash. They also sum it up by saying that *lobola* is immoral and demeaning to the woman and must be done away with. Those against the practice felt the connotations around what it symbolises may not affect some, but many women have suffered from it. Some men think they can 'discipline' wives because they paid *lobola*.

7.4 Bride Price, Migration & Modernisation

The study identified that most of the participants did not support the abolishment of the practice because it was perceived that women would lose respect and that this process was considered one of the only ways women can earn respect. A few female participants suggested the abolishment of Bride Price and recommended that Bride Price, which does not meet the cultural standards, should be scripted off, but what this meant exactly was not elaborated on. A pastor in Harare suggested that the term 'Bride Price' should be replaced with the term '*lobola*' because the former is demeaning to women. It was recommended that there should be constant sensitisation regarding the necessity of Bride Price, and special references were made to the important role that traditional and religious leaders could play in these messages. In support of the research by Chireshe & Chireshe (2010), there should be a better mutual understanding between the parties during the bargaining process. Participants in Birmingham also recognised that the changes and commercialization of Bride Price were mainly related to neoliberalism and modernisation. It was said that this corrupted the traditional value of Bride Price and created an economic burden for the groom. Better communication between parents and their children was often mentioned as well as the role of the aunties in the process (Muzulu, 2014). Another significant finding was the importance the role of aunts as agents of change. Some of my participants in the rural areas argued that aunts should continue with cultural education to impart traditional values to the daughters.

Older men who participated in the research provided some suggestions on how Bride Price could be changed and although they did not want Bride Price to disappear altogether, they suggested changes in the amounts asked for. Some participants suggested that the government must be approached to "put laws that will help reduce the burden of Bride Price at least to a cow or goat and not ten cows or ten goats".

Some other suggestions were also made regarding how to resolve the issue of Bride Price and the involvement of the government was mentioned. Such a solution however appears to increase the victimisation of poor families rather than dealing with the impact of Bride Price. Similarly, fines that involved the payment of a cow for elopement were also mentioned. Ideas on the regulation of Bride Price were brought up by a married religious leader in Harare who mentioned that this would prevent exploitation. The study highlighted that rules and regulation about Bride Price should be instituted to prevent exploitation, or even laws could potentially be put in place according to cultures. Some of the suggestions were that policies needed to be instituted to protect the traditions and the girl child against illegal marriage. The change to the monetary value of Bride Price or its flexibility was a common theme (Magezi, 2007), and it was often suggested that Bride Price must be reduced to a more affordable level. Some of the married female participants in Birmingham argued that people should reduce the Bride Price in order to make it affordable for some families or men.

The study revealed that most of my participants believed that *lobola* has no fixed price and that the practice is also known as '*lobola* negotiations'. They argued that the question of affordability is irrelevant as far as this topic is concerned. Furthermore, they asserted that it has always been relevant as it helps in the preparations for a wedding. However, those against the custom believed that they have to confront the Bride Price in the context of today, even if it means changing certain situations of a cultural nature if they hinder nation building in our society. Their argument was that *lobola* was once relevant but in their context, they fail to see its significance. They consider the problem to be that things have changed; a lack of strong family values, the weakening of the Church and inter-tribal marriages have left a huge vacuum through which people now fail to respect things like marriage or someone else's daughter. This will remain as long as a man sticks to the narrative of 'I paid cows for you'. Matembe (2002) suggests that those who did not support *lobola* were also interested in hearing from the views of those who did. They wanted to understand why it mattered so much to them.

Those who were against the practice in Harare believed that the problem arose when it was treated as an achievement for women only. But certainly, it can be a feat, albeit at a low level. The participants who supported the practice abhor the idea of treating *lobola* as some kind of a business, but they will happily pay *lobola* for the one they love as a way of appreciating their partner. But it is not just as one would gladly pay for a beer, shoes, or any other object, they think there is a slight difference between appreciating something and paying out of want. But this leaves open the question of whether they see a human being in the same light as an object. They argued that there is a difference. Appreciation is a high level of need, treasure and value. It has respect within it and that cannot be viewed as objectifying women. They are taken as objects only when *lobola* is treated as a source of wealth. The participants who are against the practice believe that mind-set change in that regard must be central to the conversation around *lobola*. Even to feminist sympathizers, the notion that gender can be quantified and equated is totally ridiculous, *lobola* should not be paid to maintain a norm.

Under African patriarchy, to be married provides status, and the majority of women do not worry about their level of education once they approach their mid to late-twenties because they come under pressure to get married. However, those against the practice believe that the payment of *lobola* has some connections in the broader context of inequalities that emanate from patriarchy. They believed that *lobola* is but a token of appreciation until one chooses to abuse it and take it as a passport to abuse his wife. My participants in Birmingham who were against *lobola* believed that the practice is patriarchal. They questioned the composition of the people who lead *lobola* negotiations; one's father, their brothers, and their aunts. So, the men from the groom's family come to negotiate for the bride with her family. They also questioned why the bride did not have a say in the whole process.

Those who are not in support of *lobola* believed that marriage should not be defined by paying *lobola*. Equally, they are against putting a price tag on a human being; everyone is priceless and *lobola* is a market where men sell a commodity (women) to other men using 'appreciation' as the justification and yet the whole process is a commercial activity. They regarded *lobola* as a way through which to sell a product. The custom then evolved into a societal norm under the guise of 'appreciation' thus leading to the commodification and suppression of women in their commodification, leading to sentiments like *'ndakakubvisira mari'* (I paid for you). The practice, which is deeply entrenched in patriarchy, is regarded as a social norm and not many people are prepared to question it. Marriage should therefore conform to the UN Convention on Consent to Marriage, Minimum Age for Marriage and Registration of Marriages, and the people abusing that must be prosecuted as stipulated in the Convention, argued those against the practice.

My participants in Birmingham, who were against the practice argued that what made Bride Price wrong was that it does not have any justification, they were just perpetuating it because it is a tradition. This also came out of the informal discussion with my participants who were against the practice. They argued that it being a tradition did not make it right. Those against the practice also believed that *lobola* gave men a sense of ownership to the extent that they cheat because they feel they can. They were also of the opinion that *lobola* was no different from an auction because women deemed as 'damaged goods' are sold off at lower prices like an old car; one could buy and sell a wife. For these reasons, they saw *lobola* as an out-dated practice, arguing that it violates the rights of women.

Some of the interviewees in the towns believed that *lobola* has no significance in this present day, because women can work and can even be richer than the men they love, and if *lobola* was to seal the bond, the bride could pay *lobola* to the groom's family. The reason no reason for it to be the man that pays. One wants to pay *lobola* but they do not really know the really value of the custom. Additionally, some of the participants said that some men have made a bad name for *lobola* by mistreating their wives and trying to justify it by saying they paid money for them. That is not what *lobola* states, they argued. The older participants. especially in rural Zimbabwe, believed that *lobola* does not allow men to abuse their wives. They believed that men needed to change their ways and stop abusing or undermining the women they marry. They also asserted that men should not blame *lobola* but should change their ways and treat their wives as equals.

But still the question remains, what are the justifications for *lobola* other than tradition? Does it have any justification? Advocates for practice believe that it is part of their tradition and that questioning it does not mean they want to embrace the Western culture. There was a suggestion by some of the participants that the *lobola* (money) should be set aside to benefit the young family, or should be saved as a bereavement fund for future use by the wife and children in the event that the husband dies and the bereaved are left with without a livelihood. It should be for future use by the wife and children. When it is given to the parents or relatives of the wife, it should be for safe keeping and not the current situation where the parents and relatives of the wife take it as a wealth generating venture, for them to enrich themselves.

From the participants, it is evident that most people do not even know what makes *lobola* right, even though they 'felt' that it is right to do because it is their tradition. But denying that there is something wrong with it does not make it right. For a couple starting out a family, they need all the support they can get, especially in a time of economic turbulence. And to expect a young groom to start off married life with a debt to his in-laws, or having to save up a lump-sum of money to pay *lobola* when he should be setting aside resources for his family is totally unfair, and very unreasonable. The participants who were against the practice believed that *lobola* objectifies the woman; the man feels like he is buying her as a commodity, which creates a very unhealthy relationship between the two, even though it might not be expressed verbally. Paying *lobola*, they argued, has become a get-rich-quick scheme for most people, and my data revealed that parents may be tempted to marry off daughters just to get some wealth through *lobola*, which opens the door to unhealthy marriages not based on love. In fact, my participants revealed that this has been happening to some unfortunate women who were married off to men chosen by the parents because they were rich enough to afford a hefty price for *lobola*. Their argument was that just as the men of the past who came together to decide in their time what was right for *lobola*, they are now the men living today and have the right to determine what system is appropriate for them to make marriages official.

The study highlighted that the male participants who support the practice argue that questioning a tradition that had been handed down and that they did not understand fully does not mean they should be ashamed of who they are. Equally, participants in Birmingham advocating for the reformation of the practice argued that merely accepting traditions that do not fit well with current times is not an intelligent thing to do. They asserted that they themselves, not their fore-fathers who are long gone, are the masters of their own destiny. They also believed that if something makes sense then they could continue with it, but if it has served its purpose and is no longer necessary in the new situation they are living, they should scrap the tradition and come up with a new one. They believed that they are supposed to be men and take charge of their affairs, and not be boys that simply follow the crowd and do things without questioning their validity.

7.5 Gender Relations at the Household Level

The study identifies the Bride Price process as potentially creating problems within the families due to the process not providing gifts for all family members. The female participants in Harare believed that Bride Price may bring misunderstandings between the family members since not everyone was considered at the time of sharing the Bride Price. Educating communities about the traditional meaning of Bride Price was mentioned by most of the participants. This n line with the research by Machinga which argued that:

> Communities should be sensitized and on the value of Bride Price according to the culture -- what it was meant for otherwise it has since lost its meaning as people are paying Bride Price for the sake of pleasing the in-laws.

(Machinga, 2011a, p.35)

The study highlights that education in general resulted in the reduction of early marriages and unwanted pregnancies. These two issues were identified as the reasons for overcharging and conflicts among family members during the process of Bride Price negotiations. My participants also asserted that the role of the Church in educating communities, including the use of weekly sermons. It was said that the gap between the Church and tradition needs to be reduced and that they should work hand in hand to improve the institution of Bride Price. Most women from the focus group in Birmingham said that they are happy with the idea of *lobola* because it confers a certain status on them in society and among their kin. However, others were not happy with the current situation, arguing that the commercialisation of *lobola* has resulted in many family problems, such as domestic violence. Essentially, this study shows that the payment of *lobola* goes together with both explicit and implicit obligations. Failing (or being perceived to have failed) to meet these obligations may result in serious problems. Indeed, most female participants stated that their husbands abused them out of bitterness resulting from the huge amounts of money that they paid to their in-laws for *lobola*.

The study also identified that conjugal rights were central in all marriages. Most of my participants concurred that men's understanding was that conjugal rights were purchased through the payment of *lobola*. However, the Zimbabwe government recognises in law that sexual rights should be negotiated and not controlled by one person (Kurebwa, 2015). But some men insist that since they paid large sums of *lobola*, this gave them the right to take all decisions regarding sex - women's rights were sadly limited in this respect. These findings reinforce Bergen's (1999, p. 4) postulation that men "are often portrayed as jealous, domineering individuals who feel a sense of entitlement to have sex with their 'property'".

The study revealed that the situation was worsened by the extreme difficulties women have when reporting cases of marital rape, even though laws have been in place in Zimbabwe since 2002 as part of the Sexual Offences Act. Bergen (1999) and the African Population Research and Health Center (2010, p. 1) found out that: "marital rape is one of the under-reported violent crimes because it is socially tolerated". My participants believed that women felt that to report such crimes would not only be a betrayal of the husband, but also a disgrace to their family.

In addition, women admitted that it is harder to press charges when the husband has paid a large sum of money to their family as *lobola*. Married men's control over sex does not only infringe women's rights, it also exposes them to HIV infection. Some married women find it very hard to negotiate safe sex because their husbands simply say '*Dzakaenda dzakapfeka macondom here?*' (Did the cattle we paid go with condoms on?). In addition, I found that men who have paid *lobola* sometimes resort to violence to 'discipline' their wives since they believe that the payment of *lobola* gave them a license to abuse their wives, who they consider to be part of their property. This situation has been worsened by the commercialisation of *lobola*. Gustafsson and Worku (2006, p. 5) noted that the payment of *lobola* is "as if the husband buys his wife".

While discussing *lobola*, it is critical to note the major role played by aunts in arranging marriages and in the lead up to the payment of *lobola*. The aunts continue to intervene after the marriage to resolve conflicts and ensure that marriages are safeguarded at all costs, even if it sometimes means sacrificing the rights of the women. Where *lobola* has been paid, it is very difficult to get a divorce because the aunts will always encourage the woman to endure. Magezi (2007, p. 41) indicated that it is very common to hear the aunts saying; "You just have to endure my niece, remember your husband paid *lobola*. If you divorce him, where will we get the money to reimburse him his *lobola*?". On the issues of superiority and power relations, the aunt has a stronger role to play than what people mistake for agency in the fight against violence; they also ensure that the bride remains in the marriage irrespective of the challenges that she faces. The aunt is also involved in negotiating the Bride Price and they collect the bride's share of *lobola* during the actual Bride Price ceremony on her behalf.

The study found that the charging of exorbitant *lobola* fees can result in hostility between the two families. Some of my female participants in Harare revealed that their husbands speak harshly every time they have an argument, including the husbands sometimes mentioning that the bride's parents had 'overcharged' during the *lobola* process. It is with this in mind that my participants felt that the traditional purpose of *lobola* - to bring two families together as postulated by Bourdillon (1976) - is sacrificed for the love of money. They further argued that in Zimbabwe, some 'bitter' husbands no longer treat their in-laws with respect since their relationship has been poisoned by the commercialised nature of the *lobola* process.

A key contribution of the study is the assertion by some of my female participants that they are happy with the current situation despite the many alleged negative consequences of the commercialisation of *lobola*. As noted by Nyambedha (2004) and Aagaard-Hansen and Nyambedha (2003), the payment of *lobola* guarantees women and their children the right to resources within the kin group, and a place within the kinship structure. This position is supported by Luyirika (2010, p. 29), whose study found that "if a large sum of money is paid [...], it shows that you have value". Most women interviewed said that if the woman is loved and has value then 'real' money has to be paid. They argued that the payment of a higher fee can denote true love. An example was given of a police officer who earns approximately US$500 per month but managed to pay US$2500 cash. It was agreed that this kind of commitment bestows value on the woman who is being paid for. Others reasoned that if you are a person with a cultured family background, then you ought to be of great value. They added that one is being used if nothing meaningful is paid for them. These results concur with the sentiments shared by Thorpe (1991) and Chireshe and Chireshe (2010), who argued that the majority of people believe that the payment of *lobola* reflects that the groom and his family are committed to the marriage. Bourdillon (1976), in his study among the Shona people, found that the payment of a high Bride Price conferred a higher status on the bride and reflected the value the husband places on the marriage.

7.6 Policy and Practice Recommendations

This first study of Bride Price in three different contexts focused on its gendered dimensions in terms of domestic violence and impoverishment and found a mix of positive and negative impacts. However, the negative effects of this traditional practice far outnumber the positives. The research identified many harmful effects for women, most of them extremely damaging and distressing in nature, and some that also affected men and children. For women, they included the cementing of gender inequality and endemic domestic violence and abuse, early or forced marriage for girls, landlessness and homelessness that could almost lead to starvation, and increased risk of HIV infection. Further impacts highlighted included debt and financial difficulties for young men leading to entrenchment of poverty. Although domestic violence and poverty were clearly identified as the over-riding issues, both of which were woven into local life at a deep and concerning level, Bride Price made each of them worse in different ways.

This research is of key importance in beginning the process of transforming views on Bride Price, and indeed transforming the lives of Zimbabwean women. It has also proved vital in introducing a gendered lens into conceptualizations of Bride Price. The practice may have functioned in the past, at least, as a helpful means of exchange, but this study and other literature demonstrate the huge cost to women in such a system (see, e.g., Baryomunsi, 2004; Matembe, 2004). The commodification of wives has led, as this research demonstrates, to deleterious social impacts, especially in terms of increased domestic violence, poverty and the entrenchment of male power over women. In situations where domestic violence is common, Bride Price introduces additional ways in which husbands may feel able to abuse and hurt their wives.

As highlighted in Chapter Five, reforming Bride Price can be seen as an important issue in moving towards gender equality, combating patriarchal notions of power and decision-making in communities, and challenging violence against women. Men remain in positions of control in the communities concerned, and reforming Bride Price would be one step towards enhancing women's human rights. It would contribute to removing Bride Price violations and abuse, and empowering women to feel they are equal members of communities, marriages and families. This is important as the custom would then serve the purpose for which it was created.

The book demonstrates that consideration must be given to the important role of Bride Price as a valuable cultural tradition. This research, as the first major investigation into the practice amongst Zimbabweans, gives rise to action to begin moving toward social change for women and for their communities. It is possible, through participatory action research, to put in place strategies to remove some of the harmful effects of Bride Price and hence begin working towards women's empowerment nationally and locally, and with some development planned at the international level. The provision of empowering services, awareness-raising, and community sensitization should be put into place through local organizations, with the aim of leading to further social change. The female participants wanted a more active role in the process of engagement in terms of reforming the practice.

On the basis of both micro-level and macro studies, this book explored Bride Price and culture. While there are several negative effects attributed to the practice of Bride Price, this book highlighted one of the reasons why a large proportion of women remain in favour of Bride Price; that Bride Price has a role in producing security and status for them in the marital household. The study showed that Bride Price is negatively linked to the level of inter-spousal violence experienced by women, and the book argued that in the study area larger Bride Prices increase marital violence partly as a result of the practice reducing the economic resources of the marital household. It can also diminish the social status of the groom and his family and serve as a source of household wealth over which a woman enjoys relatively more control. In contrast to the effect of Bride Price, women's education tends to be associated with an increase in the level of violence. While Bride Price-obtained wealth confirms the female image, it seems that an increase in women's income and educational prospects challenges a husband's authority, threatens prevailing gender norms, and manifests itself in increased violence.

While the study focused on three sites, it is likely that the findings are relevant to other parts of the country and other countries in which Bride Price is practiced, and possibly even elsewhere in places that have similar kinship arrangements. In particular, it may not be Bride Price per se that affords protection but rather the extent to which a man owns and controls a bride as 'his' asset that has a bearing on women's security. Hence, it is unlikely that a larger Bride Price will afford protection to women if women have little or no control over their Bride Price.

More broadly, the results presented in this book suggest that policies that ensure equal inheritance and property rights for women and programs that help women build and retain control over assets may be necessary in order to reduce their vulnerability to violence. However, any strategy to enhance women's ownership and control over assets, whether through Bride Price, inheritance or employment, will also have to confront existing notions of masculinities and femininities that, for instance, require men to be violent and women to be subservient.

7.7 Directions for Future Research

In light of the research findings and the limitations of the study, the book highlights some areas to that warrant further investigation. My research explored why Bride Price continues whilst comparing and contrasting how it is observed across three contexts; rural Zimbabwe, urban Harare and in the diaspora of Birmingham, UK. The emphasis was to ascertain if changes have occurred in how and why it is practised, but also to consider if any changes reflect shifts in family structures and the respective roles of married men and women. My decision to focus on Bride Price was that it represents a vehicle through which to better understand and explore changes in patterns of gender relations within family structures and more widely across society. This involved looking at the shifting make up of families across the settings of this study as well as probing the ways in which Bride Price is observed.

My study calls for future research to expand the study of Bride Price by exploring the patrilineal and matrilineal societies to ascertain the impact that the custom might have (or might not have).

Patrilineal, or agnatic, relatives are identified by tracing descent exclusively through males from a founding male ancestor. Matrilineal, or uterine, relatives are identified by tracing descent exclusively through females from a founding female ancestor. For most of history, patrilineal succession (a patrilyny) dominated family units. Names, property, titles, and other valuables were traditionally passed on through a male line. Females did not inherit, unless there were no male heirs. Even then, distant male relatives would inherit over close female relatives like daughters. Property passed from father to daughter indirectly, usually through dowries on a daughter's marriage, which was paid to and came under the control of her husband or her husband's father or another male relative.

In matrilineal succession, women inherited titles and names from their mothers, and passed them down to their daughters. Matrilineal succession did not necessarily mean that women held the power and property and titles. Sometimes, men in matrilineal societies were the ones who inherited, but they did so through their mother's brothers, and passed their own inheritances along to their sisters' children.

An example of a matrilineal society in Zimbabwe is the BaTonga people who are found in and around the Binga District, Binga village the Kariba area, and other parts of Matabeleland. They number up to 300,000 and are mostly subsistence farmers. However, the women do not own the land, but are the custodians. They decide all issues involving territory, including where a community is to be settled and how land is to be used. Unlike in other communities, the women are mandated full control of communal affairs. The community leaders are selected by a caucus of women (matriarchs) before the appointments are subjected to popular review. The BaTonga traditional 'government' is composed of an equal number of men and women. The men are chiefs and the women clan-mothers. As leaders, women closely monitor the actions of men and retain the right to veto any law they deem inappropriate. The BaTonga women not only hold the reigns of leadership and economic power, they also have the right to determine all issues involving the trying of community offenders. I have therefore raised the question of whether men would face the same kind of 'treatment' or challenges. Although we do not know for sure, the structural differences between the two types of society would be an interesting dimension to explore.

The research and strategies discussed in this book, in addressing women's issues and potential harmful cultural practices in the three sites, potentially has relevance for similar projects planned in other localities or countries and may also be of interest to Women's Studies and Development Studies in transnational contexts. For Bride Price amongst Zimbabweans, overall progress may be slow, but various key developments are already in process. It is hoped that this research will help to inform, and act as a catalyst for, future action and change that leads to reform of such traditional practices in the interest of gender equality and empowerment and the prevention of violence and abuse against women, not only across Zimbabwe but also in other parts of Africa.

7.8 A Final Word

This study has explored and discussed the contradictions in how people position Bride Price in relation to gender inequalities and forms of harm and violence. Most of my participants questioned; what made *lobola* right. In life, they argued that if we seek to explore what makes anything right, if anything is right, we will see it. Likewise, if there is anything wrong, that too will automatically show itself. My participants then went on to say that they also have to look for what is wrong, because that practice will allow us the opportunity to find out about the positives and negatives of a practice. There are flaws in their thinking because as people most believe that questioning the validity of parts of our culture means being Westernised. This is very far from the truth.

Most of these participants agreed that there was a need to question everything intelligently and that doing so did not mean they were not in agreement with the practice; if somebody can adequately justify it then it would be worth practicing. However, this might not be a very comfortable experience as it opens one up to a self-critic. I am not criticising my interviewees, I am simply interrogating them, and the intention was to elicit as much information as possible whilst also making the voice of those at the grassroots heard. If it does not come out as such, then it means that I have failed in achieving my objective. It is understandable some people are not used to being questioned regarding their culture and consider it an insult; I value all the input.

The key word I found in the interviews is 'belief', and it is a fact that beliefs change as new knowledge is acquired and understood. When one knows better, they are more likely to do better. And I think we have two primary mind-sets at work here, one is among men who have the yearning and will to shape their own destiny, just as the other men who have lived before them did in their time. Then we have another mind-set that merely accepts what has been put in place for them, whether they can justify it or not, which is definitely not a habit practised by real men. Why would a man just perpetuate a ritual set in motion by other men who lived in a different time, especially when he does not fully understand the reason behind it and also has the facts to show the detrimental effects of the ritual/tradition? What emerged from all the research sites was that attitudes are not changing; the older generations were more conservative whilst the younger generations were more liberal. However, what is emerging from my research is that though the younger generation acknowledge that Bride Price could be harmful or at least that it has harmful consequences, but they would still observe the practice to appease their parents.

There was also an expectation that the bride would conceive after settling in the marriage. My participants agreed that the failure to conceive was blamed on the wife regardless of the situation. In some cases, the bride's father would be expected to provide another daughter to the son-in-law as a compensation for reproductive rights. My data also reveal that a husband was likely to marry a second wife should the wife 'fail' to conceive. In worst-case scenarios, my participants revealed that the husband may return the wife to her parents should she not agree to the husband marrying a second wife. Whilst removing Bride Price is not going to magically transform gender relations, if that is to be achieved then it would be a signal that gender relations have already been transformed. I hope my book will make some contribution towards that goal.

Bibliography

Aagaard-Hansen, J., & Nyambedha, E. O. (2003). Changing place, changing position: Orphans' movements in a community with high hiv/aids prevalence in Western Kenya. In E. Gulløv & K. Fog Olwig (Eds.). *Children's Places* (pp. 162-176). London: Routledge.

Abrahams, N., Baluku, S., & Crispus, K. S. (2012). *An Exploratory Study of Bride Price and Domestic Violence in Bundibugyo District, Uganda.* Bundibugyo: Centre for Human Rights Advancement (CEHURA).

Alston, M., & Bowles, W. (2003). *Research for social workers: An introduction to methods.* Brighton: Psychology Press.

Alupo, J. (2004). *Bride Price and Gender Violence.* A Paper Presented to The Participants at The International Conference on Bride Price and Development. Makerere University: Kampala, Uganda.

Alvesson, M., & Sköldberg, K. (2017). *Reflexive methodology: New vistas for qualitative research.* London: Sage.

Anderson, S. E. (2003). The school district role in educational change: A review of the literature. *International Journal of Educational Reform, 15*(1), 13-37.

Anderson, S. E. (2007). The economics of dowry and Bride Price. *Journal of Economic Perspectives, 21*(4), 151-174.

Andifasi, J. (1970). An analysis of Roora. In C. Kileff, & P. Kileff, (Eds.). *Shona Customs: essays by African writers* (pp. 28-32). Gweru: Mambo Press.

Ansell, N. (2001). 'Because it's Our Culture!' (Re)negotiating the Meaning of Lobola in Southern African Secondary Schools. *Journal of Southern African Studies, 27*(4), 697-716.

Anyebe, A. P. (1985). *Customary Law: The war without arms.* New Haven: Fourth Dimension Publishers.

Armstrong, A. (1987). *Women and Law in Southern Africa.* Harare: Zimbabwe Publishing House.

Asante, M. K. (2007). *An Afrocentric manifesto: Toward an African renaissance.* Cambridge: Polity Press.

Auret, D. (1990). *A decade of development Zimbabwe 1980-1990.* Gweru: Mambo/Catholic Commission for Justice and Peace.

Barton, T. R., & Pillai, V. K. (1998). Modernization and teenage sexual activity in Zambia: A multinomial logit model. *Youth & Society, 29*(3), 293-310.

Baryomunsi, C. (2004). Gender dynamics and HIV. *AIDS: Key issues for debate on price, Uganda UNFPA.*

Batezat, E. (1988). *Women and Independence: The Heritage and the Struggle.* Basingstoke: Macmillan.

Bere-Chikara, F. (1970). *Cattle: The life blood of Shona society.* In C. Kileff, & P. Kileff, (Eds.). *Shona Customs: essays by African writers.* Gweru: Mambo Press.

Bereng, P. M. (1982). *I am a Mosotho.* Lesotho: Morija Printing Works.

Bergen, R. K. (1999). *Marital Rape*. National Electronic Network on Violence against Women, Applied Research Forum. Retrieved from http://www.ilcd vp.org/Documents/Marital%20Rape%20Revised.pdf

Bianquis, T. (1996). The Family in Arab Islam. *A History of the Family, 1*, 601-47.

Bishai, D., & Grossbard, S. (2010). Far above rubies: Bride Price and extramarital sexual relations in Uganda. *Journal of Population Economics, 23*(4), 1177-1187.

Bloch, A. (2008). Zimbabweans in Britain: Transnational activities and capabilities. *Journal of Ethnic and Migration Studies, 34*(2), 287-305.

Bradley, M. A., & Harrell, M. C. (2009). *Data collection methods. Semi-structured interviews and focus groups*. Santa Monica: RAND Corporation.

Bradley, T. (2011). The politicisation of mothering in Hindu missions. *Politics, Religion & Ideology, 12*(2), 161-177.

Breen, R., & Rottman, D. (1995). Class Analysis and Class Theory. *Sociology 29*(3), 453- 473.

Bourdillon, M. F. C. (1976). *The Shona Peoples*. Gweru: Mambo Press.

Bourdillon, M. F. C. (1987). *The Shona peoples: An ethnography of the contemporary Shona, with special reference to their religion* (vol. 1). Gweru: Mambo press.

Bourdillon, M. F. C. (1990*). Religion and society: A text for Africa*. Gweru: Mambo Press.

Bourdillon, M. F. C. (1993). *Where are the ancestors? Changing culture in Zimbabwe*. Harare: University of Zimbabwe Publications.

Bourdillon, M. F. C. (1998). *The Shona peoples* (revised ed.). Gweru: Mambo Press.

Brah, A., & Phoenix, A. (2004). Ain't I A woman? Revisiting intersectionality. *Journal of international women's studies, 5*(3), 75-86.

Budgeon, S. & Roseneil, S. (2004). Cultures of intimacy and care beyond 'the family': Personal life and social change in the early 21st century. *Current Sociology, 52*(2), 135-159.

Burn, S. M. (2000). *Women across cultures: A global perspective* (2nd ed.). New York: McGraw Hill.

Butler, J. (1993). *Bodies that Matter: On Discursive Limits of Sex*. New York: Routledge.

Caldwell, J. C., Caldwell, P., & Reddy, P. H. (1983). The causes of marriage change in South India. *Population Studies, 37*(3), 343-361.

Caplan, L. (1984). Bridegroom Price in Urban India: Class, Caste and 'Dowry Evil' Among Christians in Madraa. *Man, New Series, 19*(2), 216-233.

Chambers, R. (2007). *Who counts? The quiet revolution of participation and numbers* (IDS Working Paper 296). Brighton: IDS.

Chambliss, D. F., & Schutt, R. K. (2006). *Making sense of the social world: Methods of investigation*. London: Sage.

Chamratrithirong, A., & Cherlin, A. (1988). Variations in marriage patterns in central Thailand. *Demography, 25*(3), 337-353.

Chireshe, E., & Chireshe, R. (2010). Lobola: The perceptions of great Zimbabwe university students. *Journal of Pan African Studies, 3*(9), 211-221.

Cleaver, F. (2002) Men and Masculinities: New Directions Gender and Development. In F. Cleaver (Ed.). *Masculinities Matter! Men, Gender and Development* (pp. 1-25). London: Zed Books.

Cliffe, L., & Stoneman, C. (1989). *Zimbabwe: Politics, economics and society.* London: Pinter.

Conley, T. D., Matsick, J. L., Moors, A. C., Rubin, J., & Ziegler, A. (2009). Does monogamy harm women? Deconstructing monogamy with a feminist lens. [Special Issue on Polyamory]. *Journal for Psychology, 22*(1), 1-18.

Corbin, J., Strauss, A., & Strauss, A. L. (2014). *Basics of qualitative research.* London: Sage.

Cornell, D. (1999). *Beyond accommodation: Ethical feminism, deconstruction, and the law.* Maryland: Rowman & Littlefield.

D'Hondt, W., & Vandewiele, M. (1980). Attitudes of Senegalese secondary school students towards traditional African way of life and Western way of life. *Psychological Reports, 47*(1), 235-242.

Davis, K. (2008). Intersectionality as buzzword: A sociology of science perspective on what makes a feminist theory successful. *Feminist Theory, 9*(1), 67-85.

Dekker, M., & Hoogeveen, H. (2002). Bride wealth and household security in rural Zimbabwe. *Journal of African Economies, 11*(1), 114-145.

Denscombe, M. (2010). *The good research guide: For small-scale social research projects.* Buckingham: Open University.

Dery, I. (2015). Bride-price and domestic violence: Empirical perspectives from Nandom district in the north western region of Ghana. *International Journal of Development Sustainability, 4*(3), 258-271.

Dey, I. (2003). *Qualitative data analysis: A user friendly guide for social scientists.* London: Routledge.

Dore, L. (1970). The Uses of Cattle in Shona Society. In C. Kileff, & P. Kileff, (Eds.). (1970). *Shona Customs: essays by African writers.* Gweru: Mambo Press.

Dorow, S. K. (2006). *Transnational adoption: A cultural economy of race, gender, and kinship* (Vol. 9). New York: NYU Press.

Ekong, J. M. (1992). *Bride Wealth Women and Reproduction in Sub-Saharan Africa.* Bonn: HolosVerlag.

Ekstrom, A. M., Johansson, A., Kaye, D. K., Kyomuhendo, G. B., & Mirembe, F. (2005) Implications of Bride Price on Domestic Violence and Reproductive Health in Wakiso District, Uganda. *African Health Sciences 5*(4), 300-303.

Engel, J. W. (1984). Marriage in the People's Republic of China: Analysis of a new law. *Journal of Marriage and the Family 46*(4), 955-961.

Essof, S., & Van der Wijk, L. (1996). *Women in Zimbabwe: A Fact Sheet on Gender Issues.* Harare: ZWRCN.

Ferguson, J. (1990). *The anti-politics machine: 'development', depoliticization and bureaucratic power in Lesotho.* London: University of Minnesota Press.

Fishburne Collier, J. & Yanagisako, S. J. (1987). Toward a unified analysis of gender and kinship. In J. Fishburne Collier & S. L. Yanagisako (Eds.). *Gender and kinship: Essays toward a unified analysis* (pp. 14-50). California: Stanford University Press.

Fortunato, L. (2011). Reconstructing the history of marriage strategies in Indo-European—speaking societies: Monogamy and polygyny. *Human Biology, 83*(1), 87-105.

Fuller, R., & Petch, A. (1995). *Practitioner Research: The reflexive social worker.* Buckingham: Open University Press.

Gaspart, F., & Platteau, J. P. (2007). The perverse effects of high Bride Prices. *World Development, 35*(7), 1221-1236.

Gay, J. S. (1982). *Women and development in Lesotho.* Maseru: USAID.

Gelfand, M. (1965). *African background: the traditional culture of the Shona speaking people. With a chapter by M. Hannan.* Cape town: Juta.

Gelfand, M. (1973). *The genuine Shona: Survival values of an African culture.* Gweru: Mambo Press.

Gelfand, M. (1984). *The Genuine Shona. Survival Values of An African Culture.* Gweru: Mambo Press.

Glaser, B., & Strauss, A. (1967). *The Discovery of Grounded Theory.* London: Weidenfeld.

Goldthorpe, J. H. (1983). Women and class analysis: in defence of the conventional view. *Sociology, 17*(4), 465-488.

Goldthorpe, J. H. (1996). Class Analysis and the Reorientation of Class Theory: The Case of Persisting Differentials in Educational Attainment. *The British Journal of Sociology 47*(3), 481-505.

Goody, J. (1973). Polygyny, economy, and the role of women. In J. Goody (Ed.). *The character of kinship* (pp. 175-190). London: Cambridge University Press.

Goody, J., & Tambiah, S. J. (1973). *Bride wealth and dowry.* London: Cambridge University Press.

Gopal, G., & Salim, M. (Eds.). (1988). *Gender and law: East Africa speaks.* Washington, D. C.: The World Bank.

GoZ (2012). *Zimbabwe Population Census: Mashonaland West Province Report.* Harare: Zim Stat.

Gustafsson, S., & Worku, S. Y. (2006). *Marriage markets and single motherhood in South Africa* (Tinbergen Institute Discussion Paper No. 06-102/3). Amsterdam: University of Amsterdam.

Guy, J. (1990). *Gender oppression in southern Africa's precapitalistic societies.* London: James Curry.

Gwazane, M., & Hove, K. (2011). *A study to determine factors associated with domestic violence among concordant and discordant couples in Zimbabwe* (The Special Issue on Behavioral and Social Sciences). Mutare: Department of Public Health Africa University.

Hague, G., Thiara, R. K., & Turner, A. (2011). Bride Price and its links to domestic violence and poverty in Uganda: A participatory action research study. *Women's Studies International Forum 34*(6), 550-561.

Hamisu, D. R. I. (2000). Customary Bride Price in Cameroon: Do women have a say? *Southern African Feminist Review, 4*(2), 65-72.

Hardin, R. (2007). *The systemic anticultural of capitalism.* In V. Nee & R. Swedberg (Eds.). *On Capitalism* (pp. 21-41). Satnford: Stanford University Press.

Harris, M. J., Hoyle, R. H., & Judd, C. M. (2002). *Research methods in social relations.* Wadsworth: Thomson Learning.

Heise, L. L. (1998). Violence against women an integrated, ecological framework. *Violence against women, 4*(3), 262-290.

Heise, M. (2002). The past, present, and future of empirical legal scholarship: Judicial decision making and the new empiricism. *University of Illinois Law Review, 2002*(4), 819-850.

Hellum, A., & Stewart, J. E. (1999). *Women's human rights and legal pluralism in Africa: Mixed norms and identities in infertility management in Zimbabwe.* Harare: Mond Books.

Holleman, J. F. (1952). *Shona customary law with reference to kinship, marriage, the family, estate.* Oxford: Oxford University Press.

Hoogeveen, J. G. M. (2001). *Risk and insurance in rural Zimbabwe.* Gweru: Mambo Press.

Hughes, D. O. (1978). From Bride Price to dowry in Mediterranean Europe. *Journal of family history, 3*(3), 262-296.

Humphris, R. (2010). *Zimbabweans in the UK.* ICAR population Guides series. Retrieved from https://ec.europa.eu/migrant-integration/index.cfm?

IOM UN migration. (2018). IOM Zimbabwe Supports Government Efforts to Improve Livelihoods Through Financial Literacy. Retrieved https://www.iom.int/news/iom-zimbabwe-supports-government-efforts-improve-livelihoods-through-financial-literacy

Janhi, L. (1970). Roora and Marriage. In C. Kileff, & P. Kileff, (Eds.). *Shona Customs: essays by African writers.* Gweru: Mambo Press.

Jeater, D. (1993). *Marriage, Perversion and Power: The construction of moral discourse in Southern Rhodesia, 1894-1930.* Oxford: Oxford University Press.

Johnson, P., Look, N., Moors, A., & Nahleh, L. A. (2009). Weddings and war: marriage arrangements and celebrations in two Palestinian Intifadas. *Journal of Middle East Women's Studies, 5*(3), 11-35.

Kambarami, M. (2006). *Femininity, sexuality and culture: Patriarchy and female subordination in Zimbabwe.* Fort Hare: ARSRC.

Kethusegile, B. M., Kwaramba, A., & Lopi, B. (2000). *Beyond inequalities: women in Southern Africa.* Harare: Southern African Research and Documentation Centre (SARDC).

Kileff, C., & Kileff, P. (Eds.). (1970). *Shona Customs: essays by African writers.* Gweru: Mambo Press.

Kuperus, T. (1999). *State, Civil Society and Apartheid in South Africa; An examination of Dutch Reformed Church-State Relations.* London: Macmillan.

Kurebwa, J. (2015), A Review of Local Government System in Zimbabwe from 1980 to 2014. *IOSR Journal of Humanities and Social Sciences, 20*(2), 94-108.

Lee, R. M. & Renzetti, C. M. (1993). *Researching Sensitive Topics.* New York: Sage Publications.

Lewis, J. (2009). Redefining qualitative methods: Believability in the fifth moment. *International Journal of Qualitative Methods, 8*(2), 1-14.

Lofland, J., & Lofland, L. (1995). *Analysing Social Settings.* Belmont: Wadsworth.

Lowes, S., & Nunn, N. (2017). Bride price and the wellbeing of women. *Towards gender equity in development, 117.*

Lundgren, E. (1995). Creating bodily gender in the fields of symbol and power. *Nora, Nordic Journal of Women's Studies, 3*(2), 101-112.

Luyirika, K. (2010). Women's' Rights to Property in Marriage, Divorce, and Widowhood in Uganda: The Problematic Aspects. *Human Rights Review 11*(2),199-221.

Machinga, M. M. (2011a). The Development of Healthy Human Sexuality from a Pastoral Care & Counselling Perspective. *Testamentum Imperium International Theological Journal, 3,* 1-19.

Machinga, M. M. (2011b). Religion, health, and healing in the traditional Shona culture of Zimbabwe. *Practical Matters, 4,* 1-8.

Magezi, V. (2007). *HIV/AIDS, Poverty and Pastoral Care and Counselling: A Home-based and Congregational systems ministerial approach in Africa.* Harare: African Sun Media.

Makamure, D. M. (1970). Cattle and social status. In C. Kileff, & P. Kileff, (Eds.). *Shona Customs: essays by African writers.* Gweru: Mambo Press.

Malahleha, G. (1986). *Contradictions and ironies: women of Lesotho.* London: Chance.

Maluleke, T. S., & Nadar, S. (2002). Breaking the covenant of violence against women. *Journal of theology for Southern Africa, 114,* 5-17.

Mama, A. A. (1996). Women's Studies and Studies of Women in Africa during the 1990s (Council for the Development of Economic and Social Research in Africa Working Paper, Series 5/96). Dakar: CODESRIA.

Mandiyanike, D. (2009). The dilemma of conducting research back in your own country as a returning student-reflections of research fieldwork in Zimbabwe. *Area, 41*(1), 64-71.

Mano, W., & Willems, W. (2008). Emerging communities, emerging media: the case of a Zimbabwean nurse in the British Big Brother show. *Critical Arts: A Journal of South-North Cultural Studies, 22*(1), 101-128.

Mapara, J. (2007). Indigenous knowledge systems in Zimbabwe: Juxtaposing postcolonial theory. *Journal of Pan African Studies, 3*(1).

Matembe, M. (2002). Politics, gender and constitution making in Uganda.

Matembe, M. (2004). *The relationship between domestic violence and Bride Price.* Paper presented at the International Bride Price Conference, MP Mbarara and Pan African Parliamentarian, February, Kampala, Uganda.

May, J. (1983). *Zimbabwean women in colonial and customary law.* Gweru: Mambo Press.

Mazrui, A. A. (1993). The black woman and the problem of gender: An African perspective. *Research in African Literatures, 24*(1), 87-104.

Mbiba, B. (2012). Zimbabwean Diaspora politics in Britain: insights from the Cathedral moment 2009. *Commonwealth & Comparative Politics, 50*(2), 226-252.

McClintock, A. (2013). *Imperial leather: Race, gender, and sexuality in the colonial contest.* Routledge.

McFadden, P. (Ed). (1999). *Reflections on gender issues in Africa.* Harare: SAPES Trust.

McGregor, J. (2011). Contestations and consequences of deportability: hunger strikes and the political agency of non-citizens. *Citizenship Studies, 15*(5), 597-611.

Meekers, D. (1992). The process of marriage in African societies: A multiple indicator approach. *Population and development review, 18*(1), 61-78.

Menski, W. (2013). *Modern Indian family law.* Abingdon: Routledge.

Mesatywa, N. J. (2009*). The perceptions and experiences of African women in violent partner relationships: An exploratory study* (Unpublished doctoral thesis). Retrieved from https://core.ac.uk/download/pdf/37319758.pdf

Mohanty, C. T. (1988). Under Western eyes: Feminist scholarship and colonial discourses. *Feminist review, 30*(1), 61-88.

Mohanty, C. T., Russo, A., & Torres, L. (Eds.). (1991). *Third world women and the politics of feminism.* Bloomington: Indiana University Press.

Moore, M. (2013, January 4). Chinese Brides for Gold: Parents are Lavishing Bigger and Bigger Dowries on their Daughters. *The daily Telegraph.* Retrieved from https://www.telegraph.co.uk/news/worldnews/asia/china/9780786/Chinas-brides-go-for-gold-as-their-dowries-get-bigger-and-bigger.html

Moraga, C., & Anzaldúa, G. (Eds.). (2015). *This bridge called my back: Writings by radical women of color.* New York: SUNY Press.

Mueller, M. B. (1977). *Women and men in rural Lesotho: the periphery of the periphery.* Waltham: Brandeis University.

Mukonyora, I. (2001). Marginality and protest in the sacred wilderness: The role of women in shaping Masowe thought pattern. *Southern African Feminist Review (SAFERE),* (4.2-5.1), 1-21.

Mulder, M. B. (1995). Bride wealth and its correlates: quantifying changes over time. *Current Anthropology, 36*(4), 573-603.

Munshi, K., & Rosenzweig, M. (2005). Economic development and the decline of rural and urban community-based networks. *Economics of Transition, 13*(3), 427-443.

Murdock, G. P. (1967). Ethnographic atlas: a summary. *Ethnology, 6*(2), 109-236.

Murray, C. (1981). *Families divided: The impact of migrant labour in Lesotho.* Cambridge: Cambridge University Press.

Musisi, N. (2002). The Politics of Perception or Perception as Politics? In J. M. Allman, S. Geiger, & N. Musisi (Eds.). *Women in African Colonial Histories,* 95-115. Bloomington, Indiana University Press.

Mutizwa-Mangiza, N. D. (1986). Urban centres in Zimbabwe: Inter-censal changes, 1962-1982. *Geography, 71*(2), 148-150.

Muzulu, P. (2014) *"Zimbabwe needs Comprehensive Sexuality Education",* Newsday (6 February 2014) Available at: http:// www.newsday.co.zw/2014/02/06/zimbabwe-needs-comprehensive-sexuality-education/ (Accessed on 19 September 2016).

Mvududu, S. C. (2002). *Lobola: its implications for women's reproductive rights in Botswana, Lesotho, Malawi, Mozambique, Swaziland, Zambia, and Zimbabwe*. Women and Law in Southern Africa Research Trust. Harare: Weaver Press.

Narayan, U. (1997). *Dislocating cultures: Identities, Traditions, and Third-World Feminism*. London: Routledge.

Narayan, U. (1998). Essence of culture and a sense of history: A feminist critique of cultural essentialism. *Hypatia, 13*(2), 86-106.

Ncube, W., & Stewart, J. (1995). Parting the long grass: revealing and reconceptualising the African family. *The Journal of Legal Pluralism and Unofficial Law, 27*(35), 25-73.

Ndira, P. (2004). *Bride Price: A Rights based view*. Paper presented at the International Bride Price Conference, Kampala, Uganda.

Nicholson, L. (1997a). The myth of the traditional family. In H. Lindemann (Ed.). *Feminism and Families* (pp. 27-42). London: Routledge.

Nicholson, L. (1997b). Feminism and Marx: Integrating kinship with the economic. *Praxis international, 5*(4), 367-380.

Nyambedha, E. O. (2004). Change and continuity in kin-based support systems for widows and orphans among the Luo in Western Kenya. *African Sociological Review/Revue Africaine de Sociologie, 8*(1), 139-153.

Oduyoye, M. A. (1994). Violence Against Women: A Challenge to Christian Theology. *Journal of Inculturation theology, 1*(1), 47-60.

Oguli Oumo, M. (2004). *Bride Price and Violence against Women: the Case of Uganda*. Paper presented at the International Bride Price Conference, Kampala, Uganda.

Oyewùmí, O. (1997). *The invention of women: Making an African sense of western gender discourses*. London: University of Minnesota Press.

Oyewùmí, O. (2002). Conceptualizing gender: the Eurocentric foundations of feminist concepts and the challenge of African epistemologies. *Jenda: A Journal of Culture and African Women Studies, 2*(1), 1-9.

Pahl, J. (1983). The allocation of money and the structuring of inequality within marriage. *The Sociological Review, 31*(2), 237-262.

Parish, W. L., & Willis, R. J. (1993). Daughters, education, and family budgets Taiwan experiences. *Journal of Human Resources, 28*(4), 863-898.

Parsons, T. (1940). An Analytical Approach to the Theory of Social Stratification. *American Journal of Sociology 45*(6), 841-862.

Pasura, D. (2010). Competing meanings of the diaspora: the case of Zimbabweans in Britain. *Journal of Ethnic and Migration Studies, 36*(9), 1445-1461.

Pellauer, M. D. (1991). *Toward a Tradition of Feminist Theology*. New York: Carlson Publishing.

Penfold, M., Rotunda, R. J., & Williamson, G. (2004). Clergy response to domestic violence: A preliminary survey of clergy members, victims, and batterers. *Pastoral Psychology, 52*(4), 353-365.

Radcliffe-Brown, A. R. (1987). 1950Introduction. *African Systems of Kinship and Marriage. eds AR Brown and Daryll Forde. Oxford: OUPfor IAI.*

Rao, V. (1993). The rising price of husbands: A hedonic analysis of dowry increases in rural India. *Journal of political Economy, 101*(4), 666-677.

Rosaldo, M. Z. (1980). The use and abuse of anthropology: reflections on feminism and cross-cultural understanding. *Signs: Journal of Women in Culture and Society, 5*(3), 389-417.

Sanders, C. J. (Ed.). (1995). *Living the intersection: Womanism and Afrocentrism in theology.* Minneapolis: Fortress Press.

Schein, E. H. (1993). Legitimating clinical research in the study of organizational culture. *Journal of counselling & development, 71*(6), 703-708.

Schmidt, E. (1991). Patriarchy, capitalism, and the colonial state in Zimbabwe. *Signs: Journal of Women in Culture and Society, 16*(4), 732-756.

Schmidt, E. S. (2004). *Peasants, traders and wives: Shona women in the history of Zimbabwe, 1870-1939.* London: James Gurry.

Scoones, I. (1996). Crop production in a variable environment: A case study from southern Zimbabwe. *Experimental Agriculture, 32*(3), 291-303.

Scott, J. W. (1986). Gender: A useful category of historical analysis. *The American historical review, 91*(5), 1053-1075.

Sieber, J.E. (1992). *Planning Ethically Responsible Research: A guide for Students and Internal Review Boards.* Newbury Park: Sage Publications.

Silberschmidt, M. (1999). *"Women forget that men are the masters": gender antagonism and socio-economic change in Kisii District, Kenya.* Nordic Africa Institute.

Spiro, M. E. (1975). Marriage payments: A paradigm from the Burmese perspective. *Journal of Anthropological Research, 31*(2), 89-115.

Stanworth, M. (1984). *Gender and schooling: A study of sexual divisions in the classroom.* London: Hutchinson.

Strauss, A. L. (1987). *Qualitative analysis for social scientists.* Cambridge: Cambridge University Press.

Strube M. (1988). The Decision to Leave an Abusive Relationship: Empirical Evidence and Theoretical Issues. *Psychological Bulletin, 1988*(104), 236-250.

Tamale, S. (1993). Law reform and women's rights in Uganda. *East African Journal of Peace and Human Rights, 1*(2), 164-194.

Tamale, S. (2004). Gender trauma in Africa: enhancing women's links to resources. *Journal of African Law, 48*(01), 50-61.

Tamale, S. (2009). A human rights impact assessment of the Ugandan Anti-homosexuality Bill 2009. *The Equal Rights Review, 4*(2010), 49-57.

Tamusuza, S. (2002). Gender, ethnicity and politics in Kadongo-kamu music of Uganda. In A. Kirkegaard, & M. Palmberg (Eds.). *Playing with identities in contemporary music in Africa* (pp. 34-148). Upsala: Nordiska Afrikainstitutet.

Tesch, R. (1990). *Qualitative research: Analysis types and software tools.* London: Psychology Press.

Thelejane, T. S. (1983, September). *An African girl and an African woman in a changing world.* Paper presented at the Seminar on the Changing Family in the African Context, Maseru, Lesotho.

Thiara, K. (2012). A sensitive Cultural Matter, Bride Price/Lobola, Domestic violence and Poverty in Uganda. *The Social Work Practitioner-Researcher 24*(1), 85-102.

Thorpe, S. A. (1991). *African traditional religions: An introduction.* Pretoria: University of South Africa.

Tichagwa, W. (1998). *Beyond inequalities: Women in Zimbabwe.* Harare: Zimbabwe Women Resource Centre and Network (ZWRCN).

Tong, R. (1993). *Feminine and Feminist Ethics.* Belmont: Calif Wadsworth

Townsend, T. G. (2008). Protecting our daughters: Intersection of race, class and gender in African American mothers' socialization of their daughters' heterosexuality. *Sex Roles, 59*(5-6), 429-442.

Townshend, P. O. (2008). *A gender-critical approach to the Pauline material and the Zimbabwean context with specific reference to the position and role of women in selected denominations* (Unpublished Masters Dissertation). Retrieved from http://datad.aau.org:8080/handle/10500/2032%3E

Tracy, S. R. (2007). Patriarchy and domestic violence: Challenging common misconceptions. *Journal of the evangelical theological society, 50*(3), 573.

Tripp, M. A. (2013). Women's Movements, Customary Law and Land rights in Africa. The Case of Uganda. *African Studies Quarterly 13*(4), 1-19.

Trochim, W., & Donnelly, J. P. (2010). *The research methods knowledge base.* Ithaca, New York: Cornell University.

Tsanga, A. (1999). Criticisms against the Magaya decision: Much ado about something. *Legal Forum, 11*(2), 94-100.

Tsanga, A. S. (2003). *Taking law to the people: Gender, law reform and community legal education in Zimbabwe.* Harare: Weaver.

Tsodzo, T. K. M. (1970). *Cattle are our bank.* In C. Kileff, & P. Kileff, (Eds.). *Shona Customs: essays by African writers.* Gweru: Mambo Press.

Tumurkush, U. (2001). Fighting over the Reinterpretation of the Mongolian Woman in Mongolia's Post-socialist Identity Construction Discourse. *East Asia Journal, 19*(3), 119-146.

UNICEF (2016). *Children on the Move: Key facts and Figures.* Retrieved from https://data.unicef.org/resources/children-move-key-facts-figures/.

Verloo, M. (2006). Multiple inequalities, intersectionality and the European Union. *European Journal of Women's Studies, 13*(3), 211-228.

Wagner, N. (1999). Sexual violence against women: A key element of institutional patriarchy. *Southern African Feminist Review (SAFERE), 3*(2), 59-61.

Walby, S. (1990). *Theorizing patriarchy.* Oxford: Basil Blackwell.

Wegh, S. F. (1998). *Between Continuity and Change: Tiv concept of tradition and modernity.* Enugu: OVC Nigeria Limited.

Wekwete, K. H. (1992). New directions for urban development in rapidly urbanising countries: The case of Zimbabwe. *Habitat International, 16*(2), 53-63.

Wood, J. T. (2009). *Gendered lives: Communication, gender, and culture.*

World Bank (2017) *Governance Matters 2017* (Worldwide Governance Indicators, 2000-2016. Country Data Report for Zimbabwe). Retrieved from (http://info.worldbank.org/governance/wgi/pdf/c25.pdf)

Wright, E. O. (1999). *Foundations of Class Analysis: A Marxist Perspective.* Paper presented at the Annual Meeting of the American Sociological Association, Chicago.

Wright, K. (2000). The Stigma of AIDS. *WIPHN News, 25,* 6-7.

Zimbabwe Demographic and Health Survey (2015). *Final Report.* Rockville: Zimbabwe National Statistics Agency (ZIMSTAT) and ICF International.

Index

www.ingramcontent.com/pod-product-compliance
Lightning Source LLC
Chambersburg PA
CBHW072121020426
42334CB00018B/1676